Profile of Laird's torpedo gunboat, *Rattlesnake*, 1887. *(© National Maritime Museum, Greenwich,*

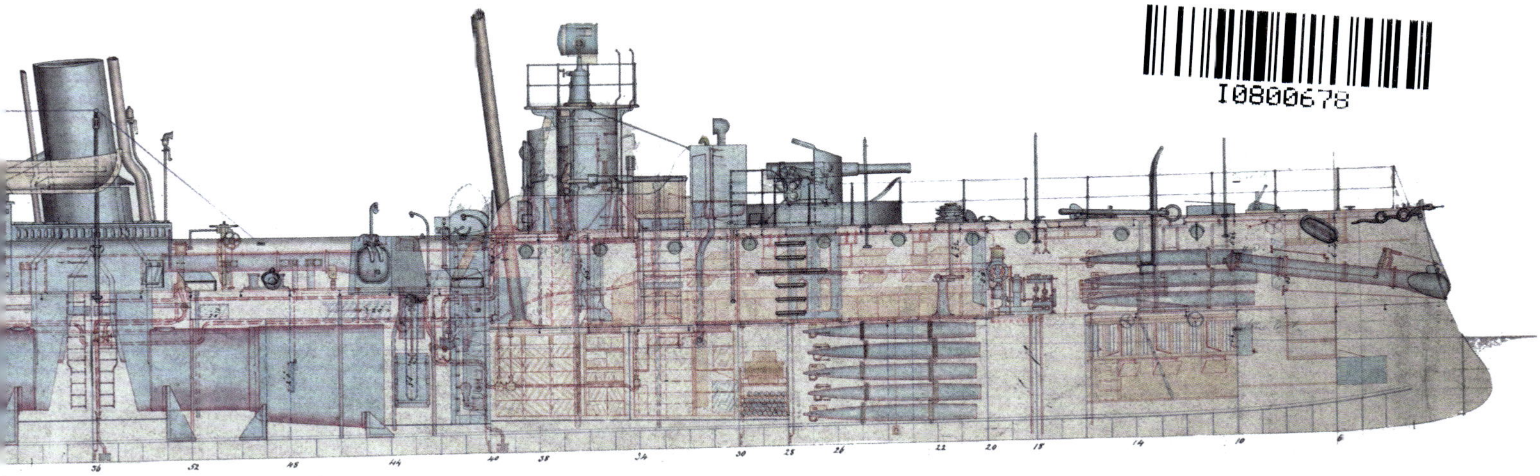

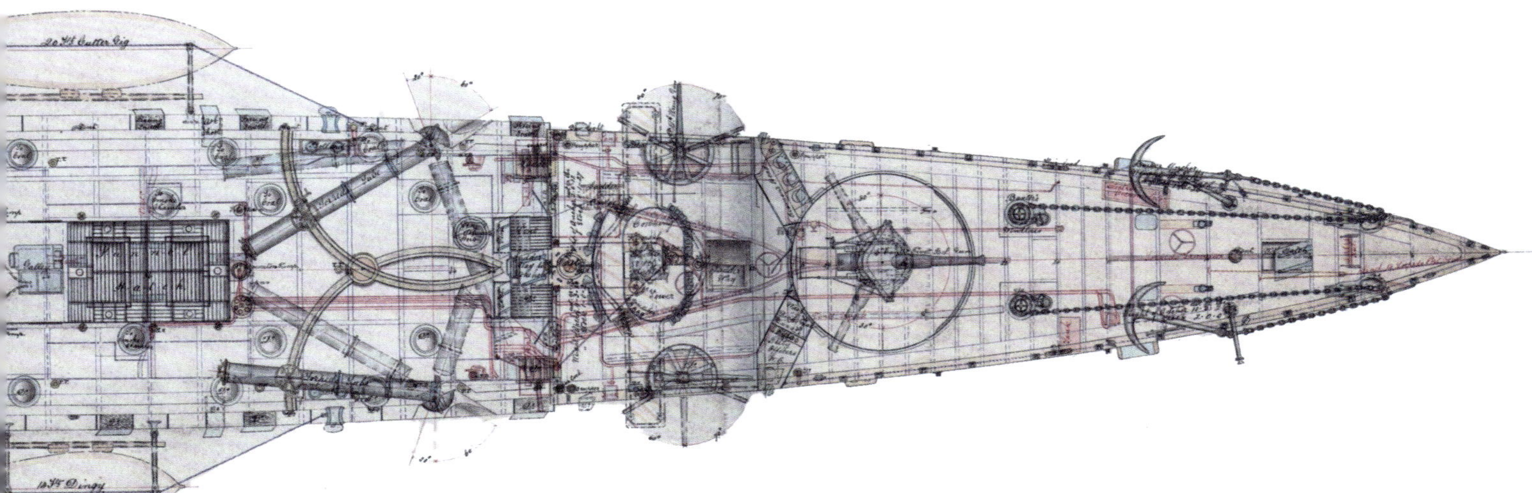

Deck plan of Laird's torpedo gunboat, *Rattlesnake*, 1887. *(© National Maritime Museum, Greenwich, London)*

ROYAL NAVY TORPEDO VESSELS

27

ROYAL NAVY TORPEDO VESSELS

1870–1914

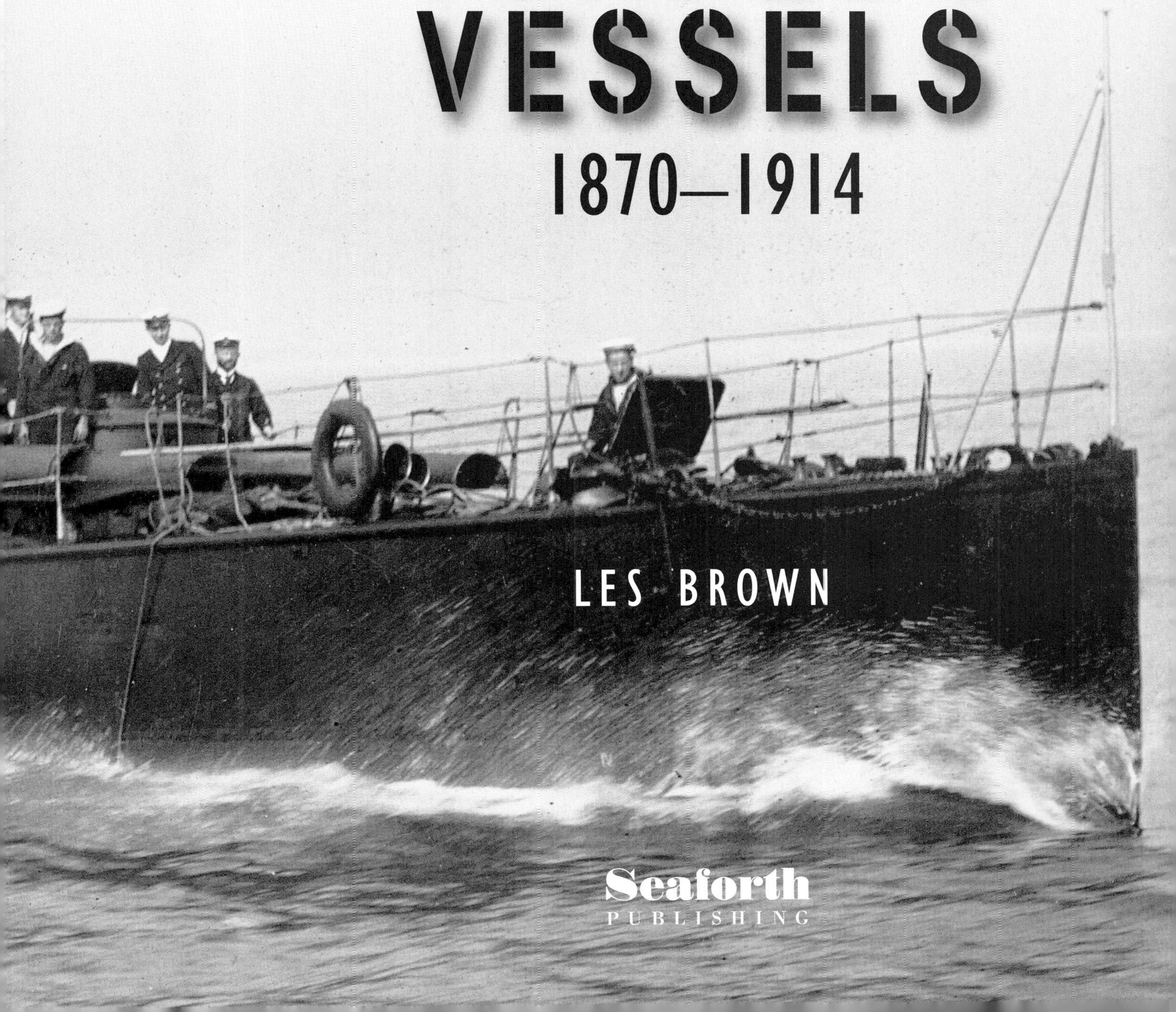

LES BROWN

Seaforth
PUBLISHING

Frontispiece: First-class torpedo boat, *TB27*, built by Thornycroft as Yard No. 219, and launched in October 1885. Note the forward twin 14in torpedo tube mounting situated over the conning tower.
(US Naval History and Heritage Command, NH 54991)

First published in Great Britain in 2023 by
Seaforth Publishing,
A division of Pen & Sword Books Ltd,
47 Church Street,
Barnsley S70 2AS
www.seaforthpublishing.com
British Library Cataloguing in Publication Data
A catalogue record for this book is available from the British Library

ISBN 978 1 3990 2285 9 (HARDBACK)
ISBN 978 1 3990 2286 6 (EPUB)
ISBN 978 1 3990 2287 3 (KINDLE)

Any uncredited illustrations are from the author's collection.

Pen & Sword Books Limited incorporates the imprints of Atlas, Archaeology, Aviation, Discovery, Family History, Fiction, History, Maritime, Military, Military Classics, Politics, Select, Transport, True Crime, Air World, Frontline Publishing, Leo Cooper, Remember When, Seaforth Publishing, The Praetorian Press, Wharncliffe Local History, Wharncliffe Transport, Wharncliffe True Crime and White Owl

Typeset and designed by ian Hughes, www.mousematdesign.com

Printed and bound by Printworks Global Ltd, London/Hong Kong

CONTENTS

INTRODUCTION

Although I have been interested in torpedo boats for many years, my interest had been primarily in the coastal motorboats (CMBs) of the First World War, the motor torpedo boats (MTBs)/ motor gunboats (MGBs) of the Second World War and the post-war Gay, Bold and Brave classes. As a volunteer at the Explosion Naval Ordnance Museum in Gosport, part of the National Museum of the Royal Navy, I was asked by Alexandra Geary, the curator, and Heather Johnson, the librarian, to catalogue the collection of annual reports from HMS *Vernon* for the late nineteenth and early twentieth centuries.

These reports contain a great deal of information, not only about torpedoes, torpedo launching systems and torpedo boats, but also about many other types of electrical equipment used by the Royal Navy. When wireless telegraphy was introduced into the Royal Navy, initially this also came under the supervision of *Vernon*, but with its rapid increase in use and complexity, a separate establishment was soon created. While cataloguing these reports, there was not time to study them in detail, but I did keep copies of the sections concerning torpedoes and torpedo boats.

A short while later, I came across a collection of CDs on eBay containing copies of the *Navy & Army Illustrated* publication of the same period. These contained many photographs and reports on mines and early torpedoes; eBay turned out to be a great source of information, containing numerous post cards and photographs, Admiralty handbooks and copies of other contemporary publications, the weekly issues of *The Engineer* and *Engineering* proving particularly fruitful.

Initially, this research was for my own personal interest, but I came to realise there was a significant gap in recent publications. On mentioning my research to Robert Gardiner, he encouraged me to continue with my work and think about putting it down in a book. The larger torpedo boat destroyers have appeared in many books, Norman Friedman's *British Destroyers from Earliest Days to the Second World War*, and the earlier *British Destroyers: A History of Development 1892–1953* by Edgar March, being the most comprehensive.

A little later, I was able to obtain the notes collected on these vessels by the late Dr Oscar Parkes. Some of these were typed but the others, in his very small, spidery handwriting, did take a while to read.

Where possible, the text of this book draws closely on contemporary documents, which does raise two points. During this period, the term 'knot' was frequently used as a measurement of distance, ie a nautical mile, and so speeds would be quoted in 'knots per hour'. However, the context is usually such that the reader can easily overcome any potential confusion. The other is the spelling of the name of the shipbuilder 'Thornycroft'. Despite the name not including an 'e', the Admiralty invariably spelt it 'Thorneycroft'.

Finally, my gratitude to Robert Gardiner for arranging for the inclusion of a selection of shipbuilders' drawings of many of the vessels described.

CHAPTER ONE

THE DEPLOYMENT OF MOORED, TOWED AND SPAR TORPEDOES

Top, the arrangement of mines in the launch ready for laying. Middle, a line of observation mines. Below the observation mine. *(Torpedoes and Torpedo Vessels)*

Prior to the invention of the self-propelled torpedo, there was much experimentation with other forms of torpedo – moored torpedoes (today, normally referred to as mines), towed torpedoes and spar torpedoes. These torpedoes did not place any great requirements on the launching vessels.

At the end of the nineteenth century, the Royal Navy were using '500lb mines' (or moored torpedoes). These comprised 500lb of gun-cotton contained in a domed cylinder, 32.2in in diameter, and made of $\frac{3}{16}$in thick Staffordshire plate. Generally referred to as 'observation mines', they were under the direct control of an operator on shore and the procedure was to fire six or more mines simultaneously as the enemy vessel passed over them. The mines were moored to the bottom by means of mooring ropes connected to 5 hundredweight (cwt) circular wrought-iron sinkers of approximately 2ft in diameter.

They were generally laid out using a general-service 42ft launch with stout thwarts fixed across the boat. If laying a line of six mines there would be four thwarts, each fitted with slips at both ends. With the boat alongside, the sinkers and mine slings were placed in position, followed by the mines, each placed with their dome aft. No. 1 mine was placed on the port end of the after thwart, then no. 2 on the starboard end. No. 3 mine was placed on the starboard end of the thwart immediately forward and no. 4 mine on the port end. The same procedure was followed with mine nos 5 and 6. The connecting cable was then laid in the boat, the domes of the mines removed and connections made to the branch cables before replacing the domes.

Having connected the mooring ropes, the mining launch and a dinghy would be towed by a steamboat to the required position, indicated by a mark buoy. The dinghy would attach a grass line, marked with bunting at appropriate points,

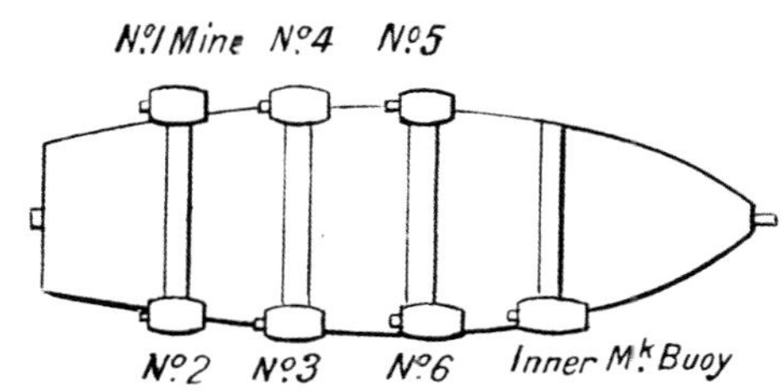

Boat loaded with Observation Mines.

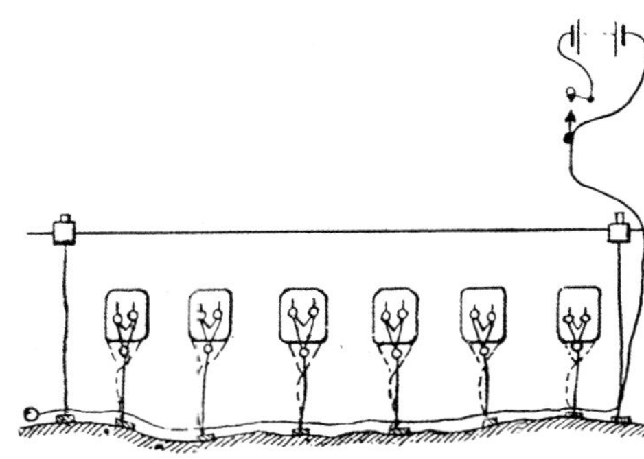

Line of Observation Mines.

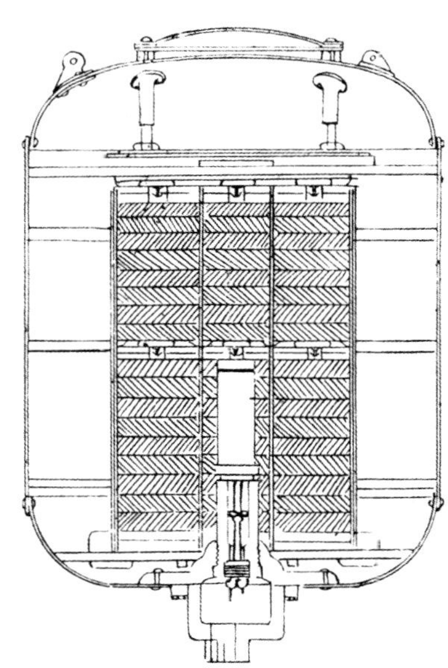

Observation Mine.

An instructor uses a model to illustrate the arrangement of mines in the launch. *(Navy & Army Illustrated)*

to the mark buoy. The crew of the mining launch would maintain the grass line taut and as each mark passed over the side, a mine would be dropped. The cable was connected to the shore station, leaving just a mark buoy at each end of the line of mines.

Mines were considered as defensive weapons and so, with Great Britain having such a powerful fleet, the Royal Navy did not show as much interest as some continental navies. However, in addition to the observation mines, they did have some electro-contact and electromechanical moored mines. Unlike the observation mines, these were intended to explode when in direct contact with the hull of the target vessel and so contained just 75lbs of wet gun-cotton. Both types operated in a very similar manner, the main difference being that the electrical supply to the electro-contact variety came from the shore, in a similar manner to that of the observation mine, and that for the electromechanical mines was provided by a battery within the mine itself.

Both comprised a cylindrical iron case fitted with eye bolts to connect to the sinkers. The charge was stowed in a copper case with a hole in the centre to receive the primer. Over the charge was situated a pedestal on a platform, on top of which was the 'circuit closer'. The circuit closer consisted of a vertical steel cylinder with an iron spindle, insulated from the body of the cylinder, pointing down into a tube. The lower section of the cylinder was filled with mercury to such a height that if the mine was tilted to an angle of 70 degrees, the mercury would make contact with the spindle, complete the circuit and explode the mine.

Electro-contact mines had a waterproof insulating plug for the electrical cables at the bottom, but the electromechanical variety were

Sailors prepare the mines before lowering them into a launch. *(Navy & Army Illustrated)*

A launch ready to lay a line of mines. *(Navy & Army Illustrated)*

fitted with a melted sugar plug which dissolved when the mine was laid, hence providing the required power. Both varieties faced problems maintaining a suitable depth for the mine below the water's surface as tides rose and fell, and with the possibility that the electromechanical mine could break free from its mooring and become a hazard to both defender and attacker, this form of mining was not considered to be desirable. In 1903 the Royal Navy decided to abandon mining.

The Russo-Japanese War increased interest in mines, and in 1906 the Navy Spherical Mine was developed. The Mark I and II mines were 38in in diameter and weighed 900lbs, 250lbs of which was gun-cotton. They were fitted with an automatic anchor, developed by HMS *Vernon* to maintain a constant depth below the water's surface, and had an arm-operated firing mechanism which released a spring-loaded striker to detonate the explosives. The Mark III

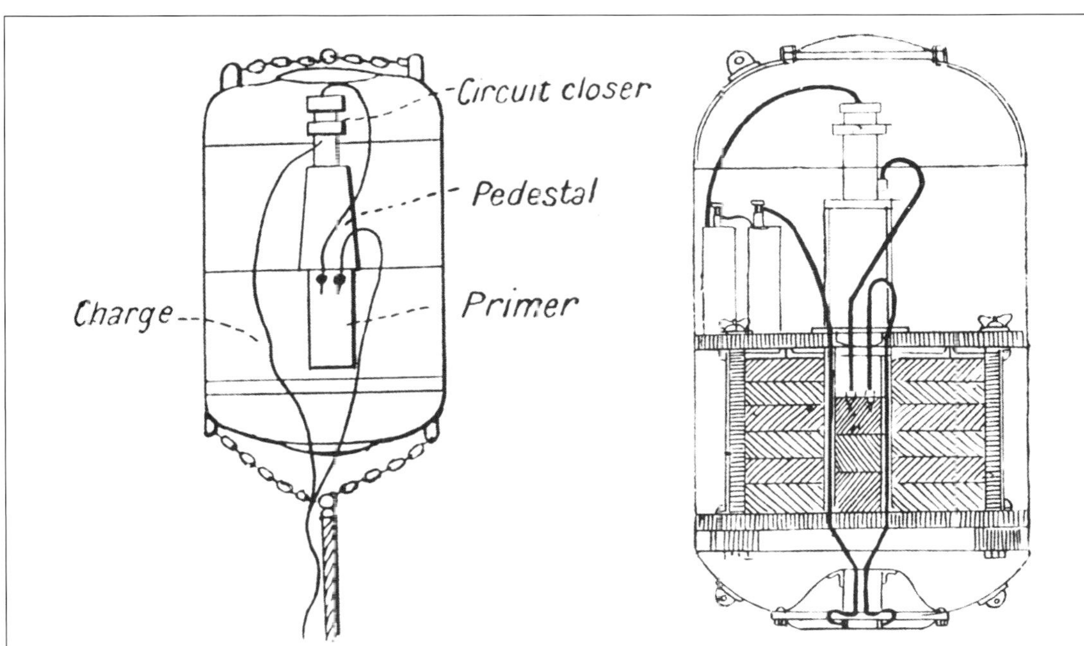

An electro-contact mine (left) and an electromechanical mine (right).

mine had a slightly smaller charge of 245lbs. One thousand mines were produced in the first year, but at the start of the Great War there were still only four thousand available.

Towed torpedoes were usually deployed in conjunction with a type of 'kite' or 'otter' float, to take the explosives away from the side of the towing vessel. This not only increased the chance of a success by allowing the towing vessel to pass further away from the target vessel, but also increased the distance between the explosion (if successful) and the towing vessel, giving it a greater chance of survival.

The Royal Navy did take some interest in the Harvey (or Otter) torpedo, which had been invented in the late 1860s by Frederick Harvey and his uncle, Captain John Harvey. In early 1870 the torpedo was tested, under the supervision of Captain Boys, commanding the *Excellent* gunnery establishment at Portsmouth. After spending more than twenty years trying to gain official recognition for the torpedo, it was agreed that they should be supplied to the Navy, but the government decided that Harvey torpedoes were to be manufactured by the Royal Arsenal at Woolwich. As a result, Captain Harvey, who had never been paid for his invention, sought compensation for his time, labour, and the loss of income that he could have made had his torpedo been manufactured elsewhere.

The Harvey torpedo involved an explosive charge contained in an Otter board which was towed beneath the surface, suspended from a cork float. When the torpedo came in contact with the hull of the target, firing levers were depressed, exploding the charge. Alternative designs were produced that permitted the torpedo to be towed to either port or starboard. Two sizes were also

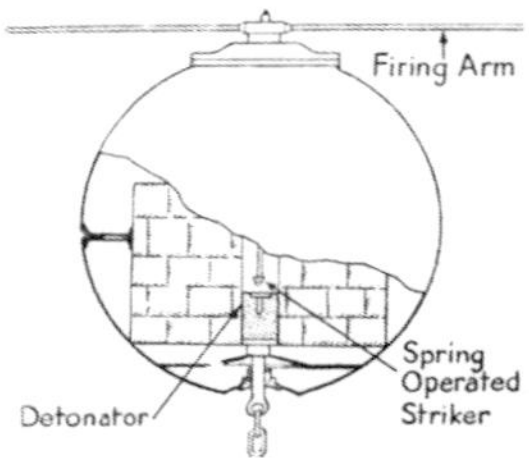

The Navy Spherical Mine with rotating firing arm.

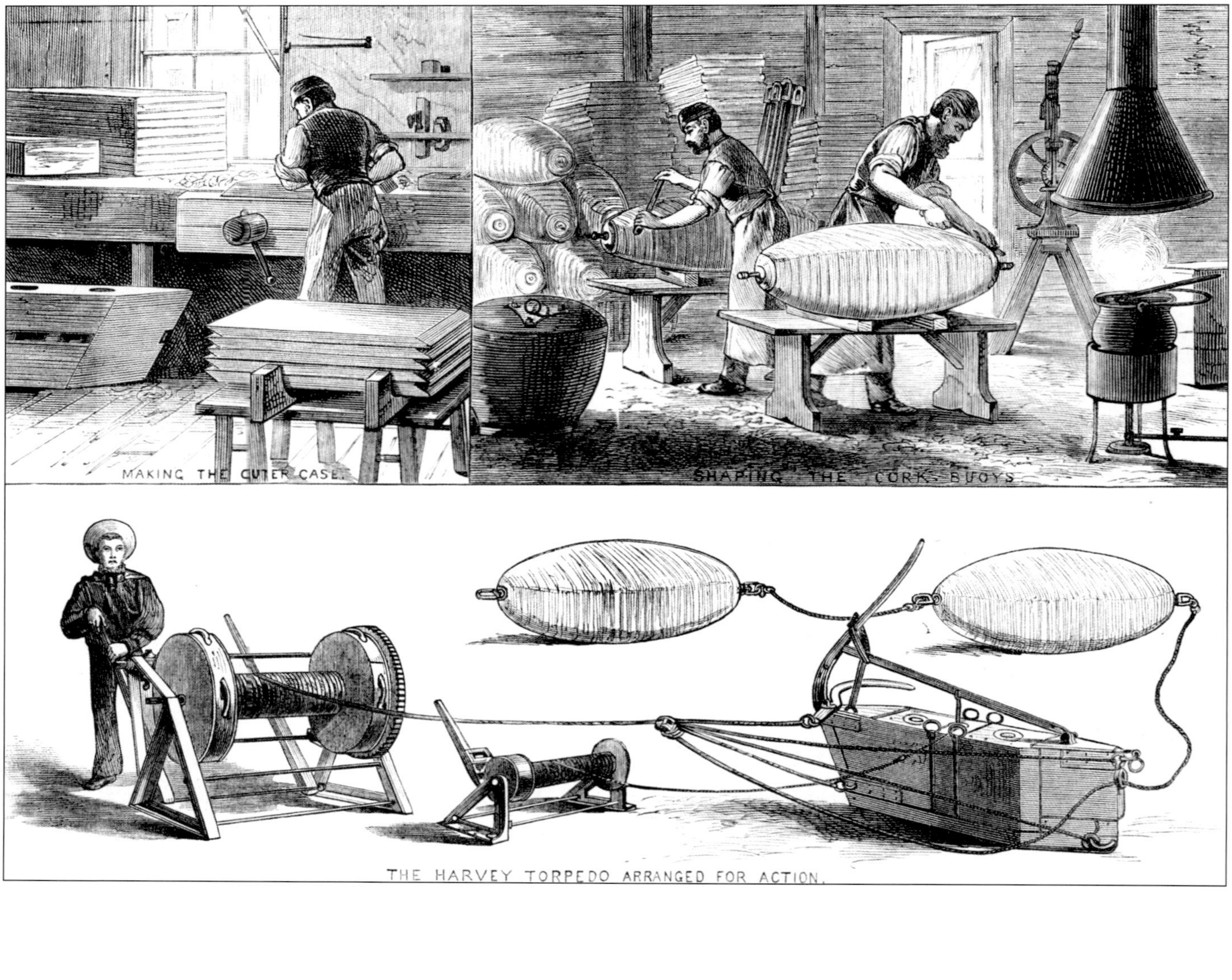

The manufacture of the Harvey torpedo at the Royal Arsenal, Woolwich. *(Illustrated London News, 5 May 1877)*

available: the larger, containing either 60lbs of gun-cotton, 76lbs of black powder or 100lbs of dynamite, was approximately 5ft long by 1ft 8¾in deep and 6in thick. The smaller version carried 22lbs, 27lbs or 35lbs, and was 3ft 8in by 1ft 6in and 5in respectively.

A trial of the Harvey torpedo was carried out, during which the torpedoes were towed out by the steam tug *Camel* to attack the turret ship *Royal Sovereign*, sent out of port for that purpose. They were fitted with a percussion head which exploded on contact with the side or keel of a vessel. The first attacks on *Royal Sovereign* were made while she was at anchor, her turrets being manned and several rounds fired at *Camel* so as to estimate the chances of getting rid of the unwelcome visitor. However, the number of rounds fired while the latter vessel was attacking never, except on two occasions, exceeded two, as only one gun could be brought to bear on her at the same time. Ten attacks were made, *Camel* succeeding in striking her enemy's side every time. The next experiment was conducted with *Royal Sovereign* under way, and doing her best to run her opponent down or to elude her by well-executed manoeuvres, without success, though handled with great skill by Commander Hill. The torpedoes were not charged with powder, the piercing of the capsule of the exploding bolt being considered sufficient evidence of their efficiency.

The image below represents the second experiment when, after vainly attempting to direct her guns so as to sink her tormentor, *Royal Sovereign* tried to run *Camel* down, but owing to the skill of her commander, Captain Mayne, and her superior speed, the latter was enabled to cross her antagonist's bows, and direct one of the torpedoes to the big vessel's starboard side. One of the torpedoes may be seen attached to the side of *Royal Sovereign*, and another is shown in the foreground. The trials were acknowledged by all who took part to be a perfect success.

The spar torpedo comprised an explosive charge fastened to the end of a spar. This spar was secured to a boat and so rigged that it could be projected forward or abeam and lowered well below the waterline of an enemy ship. The charge was exploded on contact or by means of a lanyard. This type of torpedo rose to prominence during the American Civil War when on 5 October 1863 a David-style, steam-powered, semi-submersible torpedo boat made an attack on the casemate ironclad steamer USS *New Ironsides*.

The Harvey torpedo trial. *(The Graphic, 12 March 1870)*

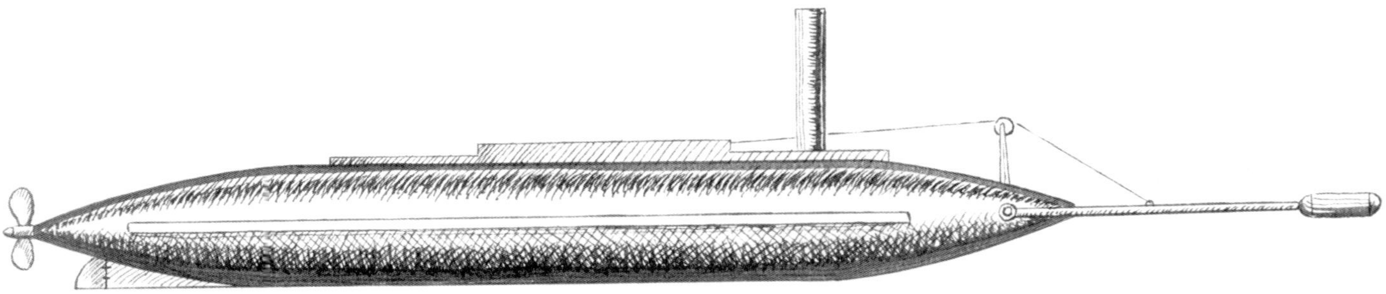

A David-style, steam-powered, semi-submersible torpedo boat. *(US Naval History and Heritage Command, NH95242)*

New Ironsides was not sunk, just damaged, but this action did show the potential of a small vessel armed with a spar torpedo. Attacks on many targets were also made by small surface vessels.

The Royal Navy's interest in spar torpedoes was limited, consideration being given primarily to their use in smaller vessels such as steam pinnaces, up to 50ft in length. Some of the early first-class torpedo boats (*TB2–12*) were used for trials of spar torpedoes and some boats supplied to the colonies were designed to carry spar torpedoes initially, frequently being replaced by dropping gear for Whitehead torpedoes after a few years' service.

Typically, the pinnace would be supplied with six spars of 42ft in length and 6in, tapering to 5in at the forward end, in diameter. Two iron bars, pivoted at the lower end and joined by a cross roller at the top with a second roller a few inches below, were positioned about 6ft aft of the pinnace's stem, and a similar frame with two rollers was fitted on the stem. The torpedo proper, comprising two iron canisters filled with 16½lbs of wet gun-cotton and a 2½lb dry gun-cotton primer, was then fitted to the end of the spar.

The spar was laid fore-and-aft with the foremost end raised on the framework. To deploy the torpedo, a purchase at the aft end of the spar moved it forward until its weight tipped it downwards. The pressure of the water would ensure the torpedo remained pointing downwards, the explosive being positioned at a depth of at least 10ft below the surface and about 33ft, horizontally, from the pinnace when fully run out. Because of the great pressure on the spar, the approach to the target was made slowly and when contact was made between the torpedo and the hull of the target, the pinnace's engines were put full speed astern and the firing key pressed.

If a swifter approach was to be made to the target, then a 'swinging' outrigger would be used. In this, a long spar would be pivoted on the deck right aft. The attacking vessel would need to pass within about 40ft of the target and the head of the spar slipped overboard. The water would swing the torpedo aft into contact with the enemy's hull and the torpedo fired.

The torpedo boats *Acheron* and *Avernus* were built for the defence of New South Wales, Australia, at a time of heightened tension between Great Britain and Russia. Tenders for the two boats closed on 17 January 1878, with £8,784 allotted for building. The Atlas Works, located at

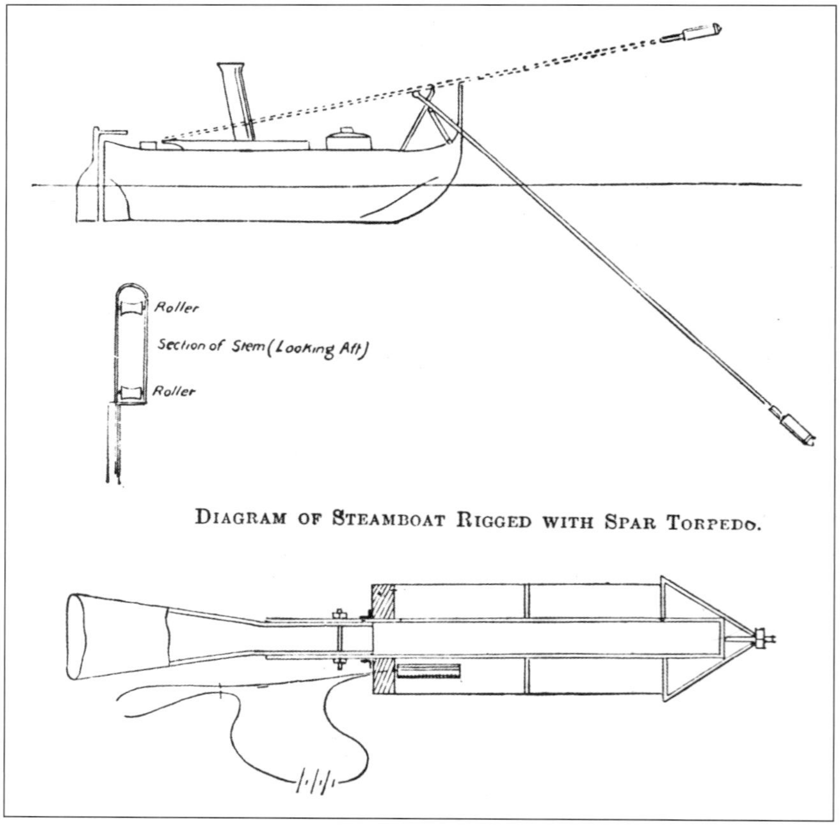

Deployment of a spar torpedo from a steam pinnace, and details of the torpedo. *(Torpedoes and Torpedo Vessels)*

A launch with a spar torpedo ready to be deployed. *(Navy & Army Illustrated)*

The explosion of a spar torpedo with the launch at a safe distance. *(Navy & Army Illustrated)*

Pyrmont in Sydney Harbour, was chosen as the successful tenderer, with completion of both vessels scheduled for March 1879. *Acheron*, the first to be launched, conducted her first trials around Sydney Harbour on 1 March 1879, the trip proving most successful. Another trial was conducted in early April; no alteration whatever had been made in the vessel since she left the slip, but the engineers were somewhat more acquainted with their work. After passing Fort Macquarie the order 'full speed' was given, and the measured mile between Pinchgut and Bradley's Head was run in four minutes and thirty-six seconds. This was not satisfactory. Twice the engines had to be lowered, owing to some oversight below, and the vessel was fetched back. In the next trial the engineers were better prepared, and she did the mile in a trifle under four minutes thirteen seconds. This was the quickest run in Australia. With a speed of seventeen miles an hour, the trial was considered very satisfactory.

Acheron was divided into ten watertight compartments:

1. the first, enclosed by a collision bulkhead bore the torpedo spar,
2. a fore cabin,
3. a small stores compartment,
4. the steering compartment,
5. torpedo compartment,
6. the boiler room,
7. the engine room,
8. the after cabin with space for twelve people,
9. two separate divisions before the stern.

The boats could be steered from the stern, or from a small sunken position directly forward of the funnel. A bulletproof steel visor protected the helmsman in the sunken position, who also had the duty of launching the torpedoes. The vessels were designed as 82ft 6in long overall, with a

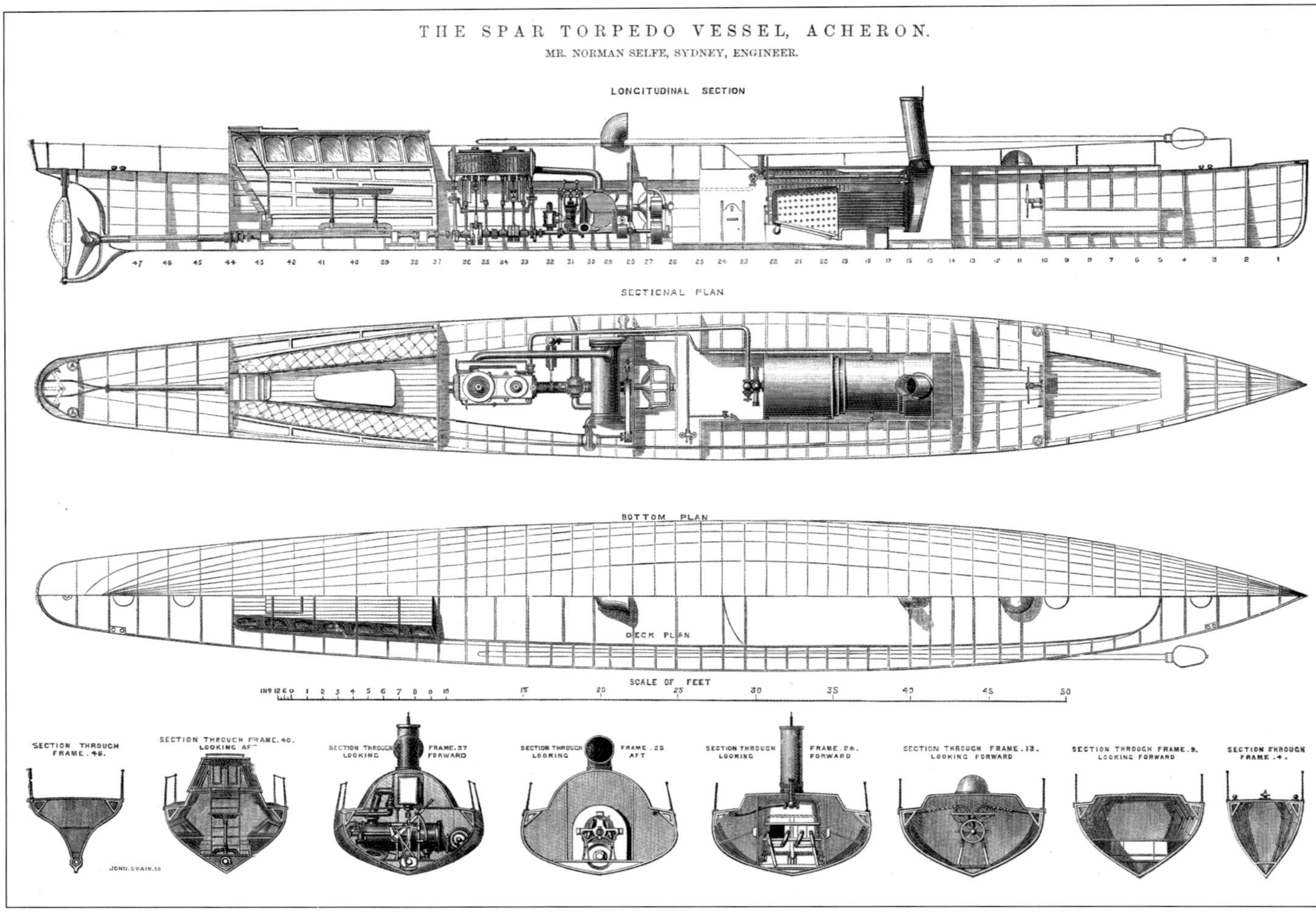

The spar torpedo vessel *Acheron. (The Engineer, 23 May 1879)*

10ft 6in beam. They were fitted with engines with cylinders 11in and 19in diameter, and 14in stroke. These engines were fitted with a surface condenser of copper, intended to run at about 350 revolutions per minute. The vessels carried 4 tons of coal.

The torpedo was to be deployed using the outrigger method, the spar being 62ft long. With a 62ft-long torpedo spar, about 45ft of the weapon would protrude over the bow, the remaining 17ft on the boat designed to keep the weapon steady. Orders to fire the explosive into the side of the intruding warship and go astern were to be given simultaneously to avoid damage

The spar torpedo vessel *Avernus. (Australian War Memorial)*

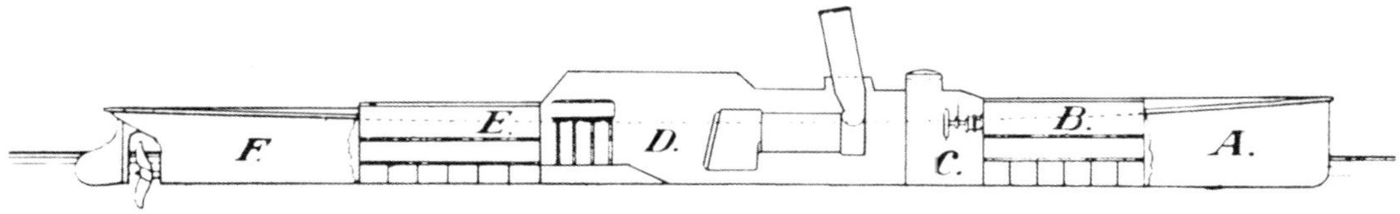

A profile of *Rap*.

to *Acheron*. Within a few years of introduction into service, the two torpedo boats were converted to carry the more modern 14in torpedoes, launched from cradles mounted along the port and starboard sides, about halfway along the vessels' length. Trials were carried out with the new weapons on 9 May 1885, after both boats had been modified in Morts Dock in Sydney.

Despite the Royal Navy not building vessels specifically for spar torpedoes, two shipbuilding companies that would subsequently become intimately involved in the design, development and construction of torpedo boats for the Whitehead torpedo, Thornycroft and Yarrow, did build such vessels for overseas governments. At that time, both companies were based on the River Thames, J I Thornycroft at Church Wharf, Chiswick, and A F Yarrow at Folly Wall on the Isle of Dogs in Poplar. Both companies had good reputations for building fast launches.

The first torpedo boat built by Thornycroft was Yard No. 23, launched in 1874 as *Rap* (or *Quick*) for the Norwegian government. At 58ft LOA (length overall), she managed a speed of 14.47 knots, one of the fastest boats afloat at the time. *Rap* was briefly used for experiments with the Harvey towed torpedo before two 50ft spars were fitted, finally being outfitted with launch racks or frames for Whitehead torpedoes in 1879. As first built, the propeller was fitted behind the rudder, but subsequently the stern was rebuilt and the rudder sited aft of the propeller. The vessel is now on display at the Norwegian Naval Museum at Horten.

Thornycroft also built spar torpedo boats for Sweden (Yard No. 29, 58ft LOA, 18kts, 1874), Austria (Yard No. 32, 67ft LOA, 18.32kts, 1874), Denmark (Yard No. 33, 58ft LOA, 15.13kts, 1874), France (Yard Nos 43 and 44, 67ft LOA, 18kts, 1875), The Netherlands (Yard No. 48, 76ft 6in LOA, 18kts, 1876), Italy (Yard No. 60, 76ft LOA, 18.27kts, 1877), Argentina (Yard Nos 114 and 115, 62ft 10in LOA, 17.16kts, 1881) and Brazil (Yard Nos 184–188, 45ft LOA, 12.8kts, 1883).

Argentine second-class spar torpedo boat, built by Thornycroft in 1880. *(US Naval History and Heritage Command, NH60527)*

THE FIRST TORPEDO BOAT

In a paper read before the United Services Institute on 11 May 1877 by Mr John Donaldson, he described *Rap* as follows:

The first Government to recognise the great advance made by Mr Thornycroft in the speed of small boats was the Norwegian, which, in 1873, gave my firm an order for our first torpedo boat. This boat was 57ft in length by 7ft 6in beam, drew 3ft of water, and the stipulated speed was 16 English statute miles, or nearly 14 knots per hour, which speed was not to be ascertained by a mere measured mile trial, but was to be 16 miles through the water in a run of one hour's duration. The hull of the vessel was constructed entirely of steel plates and angle-bars and was divided into six water-tight compartments. The compartments in the stem and stern were for stores; two others were fitted with seats for the crew, and were provided with movable steel covers; so that on going into action, or during rough weather, they might be completely covered. The two remaining compartments are for the steersman and the machinery respectively, and were covered completely by steel plating 3⁄16in in thickness – a thickness which has been found sufficient to withstand Snider or Martini-Henry bullets, fired from a distance of twenty paces. One compartment was furnished with a hood, having slits ¼in wide all round, through which the steersman could see with sufficient distinctness to direct his course easily. Motion was communicated from the wheel to the tiller by means of steel wire ropes, which it was originally intended should be encased in wrought iron tubes. The possibility, however, of these tubes being bent by a shot, and so jamming the wire ropes, led to this arrangement being abandoned, and the ropes were simply run through eyes at intervals along the side. The engines were compound, of the usual inverted double cylinder direct-acting type, capable of developing about ninety indicated horse-power, and were fitted with a surface condenser, so that the vessel could run in salt water, without danger of injuring her boiler. A small tank contained a supply of fresh water, to make good deficiencies arising from leakage, and from steam escaping at the safety valves, &c. The circulating, air, and feed pumps were driven by a separate engine, as we feared at that time that it would be impossible to run them at the same speed as the main engines. The boiler was of the locomotive type, the shell being made of Bessemer steel; the fire-box, and its stays of copper, and the tubes of solid drawn brass. The armament was not supplied by us, but I have reason to believe that it consisted of a cylindro-conical shaped torpedo towed from the top of the funnel, round which a ring was fitted with two pulleys for the towing ropes; the strain being taken off by means of two stays attached forward. The length of this torpedo was 13ft, and the diameter 9in, and with a speed of 11 knots, it has diverged to about 40 degrees from the direction of the boat's motion when running in smooth water. The torpedo is worked by means of a small winch and brake fixed on the after part of the engine-room skylight; davits are provided for dropping the torpedo overboard.

On the official trial, which took place on the Thames on 17 October 1873, the number of revolutions done in the hour was found to be 27,177, and the number required to do a mile in still water was 1,578. The distance run in the hour was, then, $^{27,177}/_{1578} = 17.22$, or very nearly 17¼ miles. The steam pressure during the trial averaged 85lb per square inch, and the vacuum 25½in.

Later, three vessels were built for Australia (Yard Nos 189 190 and 193, 62ft 10in LOA, 17.59kts, 1884) and one for Tasmania (Yard No. 191, 62ft 10in LOA, 17.21kts, 1884).

The risk of damage to a spar torpedo boat when its own torpedo exploded at short range, not surprisingly, caused considerable concern, and so the French undertook a trial with one of the Thornycroft vessels engaging the obsolete *Bayonnaise*. A somewhat colourful account of the experiment appeared in *The Times* of 13 March 1877:

> The whole squadron watched this last phase of the struggle with breathless interest and people asked themselves whether the shock of the torpedo would not infallibly destroy the little vessel which bore it. The Thornycroft put on a last spurt and struck the *Bayonnaise* with its whole force on the starboard bow. The sea was terribly agitated, a deafening report was heard and the *Bayonnaise*, with a rent as big as a house, sank with wonderful rapidity. As for the Thornycroft, rebounding by the shock about fifteen metres off, even before the explosion occurred, it went round and round for a few moments and quietly resumed the direction of the squadron.

Yarrow first mounted a spar torpedo on a fast launch in 1873, and in 1877 he received a contract from the Russian government for working drawings of a torpedo boat, 75ft in length, 10ft beam, to be built in Russia, together with up to a hundred sets of machinery, but only four sets were actually provided. The majority of these boats were originally armed with spar torpedoes. In 1878 Yarrow also built two slightly larger, double-funnel torpedo boats for Russia, but these were taken over by the Royal Navy, despite the Russian crew already being in Great Britain, preparing to sail them to the Black Sea. The two boats were originally offered to the Admiralty at the same price as was to be paid by

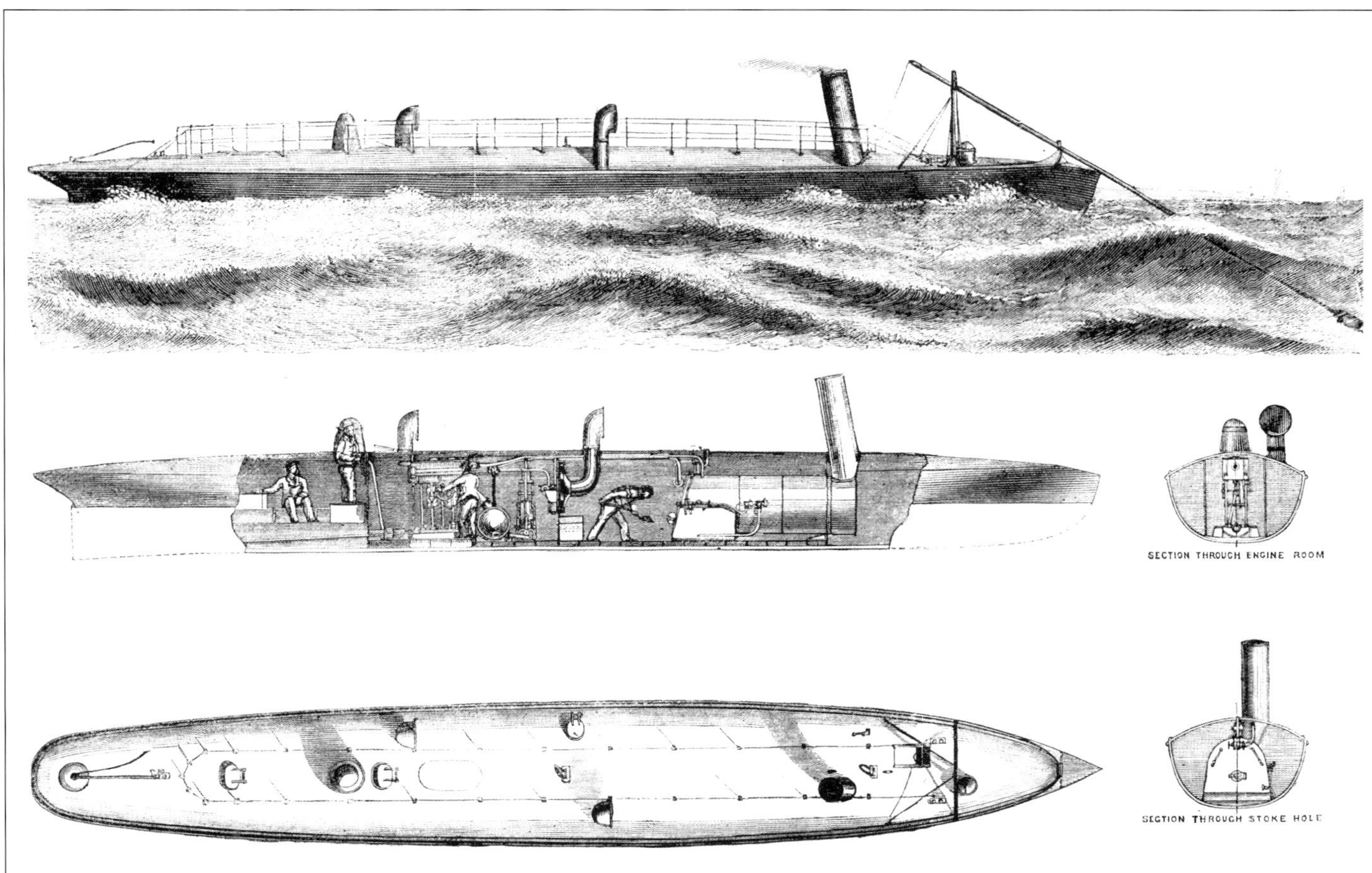

The Yarrow-designed torpedo boat, of which 100 were built in St Petersburg. *(The Graphic, 13 April 1878)*

the Russians. This was considered too high and so Yarrow offered them at the same price as the Admiralty were paying Thornycroft for similar vessels. The Admiralty accepted the proposal, but included penalties if the trials speed was below 18 knots. Yarrow agreed, provided the Admiralty paid a similar premium for a speed in excess of 18 knots. On trials the boats made 20.8 and 20.6 knots, resulting in the Admiralty paying more than the original Russian contract price!

Subsequently, the Admiralty requested the two boats take part in the 1878 Naval Review for Queen Victoria at Spithead, and the boats sailed from Poplar with both Mr and Mrs Yarrow on board. The weather was foul and so Mrs Yarrow could not leave the boat at Gravesend as planned, but remained onboard all the way to Portsmouth, the weather generally getting worse rather than better. On the day of the review, despite the 'boisterous' weather, the two boats sailed from Portsmouth to Cowes and escorted the Royal Yacht from Osborne and during the review – a serious breach of etiquette! The performance of the two boats so impressed the Prince of Wales, later to become King Edward VII, that later in the month he arranged to take a trip onboard.

The boats built in Russia experienced problems with leaking boilers when using forced draught. As in numerous other vessels, the union between the boiler tubes and plates was unable to stand the increased pressure, resulting in leaks that would often scald the stokers. Yarrow developed and patented a solution in which a light air valve was fitted between the stokehold and the fire. Air could pass easily from the stokehold to the fire, but shut off movement in the other direction, as occurred when there was a leak. This safety feature was fitted in the two boats sold to the Royal Navy, and in all subsequent boats. It was not until 1880 that the first Yarrow boat actually to reach Russia, *Batum*, was launched, by which time she was fitted with tubes for Whitehead torpedoes.

Others of Yarrow's customers included Argentina (55ft LOA, 12 5kts, 1875), Spain (33ft LOA, 15kts, 1879), Brazil (63ft LOA, 20.4kts, 1884) and Greece (100ft LOA, 19.5kts, 1881).

During the American Civil War, the use of the spar torpedo was entirely confined to those which fired mechanically, but in the Royal Navy the electrical method was adopted. It soon became evident, however, that it was very desirable that, in case of the latter missing fire by any means, as might happen if the vessel attacked were struck under the counter, that the operator should have the power of firing the torpedo at will. Such a method was invented by Captain McEvoy, of the London Ordnance Works, and called by him the duplex system.

The McEvoy torpedo was a bullet-shaped iron canister, filled with 37lbs of wet gun-cotton with a further 2½lbs of dry gun-cotton packed around an electrically activated detonator that was connected by a line running back inside the hollow spar to a battery in the conning tower. As the torpedo boat closed her target, the spar would be run out, the weight of the torpedo causing it to drop into the water until it was at least 10ft below the surface and at least 33ft in front of the boat. When the torpedo was in contact with the enemy vessel's side below the waterline, the torpedo boat's engines would be thrown into reverse and the torpedo detonated.

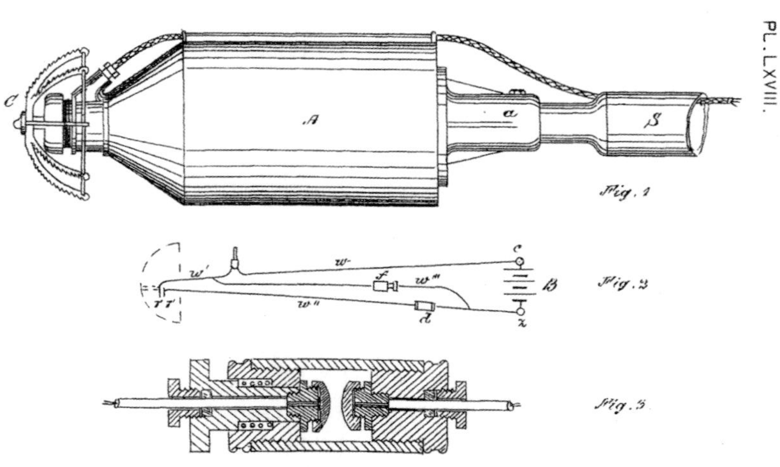

The McEvoy spar torpedo.

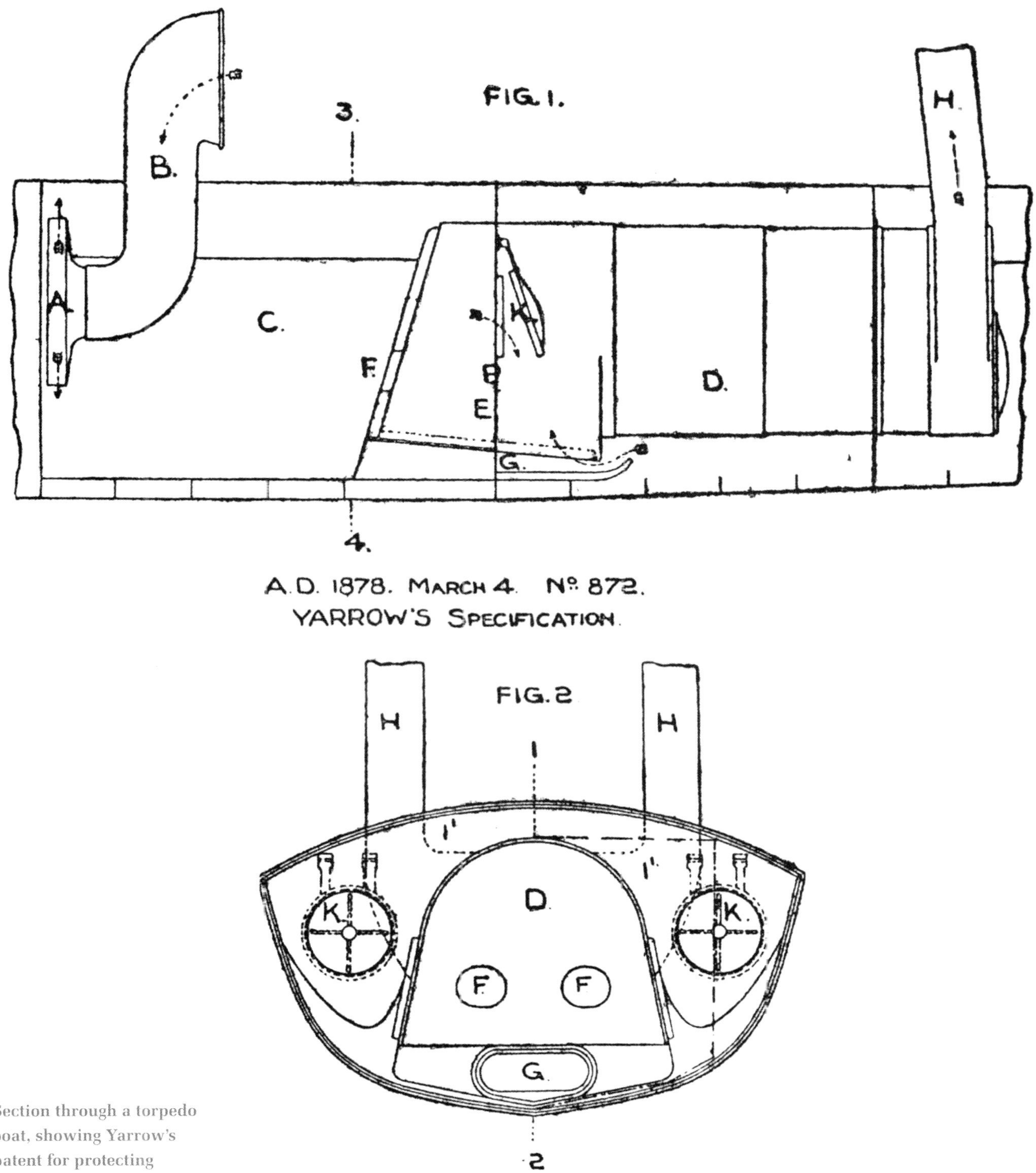

Section through a torpedo boat, showing Yarrow's patent for protecting stokers. *(Alfred Yarrow, His Life and Work)*

Russian torpedo boat *Batum*, built by Yarrow in 1880: note the folding stacks, *Steam Launches and Torpedo Boats by Yarrow & Company*, trade catalogue, published about 1888. *(US Naval History and Heritage Command, NH70400)*

First-class torpedo boat, built for the Spanish government. Note the spar torpedo at bow and torpedo dropping apparatus on each side. *(US Naval History and Heritage Command, NH70398)*

One of six improved first-class torpedo boats built for Greece by Yarrow in 1881, fitted with Whitehead and spar torpedoes. *(US Naval History and Heritage Command, NH70404)*

CHAPTER TWO

LAUNCHING THE WHITEHEAD TORPEDO

The introduction of the self-propelled torpedo, in particular the Whitehead torpedo with its rapid development, required a number of changes in the warships deploying them: first, the installation of equipment by which the torpedoes could be deployed, and secondly, the introduction of new types of warship, which required significant developments, both in terms of naval architecture and in propulsion machinery.

Robert Whitehead's involvement with torpedoes started in 1864 when, at Fiume, he was approached by Captain Giovanni de Luppis of the Austrian navy, who was developing an idea to control a spar torpedo boat remotely. Whitehead had been born in Bolton, Lancashire, in January 1823 and was apprenticed to a Manchester engineering company aged sixteen. After working in France as a marine engineer, in 1856 he had become chief engineer of an engineering company that built warships for the Austro-Hungarian empire. After lengthy consideration and some experimentation, he thought Luppis' idea not to be practical and, shortly after ending his arrangements with Luppis, Whitehead began to develop his own underwater explosive weapon. He worked only with his son, John, just twelve years old, and one trusted workman in order to maintain complete secrecy. The first model was tested in 1866 and was just over 11ft long and 14in in diameter.

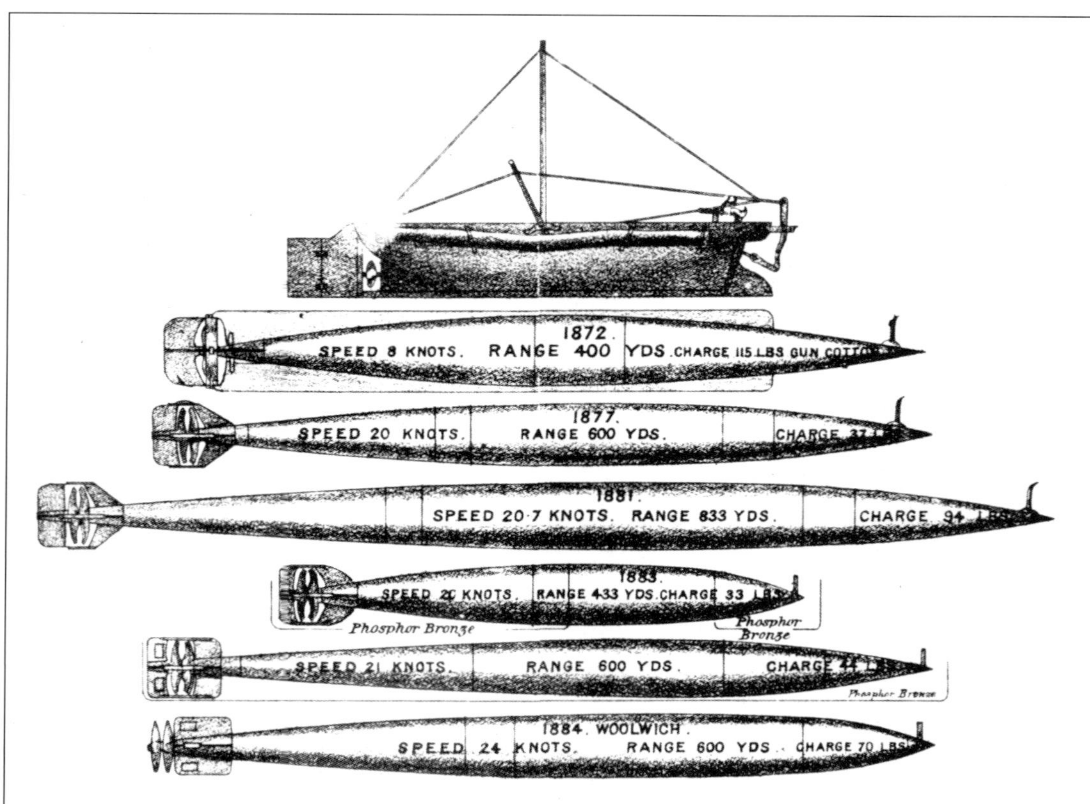

The original idea for a locomotive torpedo and its early development. *(US Naval History and Heritage Command, NH84470)*

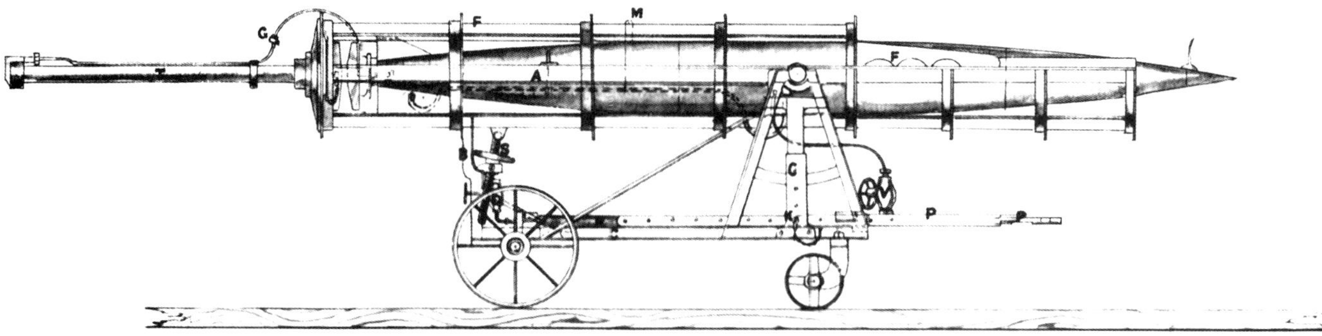

Apparatus for discharging the 16in or 14in RL torpedo from above water. *(Torpedo Manual, vol III, 1881)*

The trial was not a complete success, the compressed-air, two-cylinder engine driving a two-bladed propeller giving a speed of just 6.5 knots for 200yds, and the depth-keeping being compared to the actions of a dolphin. Nevertheless, improvements were swiftly made in speed, range and depth-keeping and the later introduction (1896) of gyros greatly enhanced azimuth control.

In 1869 the Admiralty instructed the commander-in-chief in the Mediterranean to appoint a committee to evaluate this new weapon. Following the committee's assessment, Whitehead was requested to bring two torpedoes to England. He came to England in August 1870 with two torpedoes, one 14ft long with a maximum diameter of 16in and the other 13ft 10½in long with a maximum diameter of 14in. They contained 67lbs of gun-cotton and 18lbs of dynamite explosives, respectively. Trials were carried out onboard the iron paddle-wheel sloop *Oberon* using a submerged torpedo tube in her bow, the outer end of the tube being closed with a sluice valve and bow cap to allow for reloading. The torpedoes were ejected by means of an impulse rod worked by compressed air. A framework was also fitted rigidly in line with the keel and about 3ft below the keel. Firing was effected by means of two levers worked by lines from the gunwale.

The Admiralty decided to purchase both the torpedo's 'secret' and manufacturing rights and in 1871 paid Whitehead £15,000. Manufacture of 16in torpedoes began at the Royal Laboratory in Woolwich the next year and a submerged tube, fitted to the broadside of the wooden corvette *Actaeon*, was used for trials. The torpedo was launched by means of a piston, operated by compressed air. Later an improved submerged tube was fitted to the turret ship *Glatton*. Torpedoes were initially housed in the tubes by a single T-piece side suspension but this was superseded by 'hook brackets' in 1889.

From March 1875 trials were undertaken to launch torpedoes from above water, the first being the positioning of a table, inclined at about 20°, inside one of *Actaeon*'s ports. The torpedo was then simply slid off into the water. A boat's frame was fixed in a main deck port of the iron frigate HMS *Shah*, in order to experiment further with above-water launching, and, as a result of these trials, the first above-water tubes for 16in torpedoes were made. These tubes included an 'underlip'.

One significant improvement quickly introduced by the Royal Laboratory was the use of contra-rotating propellers which countered the propeller's torque, hence reducing the tendency of the torpedo to veer off-line.

The first Royal Navy vessel to be fitted with

Above: *Glatton*.

Opposite above: *Inflexible*.

Opposite below: *Devastation*.

torpedo tubes was the masted turret ship *Inflexible*, completed in 1881, which received two submerged tubes for 14in torpedoes and two torpedo carriages, for above water launches. Prior to this, in 1879, *Devastation* was supplied with a steam cutter fitted with torpedo dropping gear. Two years later, her sister-ship *Thunderer* also received a steam cutter. Both ships also had a port cut in their breastwork armour, port and starboard, so as to be able to use torpedo carriages.

The Dreadnought Project describes torpedo carriages as 'trainable torpedo tubes on a circular rack-and-pinion system'. It also states that the Royal Navy developed a number of different models – Marks I, II, II converted, III, IV, IV$_A$, IV$_B$, IV$_C$, V, V$_A$, V$_B$, V$_C$, VI and VI$_A$, but gives no further details. Apart from a brief reference to 'improvements' being incorporated in the Mark V and VI torpedo carriages in the third annual report (1882) from HMS *Vernon*, this term appears to have only been used for a short time and applied to upper deck installations only. Below-deck installations were referred to as torpedo tubes, and this was soon adopted for all installations.

The twenty-one second-class cruisers of the *Apollo* class (launched 1890/91) each had four 14in tubes. There was one in the bow at upper deck level, two Mark V$_{D2}$, also on the upper deck abreast the mainmast, capable of firing from 70° before the beam to 10° abaft the beam, elevation from +4° to –6°, and one at the stern at main deck level. The beam tubes each weighed 1 ton 16cwt 3qtrs 23lbs and were mounted with a 2ft 1in diameter ball and socket joint at the ship's side. The two third-class cruisers of the *Barham* class

The torpedo room of HMS *Inflexible*. (*Harper's Weekly*, 26 November 1881)

(launched 1889/90) each had two Mark VII_B broadside tubes, each weighing 1 ton 5cwt 2qtrs 19lbs. These were not capable of training, but had elevation of from 0° to –6° with a canvas diaphragm. The eleven third-class cruisers of the *Pelorus* class (launched 1896–1900) were fitted with the same mark of torpedo tube (although 5cwt lighter), but which could train from 15° to 30° before the beam.

There were thirteen vessels in the *Sharpshooter* class of torpedo gunboats (launched 1888–90) and these were fitted with five 14in tubes, one in the bow and a paired Mark VII_B mounting on each beam. Each pair were on a central pivot, weighed 1 ton 14cwt 1qtr 19lbs, could train from 50° ahead to 50° abaft the beam, elevation from 0° to –6°, and were fixed 5° apart.

Mark V_{D2} and VII_B tubes were also constructed for 18in torpedoes. The Mark V_{D2} was fitted to the eight second-class cruisers of the *Astrea* class (launched 1892/3) in an arrangement similar to that of the *Apollo* class, but with training from 65° before to 15° abaft the beam, elevation +4° to –1°. They weighed 2 tons 15cwt 3qtrs, and had a 2ft 6in diameter ball at the ship's side. The majority of the *Alarm* class of torpedo gunboats (launched 1892/3) received the same arrangement of 14in VII_B tubes as the *Sharpshooter* class, but HM Ships *Speedy*, *Jason*, *Niger*, *Jaseur* and *Onyx* received single 18in VII_B tubes instead of the paired 14in tubes. The training and elevation ranges were the same as that of the paired tubes and they each weighed 1 ton 16cwt 3qtrs. The five torpedo gunboats of the *Halcyon* class (also launched 1892/3), received five 18in tubes, the paired Mark VII_B tubes having the same range of movement as the single tubes of the *Alarm* class, and weighing 3 tons 8cwt 2qtrs 14lbs.

In 1896 there were no less than sixteen different patterns of 14in above-water tubes and three different patterns of 18in tubes in use in the Royal Navy. A similar system, the Canet system, was used by the French.

The General Engine and Boiler Company, London, manufactured 'impulse tubes' which, if fitted in a similar installation as used in American battleships, would appear to match the brief description. These were manufactured to accommodate torpedoes of the usual size, 14in diameter (the manufacture of 14in torpedoes at Woolwich began in 1877) and about 15ft long, and weighed about 6cwt. Before the torpedo was launched, the tube's air reservoir was charged with air at 1,200lbs or 1,500lbs pressure. The air reservoir was placed underneath and connected to the tube in such a way that by pressing a small pin a valve was opened, admitting the air from the reservoir behind the torpedo. The firing of the torpedo was effected by hand, either by a person standing at the impulse tube, or by an electric current brought into action by pressing a button in the conning tower.

Both the submerged and internal above-water tubes fitted to battleships and cruisers, designed by Arthur Knyvet Wilson (an officer who would have a close association with HMS *Vernon*), were of very similar design, the main difference being the outer cap on the end of the submerged tube to stop water entering. The torpedoes were a snug fit in the tubes, where the torpedo's side lugs rested on narrow ledges, launching being either by compressed air (300–600psi, pounds per square inch) or by a small explosive charge (4–6½oz of powder).

The main requirement for an above-water, broadside tube was to launch the torpedo such that it struck the water, either horizontally or at a slight angle, beyond the disturbed water due to the movement of the launching vessel and so minimised the deviation of the torpedo run.

Early in 1898 Sir William Armstrong published a description of an 'improved' submerged torpedo tube, developed by Whitworth & Co, and initially fitted and trialled on *Fuji* and *Yashima*, two

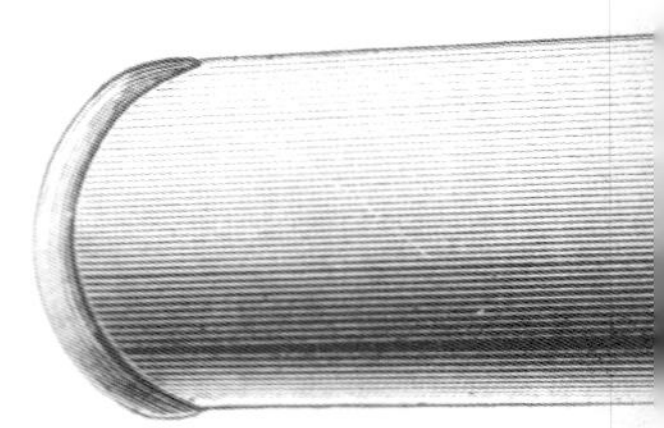

The impulse tube made by the General Engine and Boiler Company. *(The Engineer, 1 March 1889)*

ironclads being constructed by Whitworths for the Japanese. At that time, the Royal Navy submerged tube required three actions for each torpedo fired: the bar or shield was run out; the torpedo ejected; the bar withdrawn. The Elswick design was to combine all three motions, and development commenced with the construction of a quarter-size model and a water tank.

If the bar or shield (referred to as a spoon in the Elswick design) were to be ejected at the same time as the torpedo, but the shield was to be retarded and the torpedo not, then the torpedo guides would leave the grooves in the shield before it was fully deployed, risking damage to or deflection of the torpedo. Automating these two sequential motions required just a single action by the operator, hence removing (or at least substantially reducing) the risk. Cordite discharge was as used in Elswick's above-water tubes, was preferred to compressed air.

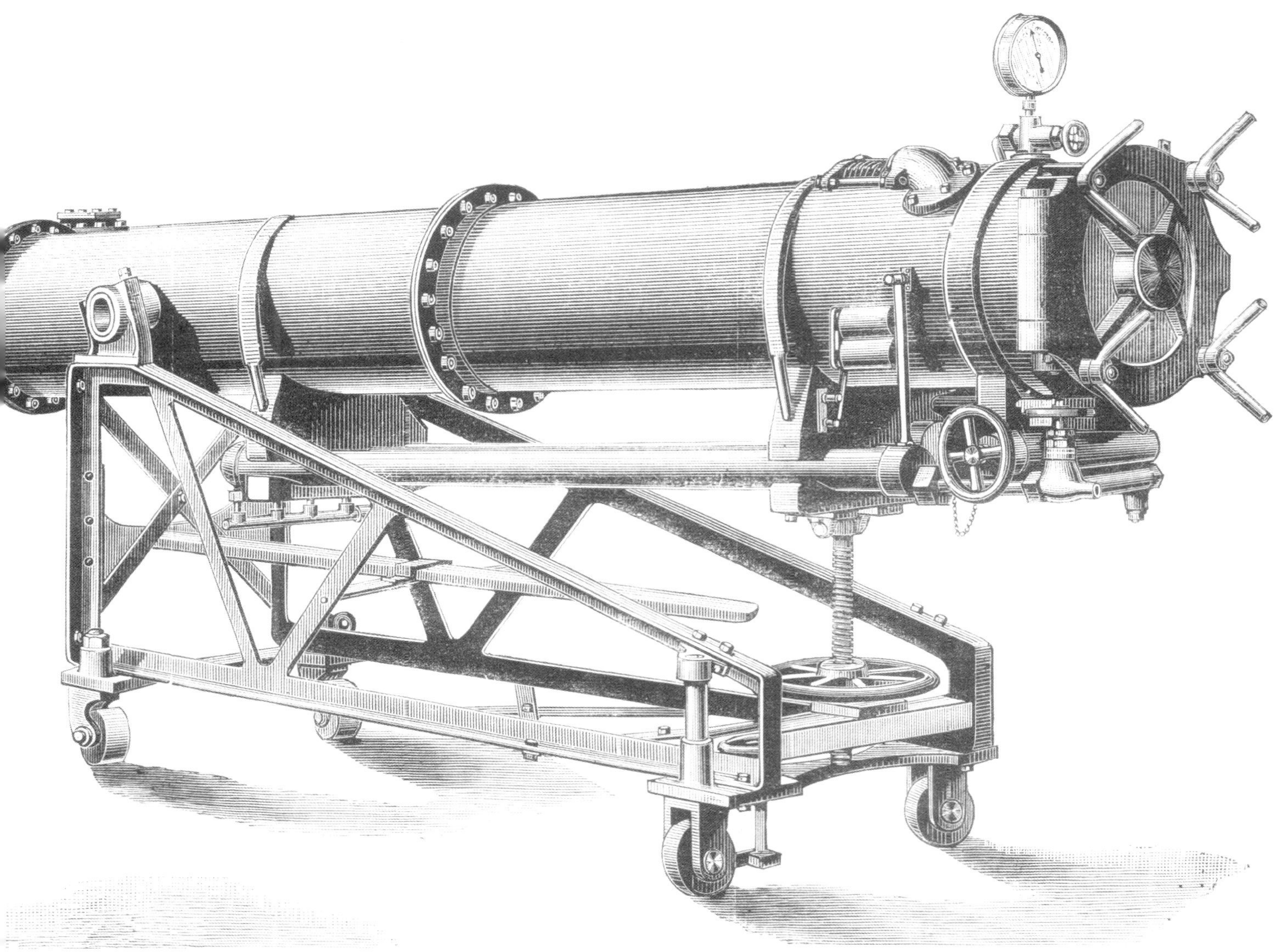

THE ELSWICK TORPEDO TUBE

The Elswick submerged torpedo tube consists of three principal parts, the outer or fixed tube A, the inner or movable tube B, and the sluice valve C. The inner tube is made in two parts, known respectively as the spoon and rear end, which are firmly bolted together – indeed, they are only separated for manufacturing purposes. The spoon is made of a special alloy of copper known as Elswick bronze, which is peculiar for strength. The rear end is made of gun-metal. When joined together the grooves for carrying and supporting the torpedo run from one end of the rear end to the other end of the spoon. The rear end is a simple cylinder in shape; it is fitted with a door at one end; this door carries the axial valve D, through which the gases pass to eject the torpedo. The spoon or shield S resembles a half cylinder, and is of such a length that the torpedo guides clear the grooves and the tail clears the sluice valve at the same moment. It is made with orifices in it wherever strength will permit, the object of these orifices being to allow water to pass through on to the torpedo, and so help to balance the pressure exerted on the head when the torpedo is being ejected with the ship steaming. The orifices also help to lighten the spoon. The outer tube is in four parts, the front outer tube A^1, the gland box G, the rear outer tube A^2, and the explosion chamber F. The front outer tube is a steel cylinder fitted with flanges at the ends; one flange bolts on to the sluice valve casing, the other to the gland box. Inside, the front outer tube has brass guides and rollers on which the inner tube travels, and outside this tube are fitted drain cocks and pipes for emptying the tube when the sluice valve is closed, also air cocks to let air escape when filling. The gland box carries the gland ring and the mechanism for externally adjusting the gland which packs the rear end of the inner tube. The rear outer tube, made of steel, is fitted at its rear end with a door known as the outer door H, in distinction to the door on the inner tube, which is known as the inner door. Like the front outer tube, the rear outer tube is fitted with guides and rollers R R R to take the inner tube. It also carries inside it the hand running-in-and-out gear, and the cam plate for regulating the axial valve D. The explosion chamber E, for use with cordite impulse, is carried on the top of the rear outer tube, a large connecting pipe being provided to convey the gases produced by the explosion of cordite into the rear outer tube.

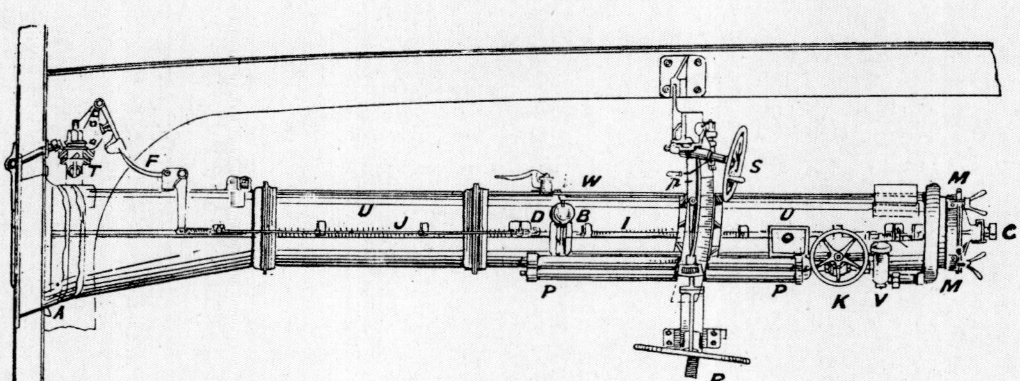

A broadside Mark VII B torpedo tube. *(Torpedoes and Torpedo Vessels)*

Key: *UU* is the tube itself working on the pivot *T*; *S* is the revolving handle which actuates the training gear. The bracket *P* acts as a carriage or supporter for the tube, which is elevated by the screw handle *R*, the amount of elevation being recorded on a graduated arc on the carriage; *w* is the 'tripper' for the torpedo. *PP* is the firing reservoir for the compressed air, and *o* is the box containing the contact maker. The little wheel *K* works the 'standby' valve for the air; *V* is the firing valve, which is worked by the firing rod *I*, which again in its turn is actuated by the magnetic firing gear at *B*. To prevent the torpedo being fired before the opening is free, an automatic locking lever *F* is connected up to a locking rod *J*, which, by means of a clutch *D*, prevents the firing rod *I* turning and discharging the torpedo. When the opening is free, the lever *F* moves so as to cause the rod *J* to move away from and unclutch the firing rod, thus leaving it free to turn, and fire the torpedo. *A* is the canvas diaphragm protecting the opening, and *C* is the pocket where the impulse charge of powder rests. *MM* is the door of the tube.

The torpedo is fired as follows: when the circuit through the wires leading to the conning tower is completed by the officer in charge, the electro magnet at *B* is put into action, and releases the heavy ball *Z*, which falls down, and in doing so turns round the firing rod *I*. The standby valve having been previously opened, the air is thereupon suddenly released from the reservoir, passes through the firing valve at *V*, and exerts its pressure in the rear end of the tube with the result that the torpedo is blown out. When using powder only the torpedo is simply ejected by the explosion of the impulse charge in the pocket *C*. The cartridges containing these charges are made in two sizes, namely, 4 and 4½oz of pebble powder, and are closed at the bottom by a varnished cardboard disc. A wireless brass electric tube containing priming composition is inserted in the centre of the cartridge case. The cartridge is fired by the fusing by electricity of a platinum wire bridge inserted in the priming charge. The cartridge is entered from the outside of the door, and is kept in its place by a hinged flap.

The cartridge is placed in the chamber t^1, which is dosed, and fired by suitable mechanism. To moderate the rush of gas resulting when the charge of cordite or other explosive is ignited, the gas is checked and baffled by being made to pass through perforations in a plate and to flow in a circuitous course. The annular space within the casing serves as an expansion chamber for the gases, and the gases when in this chamber exert a pressure in rear of the inner tube and drive it forward. If air impulse be required a reservoir of tubes is placed on the top of the rear outer tube, and the air inlet valve is fitted between the reservoir and the connecting pipe. The sluice valve is worked by the usual screwed shaft. An indicator shows the position of the valve, and an electrical safety arrangement makes it impossible to fire the torpedo unless the valve be properly opened.

The submerged torpedo tube is worked as follows: the sluice valve being closed, the inner tube of course being right in both inner and outer doors, on the rear ends of the inner and outer tubes, are opened. The torpedo is pushed into the inner tube until the guide on the torpedo takes against the stop in the tube. The air lever will be just behind the position of the air tripper. The inner door is then closed and made watertight by means of the clamps. The act of shutting this door puts the air tripper into position for engaging the air lever directly the torpedo starts in the inner tube. As soon as the inner door is closed the sluice valve may be opened, and while this is being done the outer door should be closed and secured. The cartridge with cordite charge may be placed in the explosion chamber directly the sluice valve is open. Lastly, the cartridge chamber door is closed, and all is in readiness for firing.

The electric firing circuit is arranged so that each cartridge is automatically tested directly it is placed in the chamber. Automatic indications are also given in the conning tower to show (1) when the sluice valve is opened, (2) when all is in readiness for firing. When the firing key is pressed the cordite charge will explode or the compressed air will be released with a consequent pressure in the rear outer tube, which, as already explained, acting on the rear end of the inner tube, forces it out with the spoon. As the axial valve is closed during the first part of the motion of the inner tube the gas pressure cannot act directly on the torpedo; the latter, therefore, just moves forward as an integral part of the inner tube. After the inner tube has moved forward a short distance the axial valve is allowed to open a little, thus gas passes through and starts the torpedo in relation to the inner tube. When the latter is nearly out in its extreme position, the axial valve is opened fully, the gases – very much reduced in pressure on account of the expansion which has taken place – pass through and eject the torpedo. A reaction then takes place. If cordite impulse has been used the gases cool rapidly, and the pressure in rear of the inner tube becomes reduced. The pressure due to the head of water, therefore, is unbalanced, and forces the tube in again. When air impulse is used the tube will remain out until a small valve, supplied for the purpose, is opened to allow the pressure to escape. If for any reason the tube does not automatically return – experience has shown that this contingency is very rare indeed – it is not the work of a minute to throw the hand gear into action, and the tube can then be drawn in. Arrangements are made to control the pressure in rear of the tube so that it shall come to rest gently. As soon as the tube is in, the sluice valve should be closed and the drains opened. The tube is then emptied, after which it is ready for another torpedo.

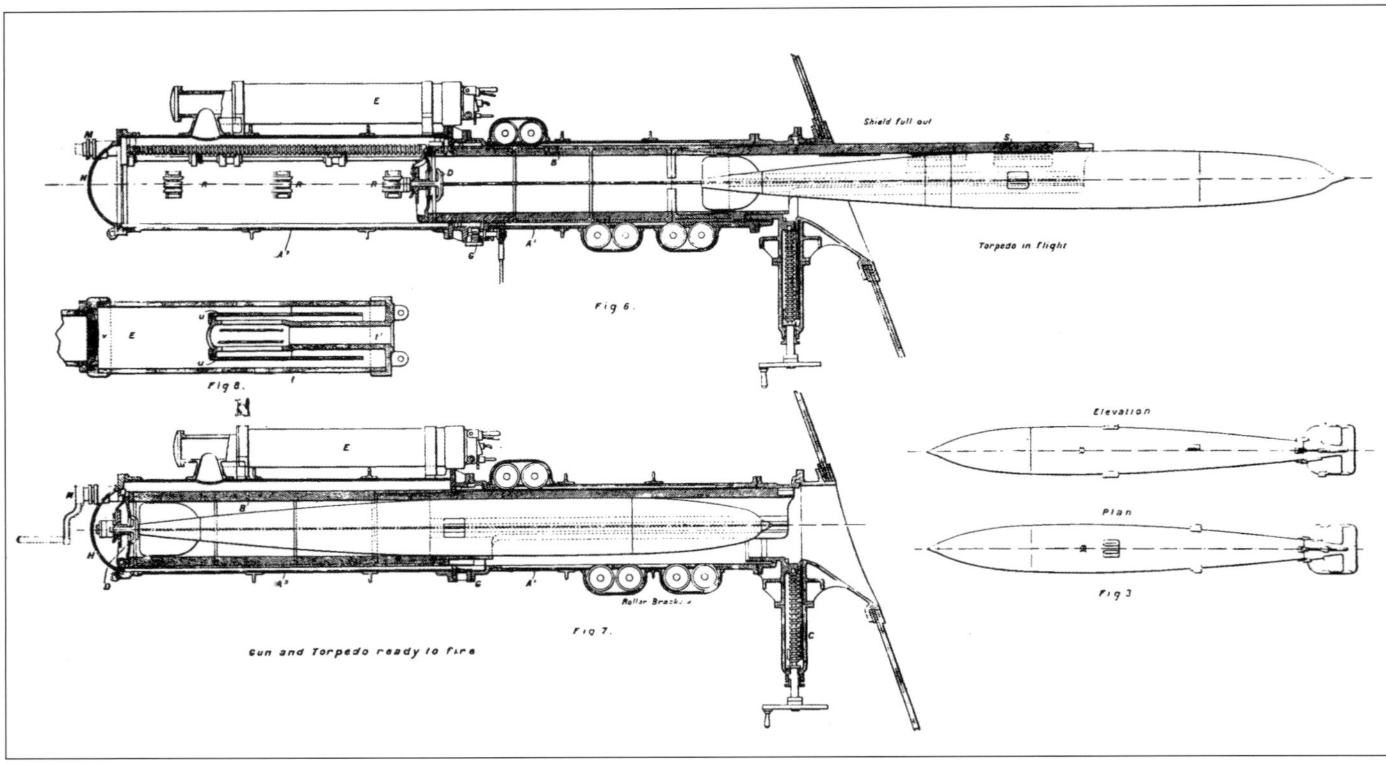

The Whitworth and Co submerged torpedo tube. *(The Engineer, 27 May 1898)*

As mentioned above, early battleships and cruisers fitted with torpedo tubes also carried small steam cutters, later to develop into second-class torpedo boats. For these smaller vessels, the torpedoes were normally launched either from a frame or by 'dropping gear', which consisted of slinging the torpedo by a pair of clip tongs supporting the ends of the torpedo. The torpedo was placed in a fore-and-aft position, clear of the launching vessel. On launch, the torpedo's engine was started as the clip tongs were released simultaneously, and the torpedo dropped horizontally into the water.

In a report from the captain of HMS *Vernon*, dated 22 March 1882, the conclusion was that dropping gear for steam pinnaces was preferable to side frames; second-class torpedo boats should retain their side frames, but have winches fitted as proposed by a Mr Gowring. This report followed a series of trials on three different types of dropping gear and five different methods of raising and lowering side frames. The systems used with the side frames were generally cumbersome and heavy, although that designed by Gowring, which used winches to raise and lower the frames, was considered to work well.

There were three different types of dropping gear. The first, the Malta type, was turned in and out by means of wheels and screws. As the wheels were turned, the ends of the screw worked down inside the boat, and it was difficult to find room for them on account of the air boxes, etc, in a service boat. This equipment was made in Malta. Second was the Portsmouth type, a screw gear somewhat similar to the Malta set, but the screws did not project into the boat. The dropping gear itself had several advantages over the old form, the principal advantage being that the same movement of the handle which released the torpedo first started the engine. The gear worked well, but in its current form was too heavy and cumbersome. The equipment was made at Portsmouth, in conjunction with experts from *Vernon*.

Thirdly, there was the Monarch type. This equipment was supported by hinged iron davits, made to top up by means of tackles. The torpedo, when inboard, rested on two crutches inside the gunwale of the boat. The use of tackles was objectionable, on account of the liability of the falls to get foul of the engines. The gear was light, easily worked and very efficient. This equipment was made aboard HMS *Monarch*. The Malta gear

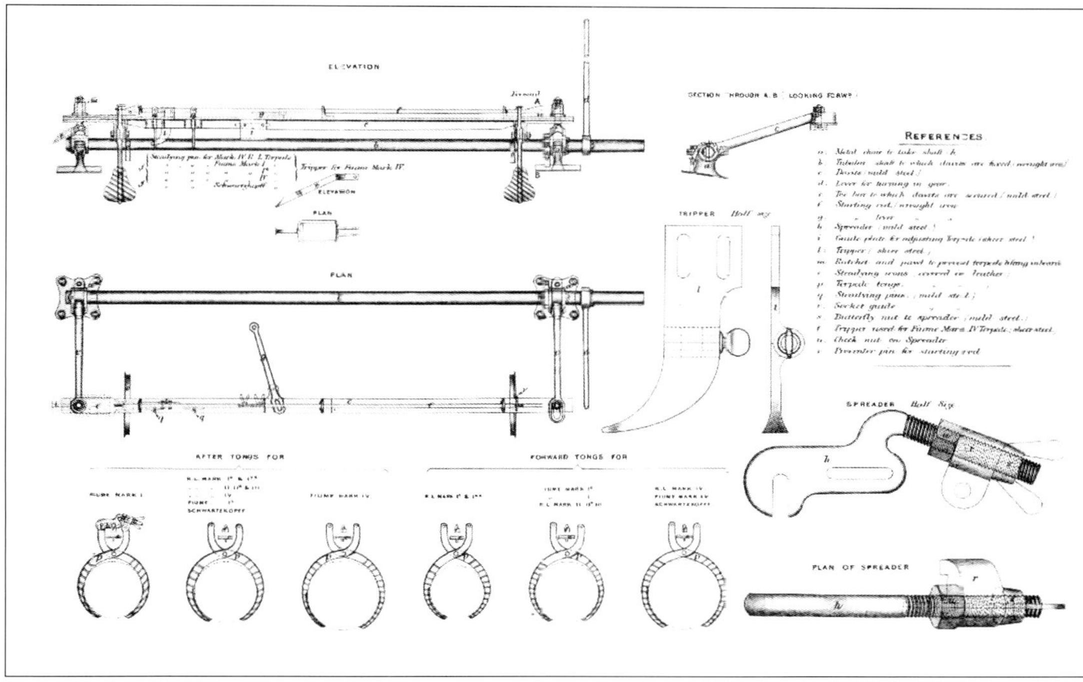

Service dropping gear. *(HMS Vernon Annual Report 1885)*

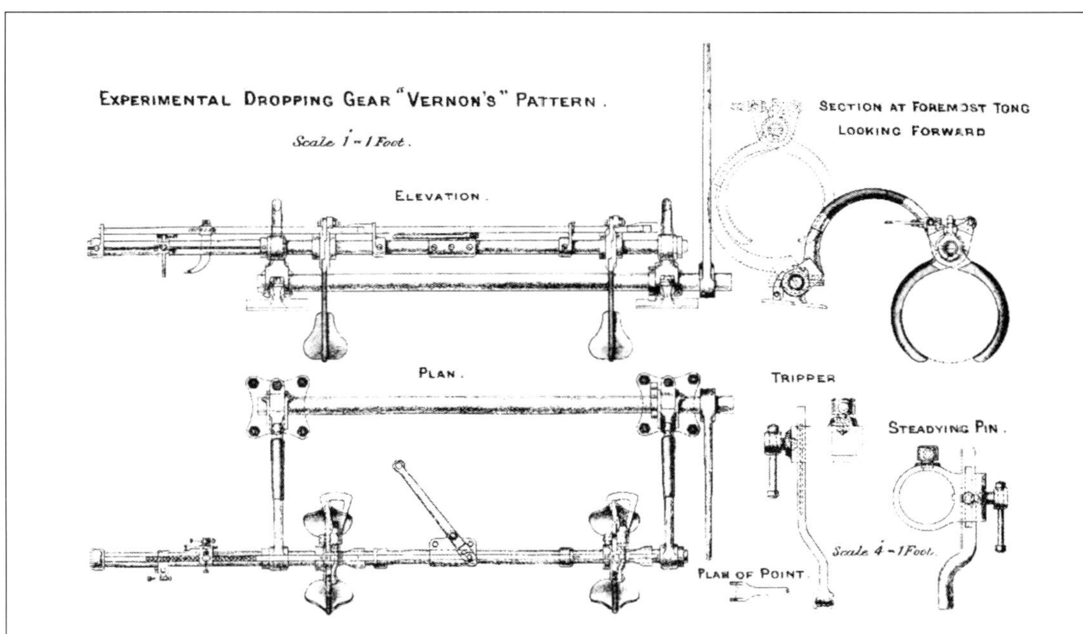

Experimental dropping gear, *Vernon* pattern. *(HMS Vernon Annual Report 1889)*

weighed 10½cwt, the Portsmouth gear 12³⁄₁₆cwt, and the Monarch gear 5cwt.

Other early trials of dropping gear in 1882 used a temporary arrangement aboard the first-class torpedo boat *Lightning*. The torpedo was launched from four different positions – 16ft, 34ft, 40ft and 44ft from *Lightning*'s stem – at various speeds from stationary up to full speed. The best results were achieved with the torpedo 34ft from the stem, with about 8–10° deflection outwards.

The second-class torpedo boats were fitted with side frames until the introduction in 1882 of the Service dropping gear, based on Corner's dropping gear which had first been tried in 1878. This dropping gear received a number of

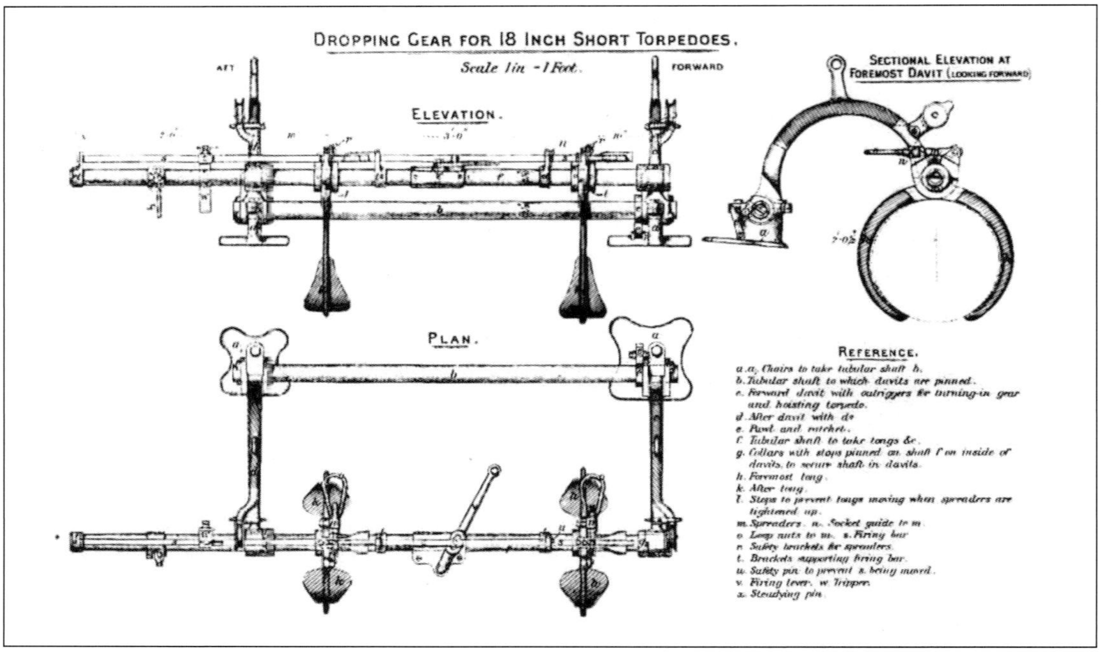

Dropping gear for 18in short torpedoes. *(HMS Vernon Annual Report 1892)*.

improvements as shown by drawings included in the annual reports from HMS *Vernon*, the first of the Service dropping gear appearing in 1885, with that for the *Vernon* pattern appearing in 1889.

Cardigan Dann, chief torpedo gunner in the Victorian (Australia) Navy, was paid £500 by the British naval authorities for his torpedo dropping gear which was invented locally and first used in the Victorian Navy. The dropping gear could hold a torpedo in three positions. The first position was when retracted for travelling to the target. The gear would be extended for firing. There were two extended positions, one for fine weather and one, higher for rough weather. The dropping gear came in a heavy pattern, which could hold 14in and 15in torpedoes. The light pattern could only hold the 14in torpedoes. Dann applied for a patent for an 'improved universal torpedo dropping-gear' on 27 February 1887, and this was granted twelve months later.

The 1882 annual report from HMS *Vernon* describes an alternative means of launching torpedoes from small boats:

> Four of the 20 second-class torpedo boats now under construction have been supplied, and two of them, Nos 79 and 80, have been tried. This type of boat is at present the latest type of second-class boat in the service.
>
> The torpedoes are carried in troughs on the forward part of the deck, and are ejected by means of impulse gear similar to the compressed air apparatus, but instead of air, steam is used from the boiler. The armament consists of two 14-inch torpedoes laid in the troughs, and arranged to be projected therefrom by means of two piston-rods in steam cylinders 4¾in in diameter by 7ft stroke.
>
> The steam is admitted to these cylinders by means of a valve, working on a face having two steam ports, one at each end, connected to the cylinders in such a way that when the valve is pushed forward, steam is admitted to the port cylinder, and when it is pulled back, to the starboard cylinder. The whole motion of the valve is ¾in, and is obtained by means of a screw passing through the valve. The spindle is connected to the stops of the torpedo troughs in such a way that when, for example, the handle on the end of it is moved to starboard, the starboard stop is withdrawn, and the valve

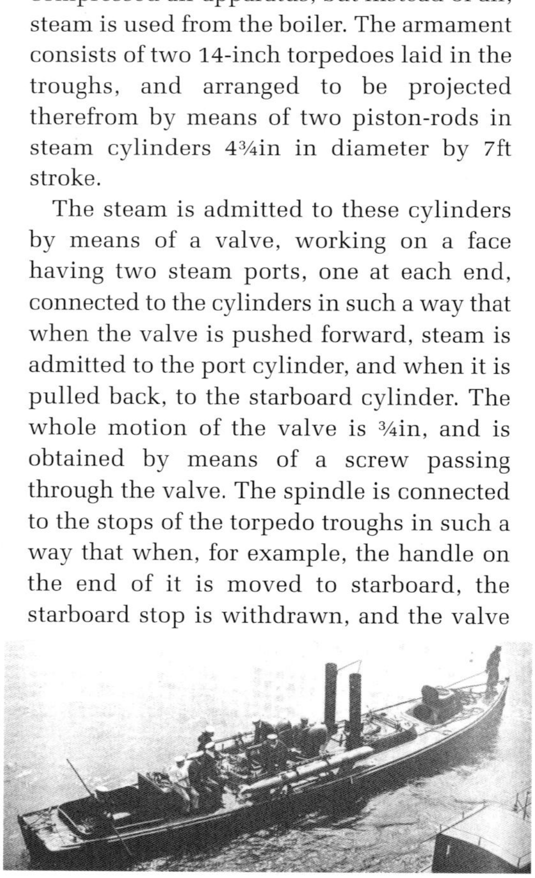

A naval picket boat armed with Whitehead torpedoes deployed using dropping gear. *(Navy & Army Illustrated)*

Dann's dropping gear.

pulled backward so as to admit steam behind the starboard piston and eject the starboard torpedo.

A stop on the handle regulates the amount of opening of the valve, so that when there is only a pressure of 60lbs in the boiler the port is opened to its full extent, and when there is a pressure of 130lbs the opening is reduced to one half.

The earliest torpedo boats, both first- and second-class, were provided with dropping gear.

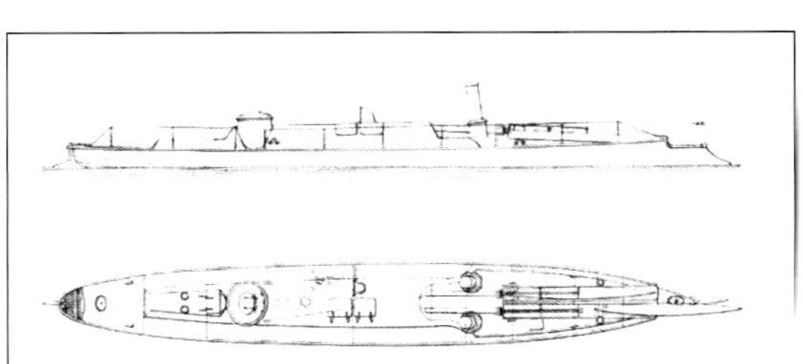

Second-class torpedo boat with torpedo troughs. ***(HMS Vernon Annual Report 1882)***

Because of their very low freeboard, problems were often experienced during the torpedo launch in anything but the calmest seas. In some cases, a single fixed torpedo tube was therefore mounted on the bow; *TB1*, *Lightning*, had hers fitted in 1879. The weight did cause some trim problems, particularly if a reload torpedo was also kept nearby. Frequently, the torpedo boats would retain their dropping gear in order to be capable of firing additional torpedoes.

Lightning was followed by eleven other similar vessels from the same shipbuilder, although these received the torpedo tube when first built. *TBs 13–20* were similar, but purchased from a number of other shipbuilders, and, according to Colledge and Warlow, were fitted with two torpedo tubes. It is more probable they were provided with two torpedoes, one in a tube with a reload or two for use with dropping gear. Other sources do record *TB17*, *TB18* and *TB20* as being built with a single tube, with reload, which was later replaced by dropping gear. The 113ft long *TB21–24*, from Thornycroft and Yarrow, were fitted with two fixed torpedo tubes in the bows and a single revolving one at the stern.

The 125ft first-class torpedo boats, *TB25–79*, were built primarily by Thornycroft and Yarrow, with a few 'turnabout' boats by Whites. These were fitted with two pairs of tubes for 14in torpedoes fitted either side of a rotating 'conning tower' which supported a 3pdr (quick-firing) QF gun. The tubes were 15ft long, fired by powder

A second-class torpedo boat fitted with dropping gear. *(Navy & Army Illustrated)*

impulse and had a depression of 2°, the mounting and tubes weighing 2 tons 17cwt 1qtr 21lbs. The height of the centre of the tube was 1ft 3½in above the deck and the tubes diverged 5° in training. Only one pair of similar tubes were fitted on the Yarrow 130ft *TB82–87* and weighed 1 ton 9cwt 1qtr (one tube only), had a depression of 2½° and were mounted 1in lower.

All torpedo boats were ordered to be fitted with doors for the wireless cartridge, and the circuit and director fittings altered, as tried out in four first-class torpedo boats in the 1889 manoeuvres and favourably reported on.

TBs 52, 54, 59, 65, 67, 68, 72, 73, 74 and *80–87* were altered before the manoeuvres, and in all cases, favourable reports of the fittings were received, with no misfires occurring. It was very necessary to keep the pocket carefully cleaned after each round to ensure a good 'earth'.

The slightly larger 140ft boats, *TB88–97*, carried 18in torpedoes and were fitted with a bow tube and one pair of rotating tubes, oriented 180° with respect to each other, their weight being 2 tons 12cwt 1qtr 2lbs, and with zero depression, ie horizontal.

Gyroscope torpedoes were issued to torpedo boats during the manoeuvres of 1900; with due care, it was found easy to keep them in a good state of preservation. The year 1907 saw the introduction of 'heater' torpedoes, where the energy of the compressed air was supplemented by that of the heat from combustion of Broxburn lighthouse oil.

The following orders were issued in one flotilla:

1. Torpedoes are to be charged to exercising pressure for 900 yards range, 10 feet deep, and in all respects ready for firing. The gyroscope is to be inserted and cocked.
2. Torpedoes are to be re-charged every day as most convenient, and the propellors turned by hand.
3. Every second day the gyroscope torpedo is to be launched back, and if circumstances admit, the main spring eased, gyroscope removed, air passages blown through, gyroscope cleaned, replaced and re-cocked.

The first-class torpedo boat *TB1*, *Lightning*, with bow torpedo tube, and a second-class torpedo boat secured outboard. Note that *Lightning* still retains her dropping gear, similar to that fitted to the second-class boat.

TB79 in 1899, showing the twin torpedo tubes either side of the rotating mount which, at that time, did not have a 3pdr gun mount fitted. *TB79* was the first command of the future King George V, who is featured in the centre.

4. In 125-feet boats the after tubes are to be coupled up, and placed on the 70° abaft bearing. In the 80 class torpedo boat the tubes will be kept fore and aft.
5. The directors are to be kept shipped, and impulse charges inserted.
6. During dark hours, or when an attack is expected, a man is to be kept stationed in instant readiness to train the tubes on the required beam for the shot

A lighter loading tray, just 1ft 9in long, was introduced in 1902, after trials on Palmer's '30-knotter' TBD *Peterel*, for use on both torpedo boats and torpedo boat destroyers.

Because of the number of torpedoes being 'lost' during practice, in 1906 the Admiralty stated that torpedoes would not have to run more than 1,000yds before reaching the target, and in no case should the range be less than 800yds. The manufacture of 14in torpedoes also ceased in 1906.

TB63, showing the gun mountings on top of the torpedo tube structures.

About to launch a torpedo from a single trainable tube. *(Illustrated War News)*

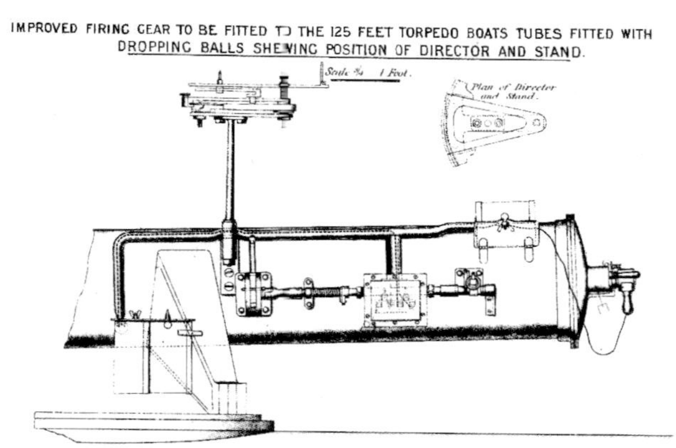

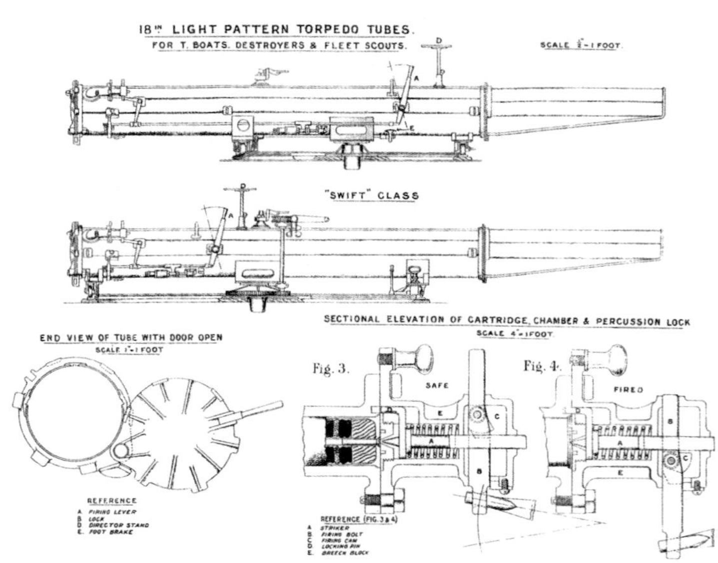

Above: Firing gear for 125ft torpedo boats. *(Vernon Annual Report 1890)*

Right: 18in light pattern torpedo tube. *(Torpedo Manual 1909)*

The broadside trainable torpedo tube for 14in torpedoes, aboard USS *Maine*, launched in 1889.

In 1911 the Admiralty issued orders to discontinue practice from stem tubes, and to dismantle the tubes as far as possible without incurring any expense.

Both revolving and fixed torpedo tubes were used by torpedo boat destroyers, double revolving tubes having also been invented by A K Wilson. Pairs were initially parallel, either pointing in the same or opposite directions, but later diverging tubes pointing in the same general direction were introduced to give a 'spread', and so increase the probability of a hit, an idea introduced by Alfred Yarrow. Loading was carried out with the tubes pointing fore-and-aft.

Triple torpedo tubes were not introduced into general service until the flotilla leaders of the *Shakespeare* class (launched 1917/18), and they were for use with 21in torpedoes, these having been introduced into service for above-water fire in 1910. Trials had previously been carried out onboard the 'V'-class leader, HMS *Vampire*. The third tube was situated on the mount's centreline, above the other two.

The bow torpedo tube of a destroyer.

The 1914 edition of the *Torpedo Drill Book*, copies of which could be sold to 'Officers and Men of HM Fleet' at sixpence per copy, listed five different marks of 14in torpedo and twenty-three different marks of 18in torpedo as being in service. The torpedo shops at the Royal Gun Factory (RGF), Woolwich, had been closed in 1911, and transferred to the Royal Navy Torpedo Factory at Greenock. Torpedoes were also manufactured at the Whitehead Torpedo Works in Weymouth. Previously, they had also been manufactured at the Whitehead Works in Fiume and by Greenwood & Batley of Leeds.

The 14in RGF design, manufactured by any of the three sources, were available as Mark IX, X, X* or XI. The Weymouth design, Mark I, was also available. The 18in RGF design, also manufactured by any of the different sources, was available as Mark I*, II*, III, IV, V, V*, V* GS, VI, VI GS, VI*, VI* H, VI** H, VI*** H, VII, VII*, VII** and VII***. Fiume designs were also available as Mark III, III*, III** and III** H, and Weymouth designs as Mark I and I*.

Images of the interiors of British warships of this time are difficult to locate, particularly those showing weapons, but similar installations were fitted to warships of other countries, like those from the United States Navy shown on page 39.

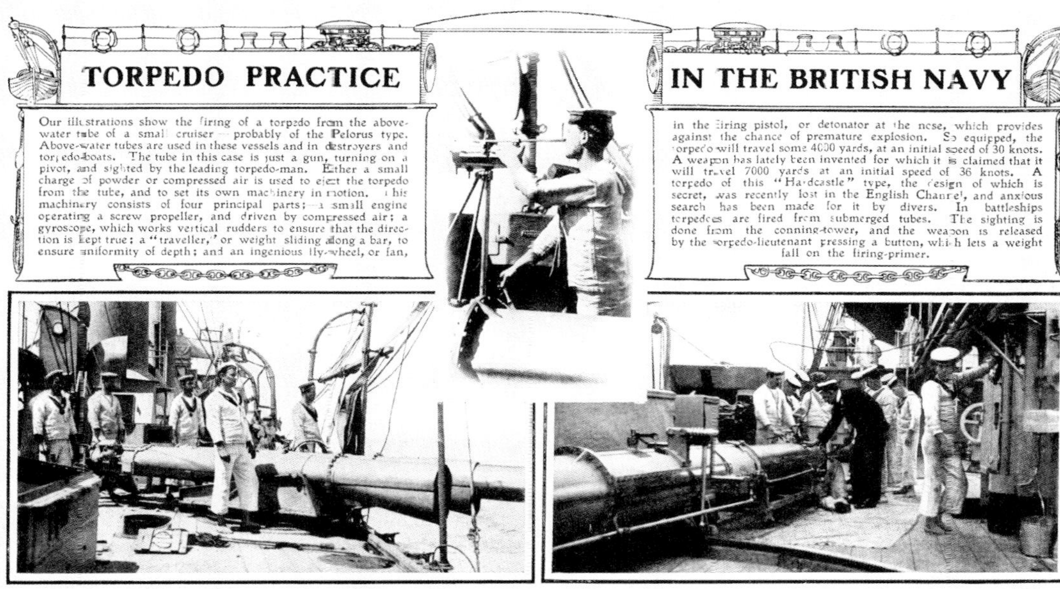

TORPEDO PRACTICE IN THE BRITISH NAVY

Our illustrations show the firing of a torpedo from the above-water tube of a small cruiser — probably of the Pelorus type. Above-water tubes are used in these vessels and in destroyers and torpedo-boats. The tube in this case is just a gun, turning on a pivot, and sighted by the leading torpedo-man. Either a small charge of powder or compressed air is used to eject the torpedo from the tube, and to set its own machinery in motion. This machinery consists of four principal parts; — a small engine operating a screw propeller, and driven by compressed air; a gyroscope, which works vertical rudders to ensure that the direction is kept true; a "traveller," or weight sliding along a bar, to ensure uniformity of depth; and an ingenious fly-wheel, or fan, in the firing pistol, or detonator at the nose, which provides against the chance of premature explosion. So equipped, the torpedo will travel some 4000 yards, at an initial speed of 30 knots. A weapon has lately been invented for which it is claimed that it will travel 7000 yards at an initial speed of 36 knots. A torpedo of this "Hardcastle" type, the design of which is secret, was recently lost in the English Channel, and anxious search has been made for it by divers. In battleships torpedoes are fired from submerged tubes. The sighting is done from the conning-tower, and the weapon is released by the torpedo-lieutenant pressing a button, which lets a weight fall on the firing-primer.

A TORPEDO CREW WAITING THE WORD TO FIRE — TAKING AIM — CHARGING THE TORPEDO-TUBE WITH COMPRESSED AIR

Torpedo practice in the Royal Navy. *(The Graphic, 16 January 1909)*

CHAPTER THREE

HMS *VERNON*, HMS *DEFIANCE*, HMS *VESUVIUS* AND HMS *POLYPHEMUS*

Crest of HMS *Vernon*.

The Royal Navy established a torpedo school in 1872 aboard the hulk of an unsuccessful ship designed by an amateur naval architect, Captain William Symonds. Although *Vernon* had not been a good gun platform and suffered from dry rot due to poor construction, she did have one advantage – a wide beam which resulted in increased deckhead height. Having been towed to Portsmouth for conversion, *Vernon* was moored on Fountain Lake, astern of HMS *Excellent*, the Navy's gunnery school which, at that time, also had responsibility for other weapons, including torpedoes. 'Jacky' Fisher was her first captain.

Vernon was not commissioned as a separate command until 26 April 1876, the first commanding officer being Captain William Arthur, who had previously been a member of the 1870 Whitehead Committee. Arthur's executive officer was Commander Arthur Knyvet Wilson, the designer of the torpedo tube used by the Royal Navy, who became the sixth captain of *Vernon* in 1889.

In order to provide accommodation both for instructors and those under instruction, a 26-gun steam frigate, *Ariadne*, was moored ahead of *Vernon*, with the lighter *Florence Nightingale*, used as running stage for torpedoes, in between. *Florence Nightingale* had been in operation since the original establishment of the school in 1872. In October 1879 another 26-gun frigate, *Actaeon*, was added to provide space for a practical workshop. January 1886 saw further enlargement when the two-deck ship of the line *Donegal* replaced *Vernon* and adopted her name. In turn, *Vernon* replaced *Actaeon*, the original frigate being scrapped.

During the 1890s, on Sunday afternoons *Vernon* was thrown open to the friends of those attached to the school, and also to those who obtained official permission to inspect the establishment – a popular time, although it is doubtful that there was much discussion about the secret work that went on there.

In 1888 the Horsea Island Range was completed. The range was under the charge of *Vernon*, but was also used by Woolwich for passing their torpedoes and by depots for re-ranging torpedoes returned for repair.

HMS *Vernon* began to move ashore at the end

The three hulks comprising HMS *Vernon*.

of the First World War, and on 1 October 1923 Gunwharf became formally known as the *Vernon* Shore Establishment.

Another torpedo school was set up at Devonport at the end of 1884, using the hulk of *Defiance*. *Defiance* was moored on the north side of the Lynher, off Wearde Quay. As with *Vernon*, space was increased by the addition of other hulks, linked by footbridges. In 1930 the wooden hull was decaying and so the original *Defiance* was replaced by a 11,000-ton cruiser which was relocated to the Hamoaze, north of Wilcove, where the water was deeper.

The range of topics taught by both *Vernon* and *Defiance* was much wider than just torpedoes and mines – it covered virtually all aspects of the use of electricity in the Royal Navy. One rapidly developing field was that of wireless telegraphy. The first ever ship-to-ship radio communications took place in 1896, from *Defiance* to her tender *Scourge*, the work of Commander (later Admiral Sir) Henry Bradwardine Jackson, who had been placed in command of *Defiance* in 1895, and was elected as a fellow of the Royal Society in 1901 in recognition of his work in the field of wireless telegraphy.

Torpedo heads and tails stored aboard HMS *Vernon*.

In January 1886 the original hulk *Vernon* was replaced by *Donegal*, renamed *Vernon*.

Crest of HMS *Defiance*.

Two views of HMS *Defiance*, the torpedo school at Devonport.

HMS *Vesuvius*, with tall funnel, after fitting-out at Portsmouth. *(Naval Photograph Club)*

In 1874 *Vernon* was allocated a tender, HMS *Vesuvius*. *Vesuvius* was the first purpose-built torpedo boat for the Royal Navy, having been ordered on 12 February 1872. She was laid down at Pembroke Dockyard on 16 March 1873 and launched twelve months and eight days later. Her cost at completion on 11 September 1874 was £17,897. She was 90ft long between perpendiculars, with a beam of 22ft and a draught of 8½ft, and displaced 245 tons. Designed for slow-speed night attacks, she had two shafts each driven by a Maudslay compound steam engine of 350ihp, giving a speed of 9.7 knots. The engines produced very little noise, the boilers were powered by coke and the small quantity of smoke produced was exhausted through vents along the side of the low freeboard hull: an early example of stealth! *Vesuvius* had a complement of fifteen.

Vesuvius was towed from Pembroke to Portsmouth for fitting out, where she was given a tall funnel to assist in raising steam. She had a single 19ft long, 24in diameter submerged bow tube, with top and bottom rollers and side guide rails, firing a 16in torpedo. *Vesuvius* could carry ten 14ft long, 16in torpedoes. She was never used in action, as the Admiralty became obsessed with speed, but was used in 1886 during trials against the old ironclad *Resistance* to establish the effectiveness of nets as a defence against torpedoes. On 21 September a 'calibration' explosion of 80lb was made, 30ft from the side of *Resistance*, causing no damage. The next day, *Vesuvius* fired a 16in torpedo with a 91lb charge against the nets, which were 30ft from *Resistance*, damaging the nets but not causing any damage to the ship. Further tests were carried out with static charges at different distances from *Resistance*, that at a distance of 15ft causing minor leaks. In June the following year, the heavier, and much more cumbersome, Bullivant net was trialled. Again *Vesuvius* fired a torpedo that damaged the nets but failed to damage the ship.

The weekly publication *Engineering*, dated 7 May 1875, contained an extensive description of *Vesuvius* and her machinery.

An illustration of the damage done to the port side of HMS *Resistance*. *(Illustrated London News, 13 November 1886)*

THE *VESUVIUS* TORPEDO SHIP, *ENGINEERING*, 7 MAY 1875

The *Vesuvius* torpedo ship is a novelty in this age of novelties. She is intended to be smokeless and noiseless, coke being used as fuel, and there being no blast or escaping steam on deck. Moreover, notwithstanding her proportions – 90ft long by 22ft beam – she was intended to have a 10 knot speed, while to secure facility in manoeuvring she is fitted with twin screws. The trials of her propelling machinery have not been altogether successful; but, nevertheless, the following account of the machinery itself, and notes of its trials, will be of interest to many.

The general arrangement of her propelling machinery will be readily understood from our outline sketches. The engines are direct-acting, inclined inverted cylinders, with single piston rods, and surface condensing. The surface condenser common to both pairs of engines, is placed between them, and receives not only the exhaust steam from the main engines, but also that from all the numerous auxiliary engines with which the ship is fitted. The cylinders are steam jacketted, and fitted with expansion valves working on the back of the slide valves, and cutting off as early as one-tenth of the stroke. The piston rods and slide valve rods are of steel, and the piston rod gland nuts are toothed to admit of their being screwed up together. There are two air pumps worked by eccentrics on the main shafts, one on each shaft, and the circulating pump is centrifugal, driven by a separate engine. A Silver's governor is fitted to each pair of engines. The propellers originally fitted are three-bladed Griffiths', but we believe that a trial is to be made with Thornycroft's propellers.

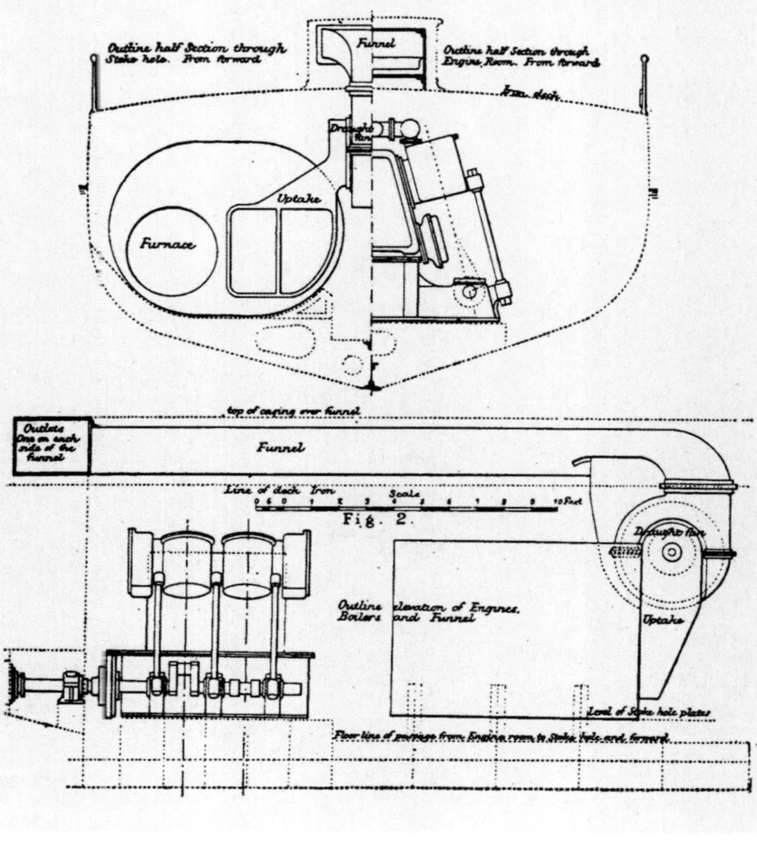

The machinery arrangements of HMS *Vesuvius*. (*Engineering*, 7 May 1875)

The boilers are nearly circular, and pressed to 70lb on the square inch. The safety valves are loaded by Salter's balances, and small test valves loaded with weights are fitted in addition. The waste steam from the safety valves is discharged below water, and relief valves are fitted to the waste steam pipe – one set opening outwards spring loaded, the other inwards, not loaded, except by their own weight. The former are not far from the starting gear, and it appears to us that if the under water waste valves should happen to be left shut, the engineer in charge will be promptly and somewhat uncomfortably reminded of the oversight by becoming enveloped in the escaping steam. It would be well to provide some way of escape for the steam in such a case other than direct into the engine room. However undesirable it is to show the 'white feather' on deck, it is more so to convert the already limited space in the engine room into a steaming stove.

There is no funnel in the ordinary sense of the term, no 'smoke stack', as our American friends would say. The products of combustion from the furnaces are carried by a flue along and close to the upper deck to a point just abaft the engine room, where they escape across the deck through openings in the sides of the flue. To maintain the necessary draught through the furnaces, a fan is fitted in the common uptake, driven by one of Brotherhood and Hardingham's three-cylinder engines, coupled direct to the fan spindle.

There are several auxiliary engines. Two are fitted to drive the draught fan, one the three-cylinder engine already referred to; another, of the ordinary kind, is in place ready for coupling to the end of the fan shaft in case of the former failing. Not that failure is at all anticipated, but as the fan must be kept going, and as the three-cylinder engine is a novelty in the Royal Naval service, it is considered advisable to prepare for any emergency.

Another auxiliary engine is fitted to drive the ventilating fan, whence air is thrown into the different parts of the ship, another as a fire engine, another as a donkey, and yet another for pumping the air into the torpedo supply tanks. The ship is essentially a box of machinery; the accommodation for the officers and crew is of the most limited description; and, indeed, the crew is limited to the smallest possible number consistent with the work to be done. The vessel is built entirely of iron, but to prevent the slipperiness and consequent danger of the iron deck when wet it is proposed to coat it with Welch's cork cement. Of the whole space in the ship a small slice aft provides cabins for the three officers, captain, engineer, and gunner; and another small slice forward accommodates the crew, very few in number. Of the remainder by far the greater part is occupied, say all but filled, by the propelling machinery, and the rest is

HMS *Vesuvius* operating as an experimental vessel with a white hull.

appropriated to the torpedo room with its launching tube, launching machinery, air-compressing engines, pumps and reservoirs, and torpedo store.

It is rather interesting, and at times amusing, to hear the account given of the attempts, successful and otherwise, made to get the steam trials carried out. The earliest and hitherto the chief difficulty has been with reference to the draught. The original design provided that the fan should be driven by a belt from an engine of the ordinary kind fixed near it. The result of the first trial was to fill the stokehole and engine-room with fumes so noxious and suffocating as to be positively hurtful to every one on board. That trial rendered it plain that to drive the fan by means of a belt was out of the question, because of its slipping; and further, that the ship must be towed to Portsmouth, as she could not steam.

Prior to the next trial the engine and fan were connected by geared shafting. The noise was very great, and quite prevented all verbal communication anywhere in the ship, while it could be heard at a considerable distance outside. That trial ended by the fan engine breaking down, and the consequent immediate loss of steam, dying out of the fires, and general tendency to suffocation. Then was fitted the Brotherhood engine, which has been in use throughout all the trials since, and has worked well. Working at a speed of 570 revolutions per minute it is absolutely noiseless and free from vibration, and seems to be the right thing in the right place.

For getting up steam, during which it is, of course, impossible to work the draught engine, a temporary vertical funnel has been fitted just over the fan. When steam is up this funnel is removed, folded down to rest on the funnel proper, and can, when necessary, be taken to pieces and stowed lower down on the deck itself.

The first trial over the measured mile took place late in November last. The result was rather disappointing; a speed of 10 knots and an indicated power of 350 were anticipated, but although the coal used was the best Welsh picked trial coal, the power was under 300 horse power, and the speed was just over 9 knots. However, seeing that the bottom was foul, the steering bad, and the vacuum low, there was good hope of a better result being attained. The *Vesuvius* does not appear to steer well at any time; but the bad steering on this occasion is easily accounted for. The vessel is intended to be controlled from a conning tower near the bow, the upper part only of which is raised above the deck. Slits are provided in the sides of the tower through which the steersman can see his way, and these serve the purpose well enough when the object towards which the ship is steered is well in sight. But the buoys which mark the measured mile course are not plain to one so near the water level, and whose range of vision is so limited; and whilst running over it, the pilot outside the tower standing on the deck, conned the ship, giving orders as necessary from time to time to the man at the wheel below him. The time lost in this way, though not in itself great, was yet ample for a vessel like the *Vesuvius* to swerve considerably from the course, and so make the distance she had to run something more than a knot.

On the next trial over the measured mile, an extra steering-wheel having been meanwhile fitted up on deck outside the conning tower, the course was singularly well kept. The steersman was then in a better position for seeing exactly what was wanted, and could move the helm to meet any apparent tendency to fall off to one side or the other.

On this trial, anthracite was used by itself as an experiment. The result was unfavourable. The speed at full power was only 8.362 knots with an indicated horse power of 230, and the disagreeable and suffocating fumes from the sulphur in the fuel found their way into every part of the ship. It was plain that that would not do.

The next trial was ordered to be made with a mixture in equal parts of the best Welsh trial coal and anthracite. The weather was too stormy for the measured mile to be run; but the result as to power was better than any previously obtained.

The last trial of this series was the most successful of all. The fuel used was a mixture of best trial Welsh coal and coke, in the proportion of five of the former to three of the latter. The better result is not, however, attributed altogether to the fuel, but in part to the better working of the air and feed pumps, which had meanwhile been overhauled. We append some results of the later trials:

Date	**Nov '74**	**Jan 12, '75**		**Jan 18, '75**	**Jan 20, '75**
No. of days out of dock	84	130		136	138
Weather	Fine	Fine		Stormy	Moderate
Steam pressure		2 boilers	1 boiler		
	52	57	50	62	
Revolutions	135	122	84	140	142
IHP	300	223	95	335	380
Speed	9	8.362	6.273	Not tried	9.423
Fuel	Welsh	Anthracite		½ Welsh	⅝ Welsh
				½ Anthracite	⅜ Coke

The *Vesuvius* appears on the whole to be a disagreeable ship to have anything to do with. We saw her on her arrival from her trial of the 18 January, and as we looked down on the low smoke-be-grimed deck, unprotected by bulwarks, and on the salt-whitened funnel, and then looked out seawards, we quite understood how well drenched the people on deck must have been during the trial. They looked it, and we wondered not that they growled over their ducking. We could quite understand, too, that the ducking was not the only discomfort. The hot gases from the funnel are, as already noted, discharged from openings in the sides of the flue. These openings are 8ft from the ship's sides, and the hot vapour and soot, if any, is left to find its way across the deck as best it may, or as best suits the wind then blowing. At all events there is no free-from-suffocation standing room abaft these openings, and the result with respect to deck passengers on a day like that was that if they moved one way they got swamped by the seas falling on board, if in the other they were exposed to all the noxiousness of the funnel mixture, while, if amidships, they had a share of both.

We do not quite see why the flue should not be split and extended, one branch to each quarter, each having a hanging door. The door on the weather side could be lowered, and so make the vile compound issue on the lee side only. Of course on actual service there will be no deck passengers, but before she is fit for any such service, and we hope long before any is required, there are many experiments to make, and if only for the comfort of those who must be on board during these experiments, it would be well to fit something of the kind.

Vesuvius remained with *Vernon* until sold to the shipbreakers Cashmore for scrap on 14 September 1923, hence becoming both the first and the last torpedo boat in Royal Navy service. She foundered while being towed to Cashmore's yard at Newport.

In 1872 the Director of Naval Construction, Nathaniel Barnaby, produced a design for a larger version of *Vesuvius* – before she was even laid down. This new vessel was to have a fast, cigar-shaped hull with five submerged torpedo tubes, a bow tube and four broadside tubes, and protected by 2in of armour over the deck. The design was modified in late 1875 into a larger vessel equipped with a ram. Early in 1876 the design was modified again into a 240ft LBP unarmoured torpedo ram, with a top speed of 17 knots. Later the design was changed yet again to have armour added to the exposed steel deck.

Polyphemus (see Plate 2) was ordered on 5 February 1878 and laid down on 21 September of the same year at Chatham Naval Dockyard. She was launched on 15 June 1881 and completed in September the following year. She was equipped with two sets of two-cylinder compound engines and a low turtle-back hull, which was almost submerged when the vessel was travelling at speed. The engines were manufactured by Humphrys & Tennant, developing 5,520ihp (7,000ihp forced) resulting in a maximum speed of 17.85 knots (18 knots). Her deck was armoured with 3in of armour plate. Normal bunker capacity was 200 tons of coal. Her complement was 146 – ten times that of *Vesuvius* – and her cost was £174,450 – again, ten times that of *Vesuvius*.

The *Engineering* publication featured three articles on HMS *Polyphemus*, the first appearing on 1 August 1879, while the vessel was under construction.

THE TORPEDO RAM *POLYPHEMUS*
ENGINEERING, 1 AUGUST 1879

The torpedo ram *Polyphemus*, now being constructed in Chatham Dockyard, appears likely to be the most extraordinary ship that has yet been built. She is novel and peculiar alike in form, structure, fittings, and arrangement of armour protection; while her weapons of attack are such as will necessitate her being

HMS ***Polyphemus.*** ***(US History and Heritage Command, NH65966)***

fought differently from any other warship. Her design was described by the late Mr Ward Hunt in the House of Commons on 12 of March 1877, as being 'of a kind as yet unknown in any part of the world, but which has been much talked about, and has been at last forced upon me by that gallant officer who stands at the head of the veteran list of the Navy, viz, Sir George Sartorius, who has shown that although his age is great, his mind is still youthful, and that he is willing to receive new ideas and able to inculcate them.'

The leading features of the *Polyphemus* are a strong ram bow, a powerful torpedo battery, great speed and handiness, moderate size, and a small extent of surface above water exposed to the enemy's fire, such portion of the vessel as is above the water line being convex in form, so as to deflect any projectile that may strike it. The appearance she will present when at sea will be that of a cylinder, floating on its side and deeply immersed, which is tapered at the ends to form a bow and stern. The top of the cylinder will be 4ft 6in above the water line, and will be flattened over a large portion of its area to form a deck. The whole of this flattened cylindrical surface will be plated over with steel armour, and will cover in and protect the ship and all her machinery and fighting appliances. The ship proper as she will thus appear will be surmounted by a light structure carrying a hurricane deck of about two-thirds her length, and upon this deck will be seen a signal mast, funnel, pilot tower, boats, and other fittings.Under water the form of the *Polyphemus* is as strange as it will thus appear above. The cylindrical curvature of the sides is carried down several feet below the water line, and armour-plated to that depth. Below this point the section assumes a 'V' form, and ends in a sharp angle at the keel. It will therefore be seen that a complete cross-section of the vessel is very similar to that of a peg-top. The flattened convex curvature of the upper part of the peg-top would represent the part of the *Polyphemus* that is above water, and the lower portion, which ends in a point, would also represent the part of the ship that is below water. If the peg-top be imagined to float in water at a depth below where its breadth is greatest and where the section thus begins to curve towards the centre line, a rough idea may be obtained both of the form and proportions of the above and under-water parts of the *Polyphemus*.

The *Polyphemus* is 240ft long between perpendiculars, 40ft in extreme breadth, and will have a load draught of 20ft. Her displacement will be 2,640 tons. The convex armoured deck will be 4ft 6in above the water line, and will be completely plated over with steel armour 3in thick. This armour will be carried to a depth of 6ft to 7ft below the water line. The *Polyphemus* will not be

HMS *Polyphemus* at sea, showing her low freeboard. *(Navypedia)*

fitted with masts or sails, but will carry a pole for signalling purposes and for making observations from. She will be propelled by twin screws, and will have two pairs of high-pressure compound horizontal engines, which are being constructed by Messrs Humphreys and Tennant, of Deptford. Each high-pressure cylinder will be 38in in diameter and the low pressure 64in. The stroke will be 45in. The boilers will be of the locomotive type, twelve in number, and will be made of steel They will work up to a pressure of 110lb per square inch. It is estimated that the engines will indicate a collective power of 5,500 horses, and that the speed of the ship will be 17 knots.

The only offensive weapons the *Polyphemus* will possess are a powerful ram bow and Whitehead torpedoes. She will have no guns at all, except a few light shell guns and Gatlings on the hurricane deck for the purpose of repelling boat or torpedo attack. The ram will consist of a very strong spur, which will project 12ft in advance of the stem of the ship, and is so placed that it will strike several feet below an enemy's armour. It will be connected to the stem and bow by deep web plates and angles on each side; the former being a continuation of the 3in deck armour, which is curved downwards at the bow and carried under water till it reaches the level of the spur. The spur is being fitted so that it may be unshipped and taken off the stem when not required for active use. Under the ram is a torpedo port, which will enable Whitehead torpedoes to be ejected right ahead of the ship. There are also two torpedo ports on each side amidships, from which they will be ejected on the broadsides. The ports and apparatus for working the torpedoes will be upon the system fitted in the *Vesuvius* and *Glatton*. All the torpedo ports are below water, but it is understood that this under-water attack will be supplemented by torpedo firing above water from the armoured deck upon the system adopted in ordinary torpedo launches.

Above the armour-plated portion of the hull a hurricane deck is fitted for about two-thirds of its length. This deck is about one-half the extreme breadth of the ship. Communication is made between the hurricane deck and the interior of the ship by openings cut through the armoured deck. The openings thus cut

HMS *Polyphemus* in dock at Malta, clearly showing the ram torpedo tube.

are protected by glacis plates and armour, and by casings, which are carried up to the hurricane deck. The boats are carried upon the hurricane deck, and the ship is steered and worked from it. An armoured pilot tower, with protected means of access to the lower part of the ship, is placed at the fore end of the hurricane deck, and fitted with steering wheel, telegraphs, voice pipes, apparatus for firing off the torpedoes, and all other appliances for conning and working the ship. A few light shell or Gatling guns will also be carried on the hurricane deck, as we have stated, for repelling boarders or torpedo boats.

The *Polyphemus* is built throughout of steel. The frames are of Bessemer, and the bottom plating of Landore-Siemens steel. She is constructed upon the usual system of transverse bracket frames and continuous longitudinals, and has a double bottom the whole length of the ship right up to the upper deck.

The subdivision of the lower part of the ship into small watertight compartments has been carried as far as appears possible. The double bottom is split up into a large number of cellular spaces, and the hold is divided by a longitudinal middle line bulkhead, and numerous transverse bulkheads. The boilers are contained in four separate watertight compartments of the hold, three being placed in each; and each pair of engines is also contained in a separate watertight compartment. The advantage of such an arrangement is sufficiently obvious in view of the possibility of one of the boilers or engine-rooms being bilged by a blow from a ram or torpedo. The double bottom is arranged so as to include the coal bunkers, as in the *Devastation* and the *Inflexible*. By these means buoyancy is gained if one of the compartments is opened up to the sea, as the water can only find its way among the interstices of the coal, and a large quantity is thus kept out of the ship.

The cabins and accommodation for the crew will all be below the armoured deck, and will be ventilated artificially, as in the ironclad monitors. They will

A stern view of HMS *Polyphemus*. (*Naval Photograph Club*)

be lighted throughout by the electric light, which is already being fitted in several ironclads, and is likely to become extensively used for this purpose. An electric light will also be fixed in the look-out on the polemast, for reconnoitring and signalling purposes.

The most remarkable and novel feature in the ship yet remains to be described. The bottom plating on each side, instead of ending in a keel, or flat keel plate, at the middle line, is formed into a recess; so that in place of a keel there is a rectangular groove, 1ft 8in wide and 3ft deep, taken out of the bottom of the ship. This groove or recess is intended to be filled with cast-iron ballast up to a weight of 300 tons. The ballast will be cast in several lengths, and will be so attached to the ship that, in the event of a compartment becoming bilged, and its being desirable to lighten the ship, the ballast can be let go and dropped from any part, as may be required. The draught and trim may thus be regulated to a certain limited extent should the vessel be damaged in action. This is a point that will probably be discussed among engineers. The object of carrying the ballast seems to be to keep the ship down in the water, and prevent the deck from becoming too much exposed when the ship is uninjured; but should she become still further immersed from any cause, the dropping of the ballast will somewhat relieve and lighten her. The utmost effect of the ballast will be to enable the vessel to float 12in to 14in lighter when it is dropped than she would do before. In other words, although her armoured deck is only 4ft 6in above the water, and this height only is exposed to the enemy's fire, the surplus buoyancy, on account of the ballast, will be the same as though the armoured deck stood 5ft 6in or 5ft 8in above the water line.

It will be obvious that this quantity of ballast, amounting to about one-ninth of the whole weight of the ship, cannot be carried about for nothing. It adds to the work the engines have to do, and a greater expenditure of engine power for a

Another stern view of HMS *Polyphemus*. *(US History and Heritage Command, NH65965)*

given speed will be required to enable the ship to drag the ballast about with her. The additional engine power that will be required to drive the *Polyphemus* at full speed, after adding the ballast, will necessitate an increased coal consumption of 9 to 10 per cent, and a corresponding reduction in coal endurance. It will hardly be considered necessary to carry about all this dead weight in time of peace; and it will be a question for practical consideration whether the carrying of it about in time of war at a cost of reduction in speed, or in coal endurance – and this in a ship whose coal supply is very small for her power will be compensated for by the armoured deck being 4ft 6in out of water, instead of 5ft 6in.

The *Polyphemus* is more or less of an experimental character, and the building of future ships possessing some or all of her characteristics, will depend upon the results of her trials. She is not likely to create a great revolution in war shipbuilding, or to show that guns are unnecessary in a fleet. Indeed, it must be evident that there are many operations – such as the bombardment of fortifications, which could only be carried out by ships armed with guns. The question respecting the *Polyphemus* is not whether such vessels as she are to supersede gun vessels, but whether she may not serve the more humble, though very useful, purpose of starting a type of war ships that will be valuable auxiliaries in action. Mr Ward Hunt, on the occasion before referred to, spoke of her as follows:

> This vessel must, of course, to a certain extent, be regarded as an experiment, and, even supposing it to be a success, I could not propose it to the House as being likely to supersede all other kinds of fighting ships, but only as a useful adjunct to a fleet in case of war. Probably it would not be desirable that she should be kept at sea for a long period at a time, but I venture to think she will prove a very formidable weapon, and, if she should be a success, she may perhaps be regarded as a sort of rival to those monster ships with tremendous armour that we hear spoken of as likely to be built in some foreign ports.

The *Polyphemus* was commenced in September, 1878, and is already far advanced, being entirely framed and plated, except at the extreme ends. Great progress is being made with her, and she could be got ready for launching in a very few months.

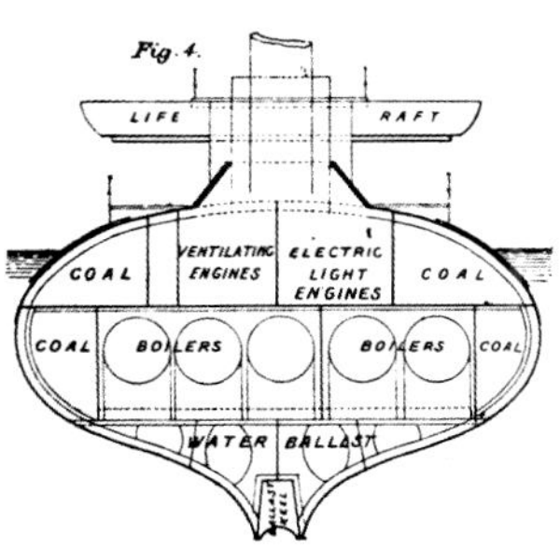

Arrangement of HMS *Polyphemus*. (*Engineering*, 8 July 1881)

The other articles appeared in June and July 1881, after the vessel had been launched and contained more technical details.

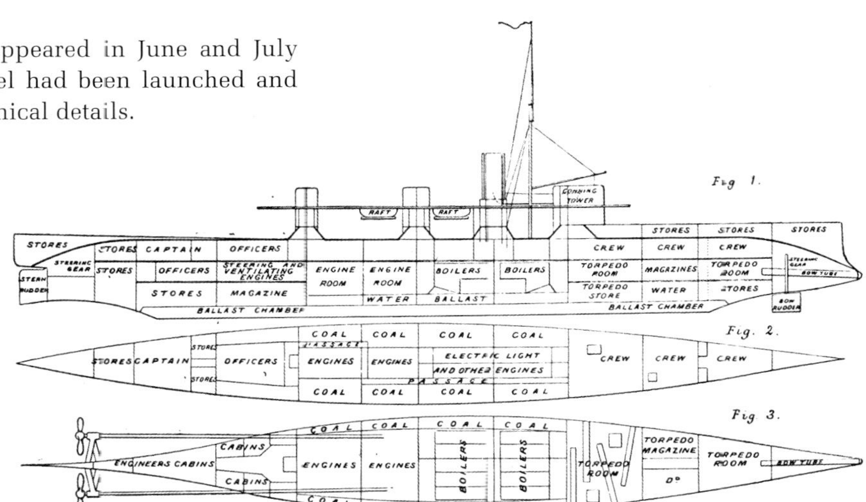

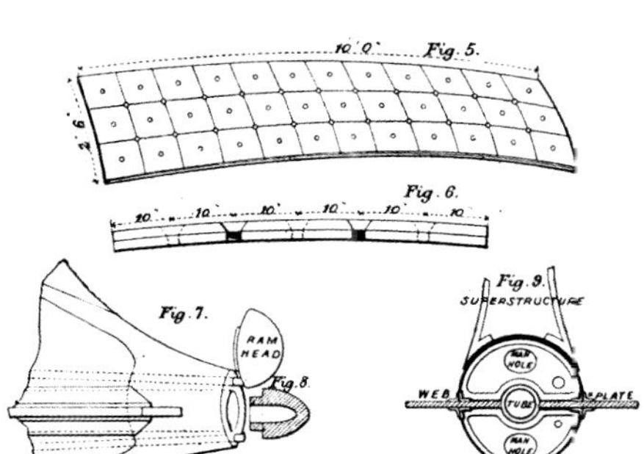

TECHNICAL DETAILS FOR *POLYPHEMUS*
ENGINEERING, 8 JULY 1881

In our issue of the 17th June last, and in a subsequent number, we described the chief elements of the construction of the *Polyphemus*, recently launched at Chatham, and discussed some of the novel features which this ship possesses. In order to make the accounts clear and to illustrate some further description which we shall now add, we give on the opposite page engravings of some sketches taken from the ship. These engravings are as follows: Fig 1 is a sectional elevation showing the positions of decks and the distribution of the various machinery compartments, magazines, storerooms, etc; Figs 2 and 3 are the corresponding plans of the main and lower decks; Fig 4 is a midship section of the ship; Figs 5 and 6 are sketches showing how the Whitworth armour is put together and worked; and Figs 7 and 8 show how the ram is constructed, and how the ram-head is carried and secured [see page 55 for diagrams].

We may again enumerate the principal dimensions of the vessel: length, 240ft; extreme breadth, 40ft; draught of water, 19ft 6in forward and 20ft 6in aft; and displacement, 2,640 tons. The upper deck, or turtle-back deck as it is called, is 4ft above the water line along its middle; but the form of the vessel is such that it curves down and enters the water at an angle of about 45 degrees, so that according to the usual acceptation of the term the ship has no free board whatever. A light superstructure forecastle is raised to a height of 4ft 6in above the turtle-back to keep the bow up when the vessel is steaming at full speed, and upon this anchors and other fittings are placed. There is also a low superstructure aft to form a platform to walk upon and to give finish to the vessel. Between these two superstructures a wash strake is fitted so as to give a good sight line and to carry hand rails.

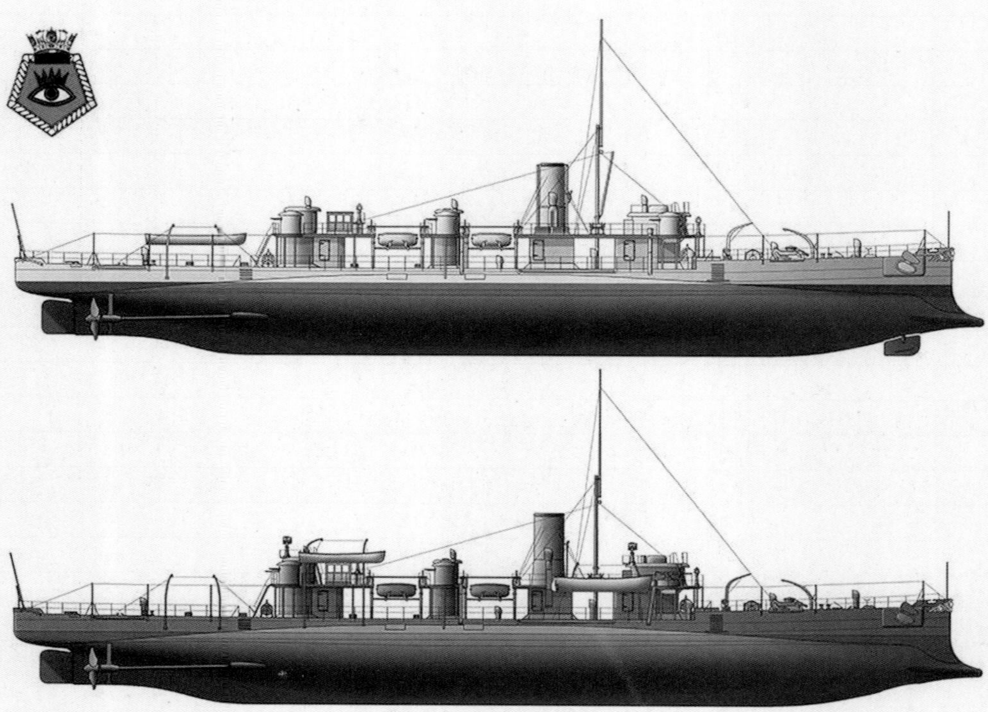

Profiles of *Polyphemus* as built and after reboilering in 1884. *(Navypedia)*

The launch of HMS *Polyphemus*. (*Illustrated London News*, 25 June 1881)

The water will sweep across the upper deck even in moderate weather; no attempt is made to keep it from doing so, but as in all the low-sided war vessels in the British Navy the principal hatchways are trunked up to a flying deck from which alone the interior of the vessel will be accessible at sea. The flying deck is 10ft 6in above the upper deck, and therefore 14ft 6in above the water, and it extends between the forecastle and the platform deck aft. There is only a handrail around the flying deck, but three of the four hatchways which are trunked up open into circular deck-houses fitted with covers or hoods 6ft or 7ft above the deck; the fourth trunk contains the funnel with its casing and air spaces which also extend several feet above the deck, and may be closed in when required. The foremost trunked hatchway is divided into three by partition bulkheads, one, by far the largest of the three ways, leading to the forward part of the ship including the torpedo-rooms and magazines, and the two smaller ones leading to each of the two forward stokeholds. The deck-house over this trunk will form the forward pilot tower, and will contain the steering wheel and the various implements for working and fighting the ship. The middle deck-house stands over a trunked way which is also divided into three by partition bulkheads; two of these lead down to the aftermost stokeholds and the third to the foremost engine-room. The aftermost trunk is divided into two, one passage leading down to the after part of the ship, and the other to the after engine-room. The deck-house over this trunk forms the after pilot tower, and will be similarly fitted to the forward pilot tower. The central deck-house may also be used as a pilot tower, but it will have no armour. The six Nordenfelt guns will be mounted in separate revolving turrets carried upon projecting framework at the level of the flying deck. There will be three of these on each side, one at the fore end of the flying deck, one at the middle, and the third at the after end.

The ship will carry four boats, two by davits from the flying deck ready for use, as on Fig 1, and two others kept lashed up under the flying deck aft. She will also be fitted with two life-rafts and gear for launching them in any weather. The position of these rafts is shown on Figs 1 and 4.

Over the side of the turtle-back deck, to a depth of from 4ft to 6ft, there are

3in of steel armour made up as follows: two ½in thicknesses of Landore-Siemens steel, one of which may be regarded as the skin of the ship; upon these is a 1in thickness of Whitworth fluid-compressed steel, which will stand a strain of 45 tons per inch and upon this again there is a 1in thickness of hard Whitworth steel, also fluid-compressed, worked in plates 10in square, which are tested to a strain of 68 tons. The two outer thicknesses of the side plating were supplied by Sir Joseph Whitworth in compound plates already bolted together and worked to shape, and only requiring to be fastened on the ship. The plates forming the under inch thickness are all 10ft long and 2ft 6in wide, so that each required thirty-six 10in squares or scales, as they are called, to cover it. The scales are secured with coned steel screw bolts placed as shown in Figs 5 and 6, viz, one at the centre of each of the plates, and one at each of the corners, so as to hold each of the four adjacent plates. Along the middle of the turtle-back deck the 10in scales are not fitted, so that here the armour is only 2in thick. The bases of the trunks from the hatchways to the flying deck are protected by a glacis of 6in steel-faced armour to a height of 3ft 6in above the deck; and the entire front of the foremost trunk is protected by 8in steel-faced armour, which also extends to a height of about 5ft above the flying deck, and gives protection to the pilot tower.

Those who are at all accustomed to considering the requirements of a vessel of this character will not be surprised to observe from the diagrams how completely filled the ship is with necessary fittings and stores, and how very little space is left for providing even requisite accommodation, to say nothing of ordinary comforts, for the officers and men. Excepting the low superstructure forecastle there is no space above water available either for the stowage of stores or for accommodation, and this in a ship of 2,640 tons, and with engines of 5,500 indicated horse power, and having an available depth of hold of about 15ft; whereas in an ordinary ship of this displacement and power, space for nearly the whole of the accommodation and much of the storage would be found above the boundary at which the hull of the *Polyphemus*

The foredeck of HMS *Polyphemus* was frequently underwater when operating at speed. *(US Naval History and Heritage Command, NH65967)*

ceases. In groping our way over the ship, along the narrow passages under the low flats and into the various compartments, we found no corner that was not appropriated. The 103 men who form the crew may manage to live in the limited spaces allotted them forward on the main deck, but they will barely be comfortable, notwithstanding the elaborate ventilators both for conveying in fresh air and for removing foul air which pass along overhead and considerably limit the area over which it is possible to stand upright. The officers also will fare but little better in their quarters on the main deck aft; their accommodation is not luxurious. The round turtle-back form of the upper deck indicated on the midship section is preserved forward and aft, indeed it is sharper towards the extremities, so that out towards the sides of the living deck both forward and aft it will be impossible to stand upright.

The whole of the central portion of the vessel over about one-third of the length is taken up by engines, boilers, and coal. As will be seen on reference to Figs 1 and 3, the boilers are placed low down in the ship below the main deck; they are arranged in four water-tight compartments, three in each of those on the starboard side and two in each of those on the port. Over them on the main deck are placed the ventilating fans, electric light engines, and various other small engines. There are two separate engine-rooms, one before the other, the forward set of engines working the port screw and the after set the starboard screw. The coal (250 tons) is carried in sixteen bunkers placed as on Figs 2, 3, and 4. The only communication below the upper deck between the compartments before the boilers, and those abaft the engines is along a passage on the main deck, shown in Figs 2 and 4, which is walled in with plating on either side and top and bottom, so as to form a water-tight tunnel. The various boiler and engine-room compartments are accessible through water-tight doors leading from this passage, as well as from above as already described. The vessel has two collision bulkheads to keep back the water in case her strongly framed bow should be strained in ramming. The chase torpedo tube extends from the ram to 2ft or 3ft abaft the inner of these collision bulkheads, and opens on the lower deck. Here the loading of this tube will be effected. Proceeding aft on the lower deck the next compartment is allotted to torpedo magazines. Abaft this again is the main torpedo chamber, where there are four tubes, two on each side. Independent air-compressing machinery will be carried in each of the torpedo chambers; each of which chambers will also carry a number of torpedoes ready for use; the main store of torpedoes will, however, be carried in the hold under the floor of the main torpedo chamber. The main magazines for the Snider and Nordenfelt ammunition are in the after hold, but it is also intended to fit a small magazine for Nordenfelt ammunition forward. Besides the keel ballast, which may be cast loose at pleasure, a considerable weight of water ballast will usually be carried in the inner bottom compartments under the boiler and engine rooms.

Whether the *Polyphemus* will be able to crush in the side of her enemy with her long pointed ram without her bow tube being so injured as to make it unfit for use, is doubted by most persons competent to give an opinion on the subject. The bow, however, is very strong, and great care has been taken to give the tube every chance of escaping uninjured. The tube proper is placed within an outer tube of great strength, against which, however, it does not rest except at its extremities; the outer tube being rigidly attached to and forming part of the framing of the bow. By continuing the armour down and attaching it to deep web plates which extend into the outer tube and out to 18in beyond the skin of the ship, an arrangement of great strength has doubtless been made. The front of the tube is a massive forging which is continued aft, above and below the tube, and is well able to take care of itself. The ram-head also is of fluid-compressed steel, and is almost solid; when in place it extends into the tube several inches, so that against all blows from the front it is firmly held by the forging just referred to. The ram-head is worked from inside the ship by a steel rod to which it is fixed, and when in place it is also held by a rod below. In the position shown by Fig 8 the ram-head is turned up clear of the tube.

Two auxiliary balanced rudders are fitted forward one on each side of the bow torpedo tube. They are carried upon strong vertical shafts by which they are worked, and when not required are drawn up into trunks within the hull. When in use these rudders may if desired be coupled up with the engine working the stern rudder, and all three rudders worked together.

It is confidently anticipated that a speed of 17 knots will be attained at the measured mile, but it can scarcely be hoped that the vessel will be able to sustain this speed for many consecutive hours. The distance she will be able to cover at her six hours' trial of continuous steaming will really be the measure of her capabilities in this direction. A consideration of vital importance in this vessel is her manoeuvring power. Her only modes of attack being the torpedo and the ram, she must necessarily constantly endeavour to come to close quarters with the enemy, or to keep out of range of his guns. With a speed 17 knots she will be able to elect whether she will fight or not with almost any ship at present afloat, and supposing she chooses to fight, the chance of her success will depend almost entirely on the rapidity with which she will be able to close in with the enemy, and having closed in with him, to manoeuvre around him, so as to bring her torpedo tubes successively into the line of fire and within range, and also to use her ram. The vessel will doubtless possess the power of turning rapidly, the powerful rudders at both ends of the ship, and the cutting away of the fore foot and the after 'deadwood' or heel will insure this, but the question of the degree of handiness can only be settled satisfactorily by actual trials.

It could be wished that her armour was thicker, but when it is remembered that the only important parts are very oblique surfaces close to the water line, and that the vital parts, the boilers and magazines, are well protected by being many feet below the water line, this can scarcely be considered altogether unsatisfactory; moreover, her many water-tight sub-divisions and detachable ballast make it probable that she might be hit at many points along the water line without being placed *hors de combat*. The *Polyphemus* is without doubt in conception a very formidable vessel, but she is novel and untried in many respects, in fact, there is scarcely anything about her which is not novel, and we look forward with much interest to her trial cruises.

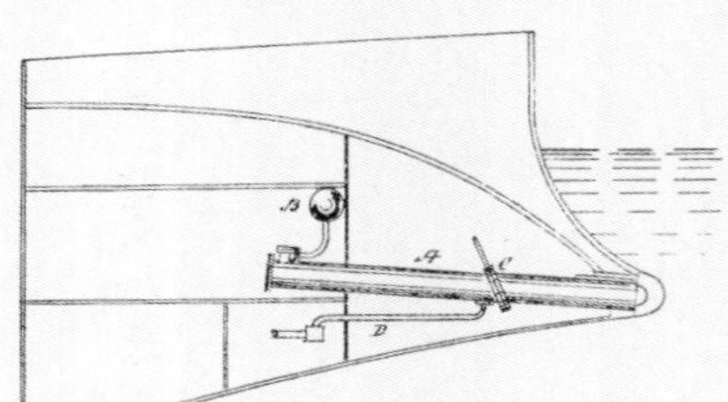

Fig. 1

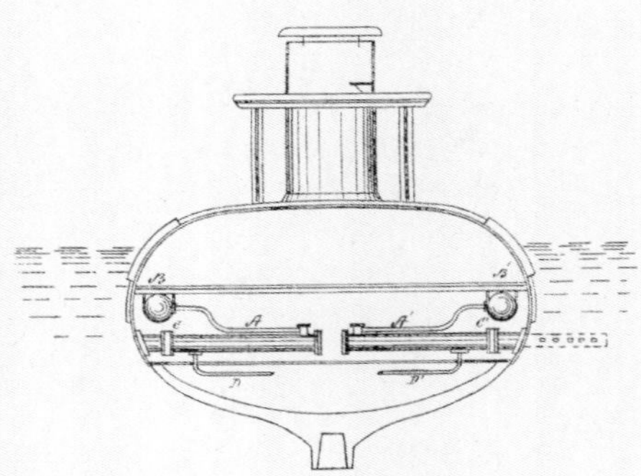

Fig. 2

The arrangement of torpedo tubes in HMS *Polyphemus* (Sleeman). Key: A – launching tube; B – air reservoir; C – sluice valve; D – drain pipe. Dotted lines represent guide bars and shield for support of the torpedo until it is clear of the tube.

The article of 17 June 1881 contained a correction to the first one, stating that the keel 'groove' was '3ft 6in deep, 2ft 6in wide at the bottom, and 2ft at the top, being formed along the whole length in the position usually occupied by the keel.' More details were also provided of the main engines:

> The engines of the *Polyphemus* were constructed by Messrs Humphrys, Tennant, and Co; they are horizontal single piston-rod compounds with high-pressure cylinders 38in in diameter and low-pressure cylinders 64in in diameter, the stroke being 39in. They are supplied from ten boilers of the locomotive type, with a working pressure of 120lb per square inch. The engines have indicated 5,500 horse power, and the estimated speed to be got with them is 17 knots. She will be propelled by three-bladed twin screws 14ft in diameter, and from 15ft to 17ft pitch.

The five torpedo tubes fired 14in Mark II torpedoes, of which eighteen were carried. The centre torpedo tube was fitted with a combined cast steel bow cap, which hinged upwards to open, and ram. The other four tubes were arranged with two on each side, as in the original concept.

Her original gun armament consisted of six twin-barrelled Nordenfelt 25mm automatic guns, although later in the 1880s they were replaced by six single Hotchkiss 3pdr quick-firing guns. *Polyphemus* was the first Royal Navy vessel to be fitted with 80V electric lighting.

She suffered a number of problems with her beam torpedo tubes which were eventually solved with the help of *Vernon*'s experts. Her locomotive boilers also gave trouble, both from priming and leaking. As a result, trials were carried out on four first-class torpedo boats, with similar boilers, which concluded that the main problems were the high rate of burning coal and the high level of draught experienced, which resulted in recommendations for modifications to the fixings of tubes to the boilers.

In 1885 the ship undertook a simulated attack on a fleet at anchor at Berehaven, County Cork. Booms and nets were laid across the channel behind Berehaven, along with small observation mines and the area covered by machine guns and torpedo boats. *Polyphemus* launched a simulated attack on 30 June, evading around ten torpedoes fired by six torpedo boats during her two-mile approach and easily smashed through the booms and a 5in steel hawser holding them in place.

Polyphemus served her entire career with the Mediterranean Fleet. In 1892 George Aston was the intelligence officer on the Mediterranean squadron and in his memoirs, *Memories of a Marine*, wrote:

> Arriving at Malta in March, 1892, I found the harbour full of ships of queer design and outline and the strangest sample of all was represented by *Polyphemus*, in which the torpedo took the place of the gun as a main armament. She sought protection from the enemy's fire by submerging nearly all her hull by taking sea-water into special compartments. Accommodation was most uncomfortable, especially at sea.

A report in *The Navy & Army Illustrated*, dated 9 April 1898, included the sentence: 'She is the only vessel of her kind in our Fleet, and, speaking generally, may be said to represent the views of certain extremists among Naval officers of twenty years ago, who at that time were loudly proclaiming the advantages of the ram as an almost resistless means of offence.' In 1884 *Polyphemus* was reboilered with eight cylindrical boilers. At that time, her armament comprised four quadruple and six twin 25/40 mountings, and two single 57/40 6pdr Hotchkiss Mk I mountings. The six twin mountings were soon removed and later this was further amended to four quadruple 25/40 and four single 57/40 6pdr Hotchkiss Mk I mountings.

Polyphemus was paid off at Chatham Dockyard in January 1900, and in April 1902 she was employed as tender to HMS *Defiance*, the Royal Navy's second torpedo school at Devonport, finally being broken up in 1903.

CHAPTER FOUR

FIRST-CLASS TORPEDO BOATS, *TB1–TB79*

In order to optimise the potential effectiveness of the Whitehead torpedo, a new type of vessel which, according to Armstrong, 'combined the qualities of great speed and extreme handiness, and was at the same time of such a size and shape as to offer the least possible target to the enemy' was required. These developed into the larger first-class boats intended for operations from naval bases, and the smaller second-class boats for harbour work and for carrying on the decks of cruisers and battleships.

The Admiralty showed particular interest in a high speed, not only for torpedo boats, and following his success with the launches *Miranda* (Yard No. 10, 1871, 16¼ kts) and *Gitana* (Yard No. 37, 1876, 20¾ kts), Thornycroft persuaded them to place an order for their first torpedo boat in 1876. The vessel, HMS *Lightning* (Yard No. 47), later to be known as *TB1*, was delivered to Portsmouth in May 1877 (see Plate 2).

In a lecture to the Royal United Services Institute (RUSI) given on 11 May 1877, entitled 'The Thornycroft Torpedo-Vessels; Their Construction, Armament, &c, And The Results Of Certain Experiments That Have Been Made With Them', Mr John Donaldson, Assoc ICE, said of *Lightning*:

> This vessel is 84ft long overall, by 10ft 10in beam, draws about 5ft of water, and is guaranteed to do a speed of 18 knots on her trial. The machinery on board the *Lightning* is similar in design to that already described, and is capable of indicating 350 horse power. The hull of the *Lightning* is made of heavier plating than we usually employ, and her

HMS *Lightning, TB1. (Vosper Thornycroft)*

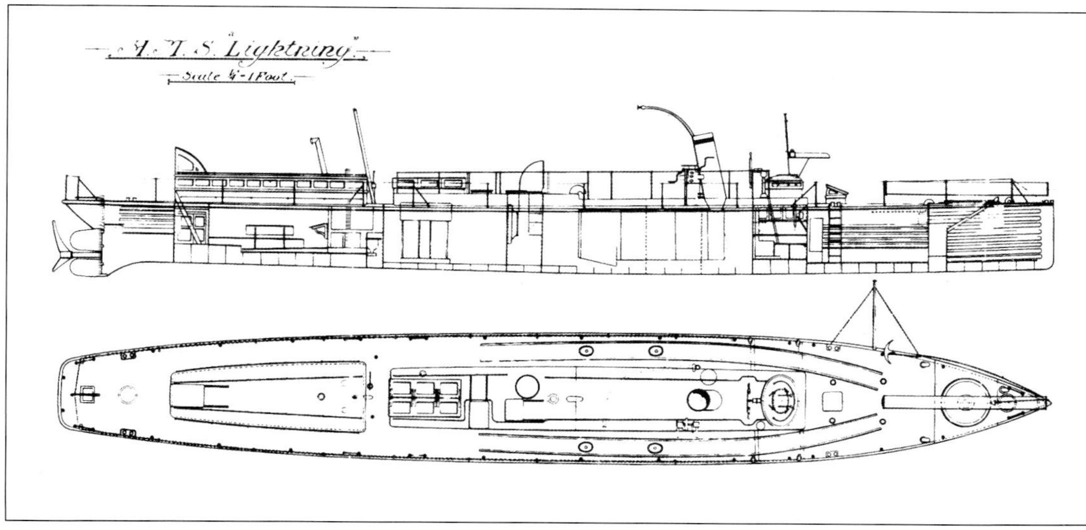

Shipbuilder's drawing of *TB1*. *(© National Maritime Museum, Greenwich, London)*

lines are fuller, as she is intended for use in a tolerably rough sea if necessary; and in order that she may be able to remain at sea for some time, cabin accommodation on a scale larger than in any of the other boats is provided for the officers and crew. The steering gear is arranged so that the vessel may be steered from the deck, or from the conning-tower, and the usual telegraph gear is fitted to communicate from the deck, or from the conning-tower to the engine-room. The top of the conning-tower is supported on three screws, so arranged that it may be raised or lowered, and the space for sight adjusted according to the range of vision required, or the risk to be run from the enemy's missiles. The *Lightning* is to be armed with the Whitehead torpedo, which will be discharged from her forward deck by means of a discharging apparatus, the details of which I am not sufficiently familiar with to be able to give a description. The torpedoes will be charged with air, by means of one of Mr Brotherhood's air-compressing pumps. The *Lightning* has not yet been officially tried, but on her preliminary runs in the Thames, she attained a speed on the measured mile of 19.4 knots per hour, a speed which will be somewhat reduced when she has her torpedoes and their gear on board, but which will leave us an ample margin on our guaranteed speed of 18 knots per hour.

Donaldson's paper indicates that the original intention was to fit a torpedo tube, but *Lightning* was completed with two torpedo frames, one on each side, and the tube was not fitted until 1879, with two reloads on trolleys being carried amidships. Donaldson also notes that 'cabin accommodation on a scale larger than in any of the other boats is provided for the officers and crew' of eleven, and is reflected by the yacht-like 'coach roof' cabin aft, a feature not included in subsequent repeat vessels.

The complement comprised one lieutenant; one sub lieutenant or warrant officer; one chief engine room artificer and one engine room artificer; a leading stoker and two stokers; one petty officer and two able seaman plus one signalman.

Lightning's entire career was spent as a tender to *Vernon*, where she undertook many experiments, connected both to the launching and running of the Whitehead torpedo and the general performance of torpedo boats. As built, the propeller was sited aft of a horizontally divided rudder, at the time thought to provide the highest speeds. The design of a propeller by Thornycroft, which was trialled on *Lightning*, was described in the 30 December 1881 issue of the weekly publication *Engineering*.

This 1/24-scale model of *Lightning* portrays her with a white hull, pristine wooden decks and shiny funnel and vents – a very unlikely condition for a torpedo boat in service! It does show the trainable torpedo tube on the bow and two spare torpedoes amidships. The propeller is aft of the rudder. *(© National Maritime Museum, Greenwich, London)*

THE THORNYCROFT PROPELLER DESIGN

ENGINEERING, 30 DECEMBER 1881

Referring to our illustrations it will be seen that the screw propeller *a* is provided with a central boss, the diameter of which increases towards the rear, this boss being as it were continued by a body *b* fixed astern of the propeller. The propeller *a* revolves within a guide tube *c*, which is continued sternwards so as also to encircle the body *b*, this latter body being connected to the guide tube by radial plates *d d*, which serve to divert the water discharged by the screw into a course approximately parallel to the axis of the body *b*. Astern of the parts already referred to is the rudder *e*, which carries a boss or body *f* forming a prolongation of the body *b*, such prolongation gradually decreasing in diameter sternwards as shown in Fig 2. The forward end of the body *f* is of a spherical form so that it can work in a corresponding hollow in the rear of the body *b* as shown. The manner in which the rudder is mounted will be readily understood from Fig 2, and it will be seen that the rudder-head *g* in addition to the ordinary tiller *h* carries also a secondary tiller *i*, the object of which we shall explain presently.

Outside the guide tube *c*, and partially encircling it, are two curved guide plates *j j*, the outline of which, in plan, is shown by dotted lines in Fig 3. The lower ends of these curved plates are pivotted on studs *k k* (see Fig 1), while their upper ends are guided by similar studs *l l*. The guide plates *j j* are operated by cranks or arms fixed at the lower ends of the two short vertical shafts *m m*, the arrangement being such that when one of the shafts *m* is rotated in the proper direction, the corresponding guide plate *j* is moved outwards and backwards,

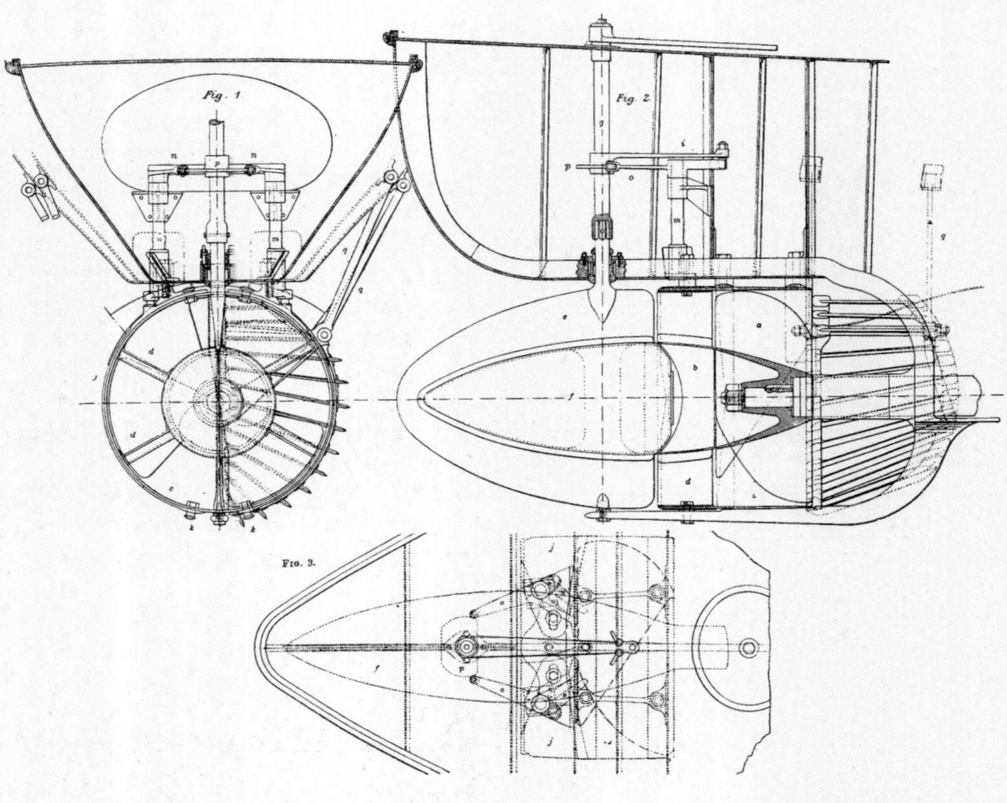

Thornycroft's patent design for a propeller for torpedo boats. *(Engineering, 30 December 1881)*

the effect being that the guide plate is first moved away from the guide tube *c*, and then carried aft so that its forward edge is pressed around the after edge of the guide tube. In this position it is so placed in relation to the guide tube as to direct the issuing water in a line approximately parallel to the axis of the body *f* in the position in which that body is at the time placed.

We have now to describe how the guide plates *j* derive their movement from the action of the tiller. We have said that the rudder-head carries a secondary tiller *i*, and on reference to Figs 2 and 3 it will be seen that this secondary tiller carries at its end a friction roller which projects downwards so that it is in the same plane as certain bifurcated levers *n n* fixed at the upper ends of the shafts *m m*. The form of those bifurcated levers *n n* can be traced in the plan, Fig 3, and it will be seen that they are formed in one piece with arms *o o* which project rearwards and carry at their ends rollers which bear against the edge of the cam or locking plate *p*, this plate being fixed on the rudder head as shown.

With the parts in the position in which they are shown in our illustrations – the rudder being amidships – the guide plates *j j* are locked in position by the locking plate *p* as just described, and it will be seen that this state of affairs is not altered so long as the rudder is moved through a moderate angle on each side of its central position. When it is desired to make a sharp turn, however, and the rudder is put hard over, the locking plate *p* is by its partial rotation carried clear of the roller at the end of one of the arms *o* (according to the direction in which the rudder is put over), while at the same time the roller at the end of the secondary tiller *i* engages with the fork of the corresponding bifurcated lever *n* with the effect of operating the corresponding guide plate in the manner already described.

If we suppose the tiller to be put over to port (the rudder being consequently deflected to starboard) the effect of the operations just explained will be to cause the guide plate *j* on the port side to be carried rearwards, when it will form a kind of curved extension of the periphery of the guide tube *c* on that side, and will divert the current of water issuing on that side into a direction approximately parallel to the axis of the rudder in its then position. The turning effect of this arrangement is remarkably powerful, the experiments on the *Lightning* showing that in making a sharp turn the bow remained practically stationary, the stern swinging round the bow as a centre. In the case of the *Lightning* a complete turn was made in this way in seventy-two seconds. The value of this power of manoeuvring in the case of a torpedo boat can scarcely be over-rated.

It will be noticed that the propeller is protected by a grid of bars which will prevent ropes, &c, becoming entangled with it. This grid is made in two parts which meet in a vertical plane near the centre line of the vessel, each part being hinged to the hull by a pair of links *q q*, of such length that the half grids may be drawn away from the screw and laid on deck without disconnecting them from their attachments. The arrangement is a very convenient one.

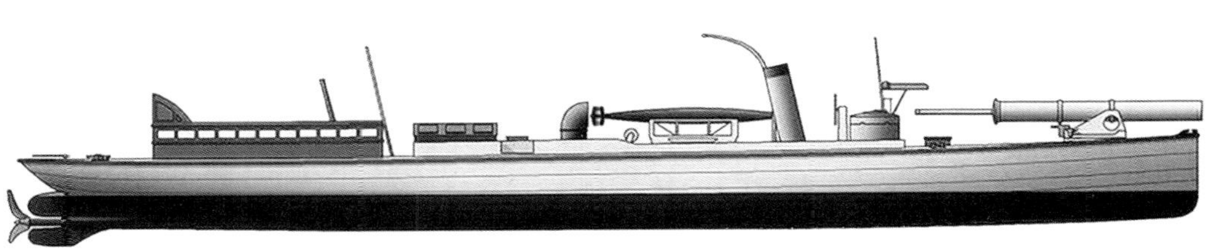

Profile of *Lightning* with bow torpedo tube. *(Navypedia)*

Lightning, *TB1*. (© National Maritime Museum, Greenwich, London, Richard Perkins Collection)

Lightning took part in the fleet review held at Spithead on 13 August 1878 and in the fleet manoeuvres at Bantry Bay during June and July 1885, finally being broken up in 1896, although her engine continued to be used to power some machinery in Portsmouth Dockyard.

Following the success of *Lightning*, eleven more similar boats were ordered from Thornycroft, *TB2–TB12* (Yard Nos 71–81). These were longer than *Lightning*, their engines developed more power, and they were not fitted with a coach roof, but they did receive a bow torpedo tube when first completed. Later, they received dropping gear for two torpedoes and some were used for trials with spar torpedoes. *TB10* had a different hull form, incorporating a ram bow. She was longer than the others and her engines delivered more power, resulting in a further increase in speed.

Details of these vessels were given in a paper, dated 10 May 1881, to the Institution of Civil Engineers by Mr John Isaac Thornycroft, entitled 'On Torpedo-Boats and Light Yachts for High Speed Steam Navigation'.

TB3 and *TB10*. (Navypedia)

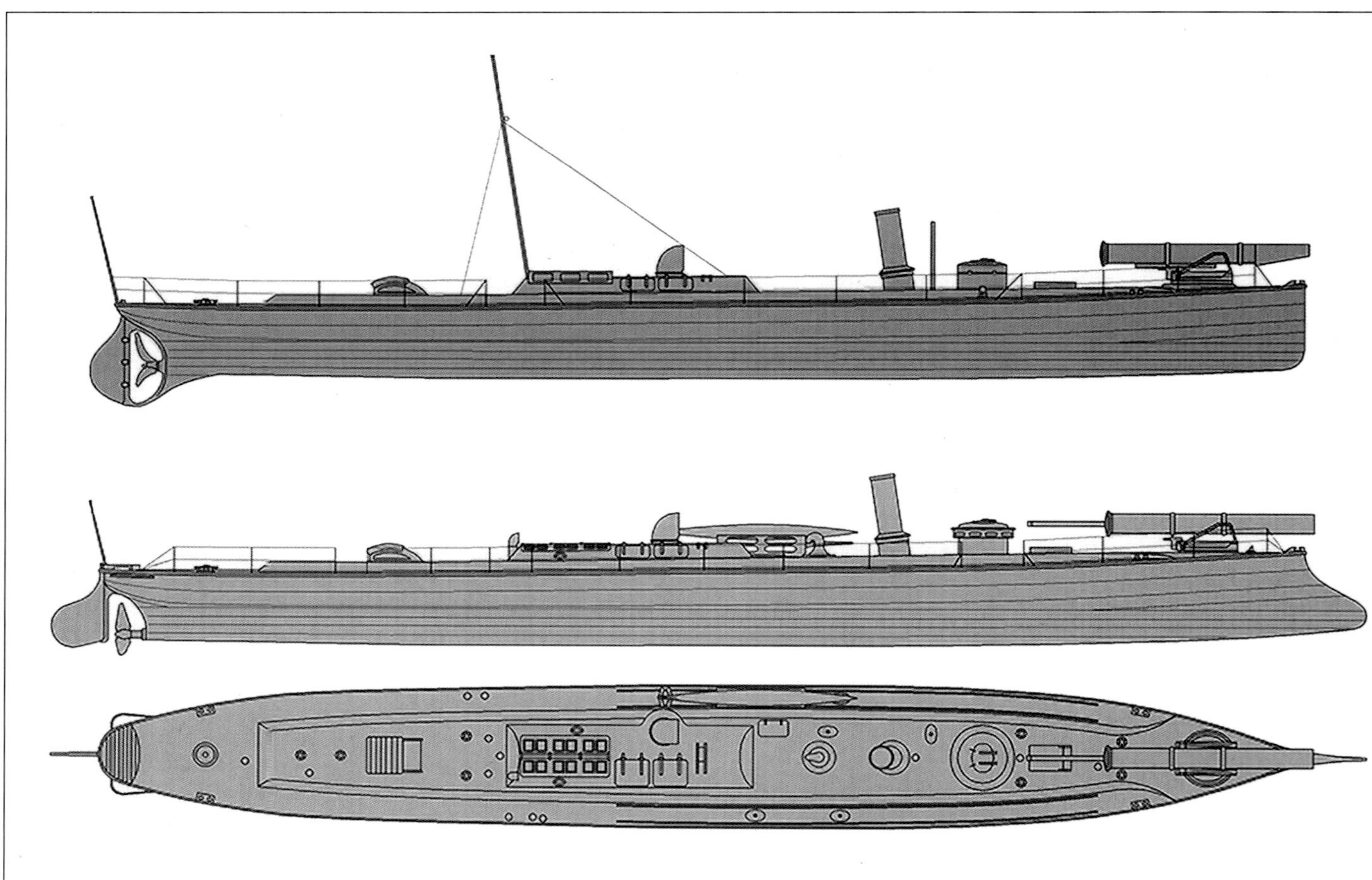

ON TORPEDO-BOATS AND LIGHT YACHTS FOR HIGH SPEED STEAM NAVIGATION
LECTURE BY MR JOHN ISAAC THORNYCROFT, M INST CE, 10 MAY 1881

This boat is 87ft in length, with a breadth of beam of 10½ft. The draught is 1ft 6in forward, and 5ft 2in aft, with a displacement of 32.4 tons. The engines are compound, with an intermediate receiver, having a 12¾in high-pressure cylinder, and a low-pressure cylinder 20in in diameter, with a stroke of 12in. The cranks are at right angles. The air-pump is worked by levers from the high-pressure cylinder, as in the engines of the *Gitana*, making, of course, the same number of strokes per minute as the engines. The condensing water is forced through the condenser by a centrifugal pump, with an auxiliary engine, assisted by a special form of grating, which, by means of gradually expanding openings, converts the external relative velocity of the water into pressure. The thrust-block is secured to the bedplate of the engine by two stays, one attached to each side, and level with the centre of the shaft: thus preventing any tendency to throw undue thrust on the lower half. The slide-valves of the engines are balanced by being placed under bridges, which are made with recesses corresponding to the ports in the cylinders, as used by Mr Wilson, of Patricroft. In order to obviate the difficulty caused by the varying deflection under varying pressures, each bridge is in section like a bowstring girder, the bow not being attached, however, to the string except at the ends; and, by connecting the intermediate space with the exhaust, the flat surface is little distorted by pressure, and does not partake of any deflection affecting the bow. This construction of Mr Wilson's valve is due to Mr J Donaldson, M Inst CE, and appears to answer its purpose well.

The packing rings of the pistons are of Perkins metal, four in each piston, in separate grooves. They are found to work much more quietly than the single wide rings usually adopted in marine engines.

The fan engine is similar to the one employed in the *Gitana*. Two feed-pumps are worked by a cast-iron four-thread worm on the engine shaft, geared into a suitable wheel of phosphor-bronze secured to a steel shaft, having cranks at the ends, to each of which a feed-pump is connected. The ratio of the gearing in the worm and wheel is as 4 to 15. The feed-pumps are 4in in diameter, with a 3in stroke. The engine-room also contains a bilge-pump, which is worked from the feed-pump shaft; and an air-compressing pump, with a separate engine, for charging torpedoes. A donkey pump is fitted in the stokehole, by which the boiler can be supplied when the main engines are at rest.

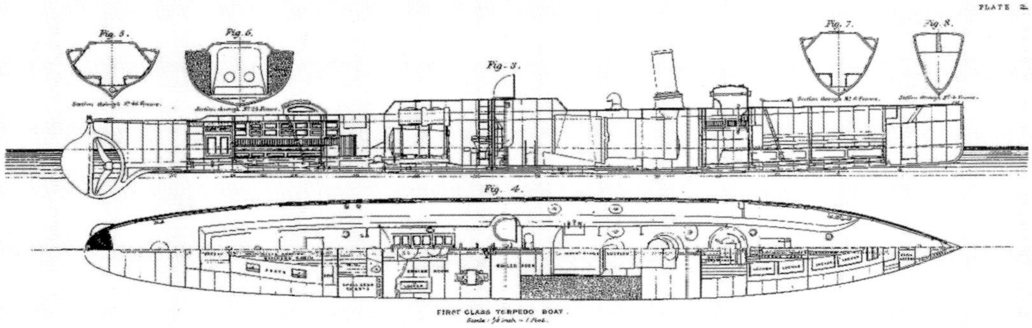

The arrangement drawing that accompanied Thornycroft's paper. *(Institution of Civil Engineers, 10 May 1881)*

The propeller is constructed with three blades, and is placed forward of the rudder. It is 4ft 6in in diameter, and has a pitch of 6ft.

The boiler is of the locomotive type, and has a total heating surface of 620sq ft, of which 56sq ft are contributed by the fire-box surface. The area of the fire-grate is 18.4sq ft. The outer shell is 4ft 5in in diameter, and 12ft 6in long. It contains two hundred and five tubes 6ft long, measured over the tube plates, and 11in in external diameter. The working pressure is 120lbs.

An important feature in the boiler is the fire-box. In the boilers of the smaller type of torpedo-boats, the roofs of the fire-boxes are stayed with ordinary longitudinal beams; but in the boilers of the larger type, where the fire-grate amounts to more than 18sq ft in area, the roof of the fire-box is stayed directly to the outer shell of the boiler, made flat for a width equal to that of the top of the fire-box, to which it is connected by vertical stays. By this mode of construction, there is the advantage of adding slightly to the steam-room, but this alone scarcely balances the extra weight of material used in construction. It is, however, more convenient for staying than the radial system when the outer shell is cylindrical over the fire-box; and there is more elasticity, to take up any unequal expansion between the fire-box and the shell. The shells of the boilers are mostly of steel. In the earlier boats, the fire-boxes were of copper; but in the boats built for the English Admiralty, the fire-box has been constructed of iron, as the boilers are liable to be fed with salt water. At the same time, iron fire-boxes possess greater strength than those of copper.

In order to extinguish the fire, in cases when it must be extinguished and cannot be drawn, a rose with an ejector is fitted, in constant communication with the sea, by admitting steam to which the fire may be extinguished in a very short time.

Provision is also made, by self-closing ashpit-doors, for preventing the return of vapour to the stokehole. A passage to the deck is also provided to facilitate the escape of the steam discharged in the event of a tube giving way.

Amidships, the deck is raised, so as to give room to work the fire and the engines, the depth of the vessel otherwise not being sufficient for this purpose. On either side of this raised deck, the torpedo-davits are fixed, and the torpedoes are so carried as to hang within the width of the boat, for security. Air for the fire is taken in at a cowl, situated just astern of the after bulkhead of the engine-room, against which may be seen the disk of the blowing fan.

The deck forward is much rounded, so that any water that may come on board can run off with facility. The stepped section amidships partially gives

TB2 underway; note the 14in torpedo tube at the bow. *(US Naval History and Heritage Command, NH54986)*

Another view of *TB2*. *(Naval History & Heritage Command Navypedia)*

the same result. It affords much better foothold than the rounded surface, which is very necessary for the men at this place.

The stern-frame extends considerably below the rest of the vessel, and carries the rudder abaft the screw. This frame is a Bessemer-steel forging, carefully shaped to a long elliptical outline in horizontal section, parallel, of course, to the direction of its intended motion through the water, in order to reduce, as far as possible, its resistance. The boat is fitted with a bilge suction-pipe to each of the principal compartments. Indexes on deck show what communicating valves are open. The boiler is placed lower at the forward end than at the fire-box end. The boilers, however, assume a horizontal position when the boats are at full speed, in consequence of the change of trim. This change amounts to about 3ft 10in in 100ft, according to the results of experiments on the *Miranda*. By Mr Froude's model of the *Lightning*, at a speed corresponding to 19 knots, it was shown that the vessel inclined 3ft 5in in the same length, 100ft; an inclination which does not differ much from that of the *Miranda*.

The paper also included a table comparing particulars of some of the boats.

TB2–TB9. *(© National Maritime Museum, Greenwich, London, Richard Perkins Collection)*

Name of vessel	Date	Length on WL (ft in)	Displacement (tons)	Indicated HP	Speed in knots per hour
First-class torpedo boat No. 1	1877	81 0	28.7	400	18.55
First-class torpedo boat No. 6	1879	83 9	32.43	425	20.00
First-class torpedo boat No. 10	1880	88 3	29.73	460	22.01
First-class torpedo boat No. 10	1880	88 3	32.5	469	21.756

In June 1884, whilst stationed at Devonport, *TB2* was allocated for torpedo trials with the Channel Squadron in Bantry Bay. On 18 July 1889 she formed part of a combined fleet that was reviewed by the German emperor and then took part in the annual manoeuvres, being paid off on 31 August at their conclusion. *TB3* was a tender to *Vernon* from May 1899 to February 1904. *TB4* was a member of the Medway Stream Reserve from 1885 to 1889, but in 1908 she appears in Lloyd's Register as being registered in Gibraltar in 1906, with M H Bland as her owner. *TB5* was commissioned in June 1884 for torpedo experiments with the Channel Fleet in Bantry Bay, whilst stationed at Devonport. Together with *TB6* and *TB7*, she took part in the annual manoeuvres in Bantry Bay in June and July 1885 and was sold in 1898/9 for £25. In early 1900 *TB6* acted as a coastguard vessel, and in January 1901 became a tender to the cruiser *Doris*, which was flagship on the Cape station. In April 1901 *Doris* was relieved by *Gibraltar* and *TB6* continued as her tender until May 1904. In 1908 *TB7* appeared in Lloyd's Register as being registered in Gibraltar in 1904. *TB8* was sold in 1902/3 for £29 10s. In early 1886 *TB9*, *TB10* and *TB11* were commissioned for service in the Mediterranean. On 7 August 1901 *TB9* collided with *Contest* in Torquay Harbour and was sold for £39. In September 1885, in the process of attacking the central battery HMS *Alexandra* in St Pauls Bay, *TB11* struck a rock whilst proceeding at 18 knots and was considerably damaged.

All had been sold for breaking up by 1906. Although these vessels were not considered to be ocean-going, many did travel significant distances to their base for operations; *TB6* went to the Cape, *TB7* to Gibraltar and *TB8*, *TB9*, *TB10* and *TB11* to Hong Kong.

On 17 December 1880 the publication *Engineering* published further details of these boats with particular reference to *TB10*.

A view of *TB3*. *(US Naval History & Heritage Command Navypedia)*

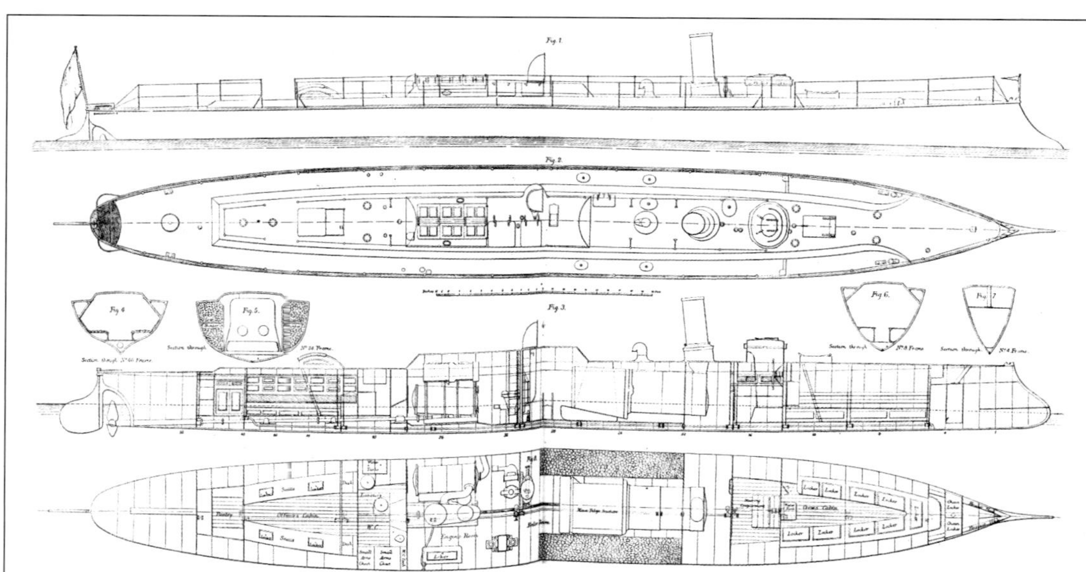

A general arrangement drawing of *TB10*. *(Engineering, 17 September 1880)*

EARLY TORPEDO BOATS, WITH PARTICULAR REFERENCE TO *TB10*

***Engineering*, 17 December 1880**

The hulls of these torpedo boats are made of Bessemer steel galvanised, the majority, as built for the Admiralty, being fitted with upright stems, and having the stern-post continued in a hoop below the propeller, with a view to its protection. In the boat illustrated, however, a ram bow was fitted and the hoop done away with, thus apparently exposing the propeller to damage. The contrary, however, is the case, as anything likely to injure the screw would certainly injure the protecting hoop, and in all probability bend it sufficiently to prevent the propeller from revolving. If, however, the propeller blade were alone injured, the propeller would in the absence of the hoop still be able to revolve, and the boat could proceed at perhaps a somewhat reduced rate of speed.

TB10. (© National Maritime Museum, Greenwich, London, Richard Perkins Collection)

The hull is divided by bulkheads and semi-bulkheads, akin the manner first proposed by Mr John Donaldson, into a large number of compartments, so that in the event of one or more of them being filled the boat would still float. In the forward end of the vessel accommodation is provided for the crew, the space being fitted up with lockers, and having hammock hooks attached to the decks. Immediately aft of this cabin is the steering compartment fitted with a conning tower, in which are arranged the telegraph gear, the voice pipe communicating with the engine-room, and the starting gear for the torpedo discharging tube. Aft of the steering compartment is the boiler-room with the coal bunkers fitted on either side. The stokehole is so arranged that the only exit for air blown into it is through the boiler, thus forming an arrangement of artificial draught without which it would be very difficult to get the power necessary for propelling these boats at the high speeds which have now been attained

Separated by a bulkhead from the boiler-room, is the engine-room, in which the necessary pipes and machinery are very skilfully arranged within uncommonly close quarters. Accommodation for the officers is provided aft of the engine-room, and is of an ample, not to say luxurious, character.

The decks of these boats are of steel, covered where foothold is necessary with Welsh's cement, and having hatchways leading to the different compartments. Those leading to the engine-room, boiler-room, and forward compartment being fitted with springs which throw the hatches wide open on withdrawing the fastening, and so give ample space for egress in an emergency.

The torpedo boats we are describing are armed with the 14in Whitehead torpedo, which is discharged through a tube mounted on a revolving carriage on the forward deck. Three torpedoes are usually carried, one in the tube, and two on transporting carriages mounted on rails on either side of the vessel, and so arranged that they can be run forward when the discharging tube is to be loaded. The impulse tube for discharging the torpedoes is attached to the cover of the after-end of the discharging tube, and consists of two pistons with hollow rods arranged telescopically, and capable, when compressed air is admitted behind them, of expelling the torpedo at a speed of 16ft per second.

The boat illustrated was tried in Long Reach on 15 January last with a load of 3.25 tons on board, making her total displacement equal to 29.73 tons, when the engines developed 460 indicated horse power and the vessel attained a speed of 22.01 knots per hour as a mean of six runs on the measured mile. Full particulars of this trial are given in Table No. 4.1.

Table No. 4.1.

Number of runs	Pressure in boiler	Vacuum in condenser	Pressure in receiver	Revolutions of engines per mile	Revolutions of engines per min	Observed time (min sec)	Speed due to time (knots per hour)	First mean speeds (knots per hour)	Second mean speeds (knots per hour)
1	124	24	37	1357	412	3 4	19.56	22.02	
2	123	24½	36	1061	433	2 27	24.49	21.87	21.94
3	123	24½	36	1375	440	3 7	19.25	22.13	22.00
4	124	24½	36	1064	443	2 24	25.00	22.17	22.15
5	122	25	35	1358	438	3 6	19.35	21.75	21.96
6	122	25	35	1080	435	2 29	24.16		
Mean	123	24½	36	1198	438.5				

True mean speed 22.01

The trial above recorded, however, was only a preliminary trial, and the full stipulated load was not on board. The official trial took place at Long Reach with a load of 6.65 tons on board, and a total displacement of 32.50 tons; on this occasion the power developed was 469 indicated horse power, but the speed fell, doubtless on account of the extra load, to 21.756 knots, as per Table No. 4.2.

Table No. 4.2.

Number of runs	Pressure in boiler	Vacuum in condenser	Pressure in receiver	Revolutions of engines per mile	Revolutions of engines per min	Observed time (min sec)	Speed due to time (knots per hour)	First mean speeds (knots per hour)	Second mean speeds (knots per hour)
1	135	24	41	1382	445	3 6	19.355	21.759	21.785
2	135	24	40	1092	440	3 6	24.162	21.810	21.770
3	135	23¾	41	1392	447.8	2 29	19.459	22.730	21.678
4	128	24	38	1088	435.2	3 5	24.000	21.626	21.790
5	135	23¾	41	1394	447	2 30	19.251	21.955	
6	135	23½	42	1078	443	3 7	24.658		
Mean	133.8	23.8	40.5	1220	443	2 26			

True mean speed 22.756

Experiments have been made by the Admiralty with a view to finding the coal consumption of these vessels; the result being that in one vessel, at a speed of 17½ knots, the engines developing 340 horse power, the consumption was 3.96lb per indicated horse power per hour; in another, doing 18¾ knots, the engines developing 340 horse power, the consumption was 3.92lb per indicated horse power per hour; the difference in speed between the two boats with the same horse power being due to the condition of their bottoms.

The following week, 24 September 1880, *Engineering* provided further details of the engines and boilers.

ENGINES AND BOILERS IN EARLY TORPEDO BOATS
ENGINEERING, 24 SEPTEMBER 1880

The engines are of the vertical compound intermediate receiver type with cranks at right angles, the high and low-pressure cylinders being respectively 12¾in and 20in in diameter, and the stroke in both cases being 12in. The cylinders, which are steam jacketted, are both cast in one piece with their valve chests, each cylinder being fitted with a liner, the space between which and the cylinder casting proper forms the steam jacket.

The slide valves are a modification of Wilson's balanced slides devised by Mr John Donaldson, and they are found to work extremely well. As will be seen from Fig 2 each valve works between the face on the cylinder and a rigid backplate or bridge piece which spans the valve, resting on the cylinder face on each side of the valve it covers, and being kept up in its place by a spring at the back. The cylinder faces are double ported, and the valves are arranged to give double openings for both steam and exhaust. The pistons are very light, and have single webs coned to give the necessary stiffness, as shown.

The cylinders are connected to the bedplate by eight vertical standards, as shown, these standards being braced together at about the middle of their height. The crossheads have slipper guides, and the bearing surfaces provided to all moving parts are very large, the crank-pins, it will be noticed, being unusually long. The valve gear is the ordinary link motion, the reversing shaft carrying a toothed quadrant geared into by a worm on a transverse shaft carrying the hand levers.

The air pump, which is single acting, is of unusual proportions, it being 12in in diameter with 3in stroke. It is worked by levers coupled to the cross-head of the low-pressure cylinder, so that it works at the same number of strokes as the engines, namely, considerably over 400 double strokes per minute. This is a very high number of reciprocations for an air pump, but arranged as they make them Messrs Thornycroft find their pumps give no trouble. The large diameter enables

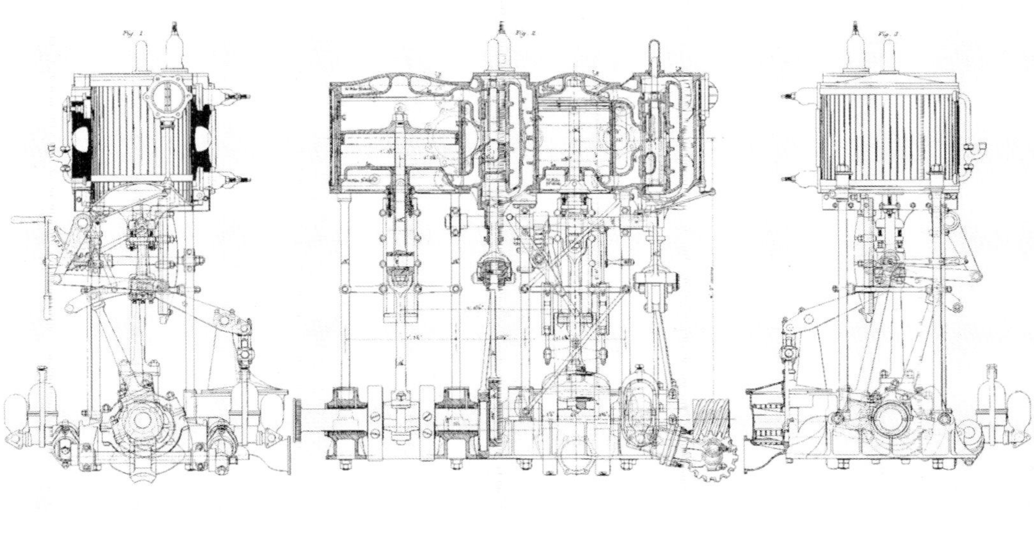

The engine for a first-class torpedo boat. (*Engineering*, 24 September 1880)

a large valve area to be obtained, the arrangement of the foot, piston, and delivery valves being alike, as will be seen from Figs 3 and 4, the latter view being a plan showing the form of the valves. From this view it will be seen that the latter are triangular, each valve being held by a guard which clips it along its radial centre line, leaving the sides free to rise. This form of valve is a convenient one to apply, and it gives a very free discharge for the water, etc. The feed pumps are plunger pumps fixed to the bedplate and driven from cranks formed at the ends of a cross shaft which carries a wormwheel geared into by a worm on the forward end of the crankshaft, as shown in Figs 1 and 2. From this cross shaft the bilge pump is also driven.

The surface condenser is cylindrical, and is distinct from the engines. The condensing water is forced through this condenser by a centrifugal pump driven by an independent engine. The engine-room also contains another independent engine, namely, one for driving a fan situated in the stokehold, by means of which a supply of air is forced into the latter. This engine is coupled direct to the fan shaft, and is sometimes driven at over 900 revolutions per minute. In the engine-room is also placed an air compressing pump for supplying compressed air to the torpedoes and to the impulse tube for discharging them. The donkey engine is fitted in the boiler-room.

The engines are supplied with steam by a boiler of the locomotive type. The shell is of Bessemer steel and the inner fire-box and tubes are of Lowmoor iron. The fire-box casing is of the Belpaire pattern, its top being stayed direct to the crown of the fire-box as shown. The boiler contains 204 tubes, 1¾in in diameter, the total heating surface being 618sq ft, of which 57sq ft is fire-box surface and 561sq ft external tube surface. The fire-grate area is 18sq ft, the firebars not extending the whole length of the fire-box, but there being a transverse firebrick bridge a short distance from the tubeplate. The flue area through the tubes (disregarding the ferrules at the fire-box end) is 2.7sq ft or $^{1}/_{6.6}$ of the grate area.

The boiler is fitted with Mr Thornycroft's patent apparatus for preventing accidents to the people in the stokehold, in the event of any of the tubes giving out while the boiler is under steam. This arrangement consists of a series of wrought-iron flaps hinged to the front of the ash-pan in such a way that they will be closed by any excess of pressure within the ash-pan, while in order to prevent the ash-pan being damaged by an excessive pressure, a passage is formed at one side leading up to the deck and fitted with a door with a spring fastening, so arranged that the door may be blown open by a comparatively slight pressure from within. The steam, etc, from the ash-pan would thus escape into the air and the people in the stokehold would be safe. Inasmuch as the stokehold is closed, the air being forced into it to produce the necessary draught through the boiler, an arrangement of the kind we have just described is most essential for safe working.

In April last the Admiralty carried out some most interesting experiments on the boiler of Messrs Thornycroft's torpedo boat No. 3 to determine the rate of evaporation obtainable with different pressures of air in the stokehold. The boiler experimented upon was of the class and dimensions of that we now illustrate, but the grate area used during the trial is given in the Admiralty reports as 18.9sq ft. The experiments were conducted by Mr Edward Newman, chief engineer, and Mr A Morcom, second assistant, the mode of carrying them out being as follows: the coal used was Nixon's navigation, and it was weighed into the bunkers at the commencement of each trial, the coal not used being weighed out again when the trial was finished. The fire-grate was not cleared at the commencement of each trial but the state of the fire was noted, and in cases where the condition of the fire at the end of a run was not the same as at the commencement, allowance was made for the difference in calculating the fuel consumed. It is stated by the experimenters that owing to the shape of the grate and the datum afforded by a line from the bottom of the furnace mouths to the top of the bridge, the condition of the fire could be very closely estimated. The thickness of fires was varied in the different trials. The stoking was very good and the same stokers were employed in all the runs.

The water used was measured by means of a tank containing 202 gallons placed on deck and connected with the extra supply tank by a pipe fitted with a cock which was closed when the measuring tank was being refilled. The donkey pump drew its supply direct from the extra supply tank. The height of water in the gauge glass was marked at the commencement of each trial, so that any difference of water level in the boiler at the commencement and end of an experiment might be allowed for.

To get rid of the steam generated, the filling nozzle was fitted with a pipe for blowing off the steam overboard, this pipe being fitted with a valve by which the discharge could be regulated. The pressure gauge was brought on deck close by the discharge valve, so that the man controlling the latter could readily maintain a steady pressure in the boiler. The discharge pipe was fitted with a small pipe for testing the dryness of the steam, but no trace of priming was found, and it is believed that the evaporations recorded were not exaggerated to any material extent by wetness of the steam.

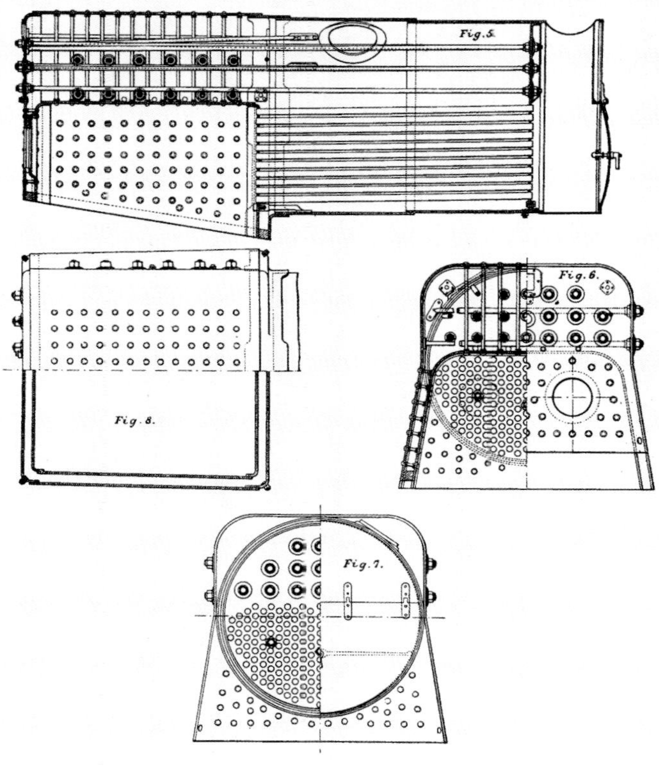

The boiler for a first-class torpedo boat. *(Engineering, 24 September 1880)*

The pressure of air in the stokehold was kept steady throughout each run by an artificer in charge of the fan engine, while water gauges to indicate the air pressure were fitted not only to the stokehold, but also to the ashpit, furnace, and funnel, the last-mentioned gauge, however, showing that the pressure in the funnel was practically nothing.

The pyrometers were placed in the funnel close above the top row of tubes, and were long enough to stretch across the mouth of the funnel. Their accuracy was tested by means of lead heated up to the melting point of antimony, both before and after the trials, the slight errors shown being allowed for in the records of the experiments. The pyrometers were stated to be found sensible throughout the trials.

The experiments made were four in number, the air pressure used in the stokehold being respectively equal to 2in, 3in, 4in, and 6in of water. There was in all cases a loss of air pressure between the stokehold and the ash-pit, amounting to from about ½in to ¾in of water. As far as can be judged from these experiments, the thickness of fire has far more effect on the loss of pressure between the ash-pit and furnace than the increase of velocity of air through the fire required to maintain the higher rates of combustion. It also appears clear that with high rates of combustion the high blast pressures are required mainly to overcome the frictional resistance experienced in the tubes, so that an increase in the flue area through the latter would very materially affect the degree of blast pressure required to maintain a given rate of combustion. In the testing boiler the combustion took place at the rate of 25.65lb of coal per square foot of grate, or 0.913lb per square foot of heating surface per hour, while the evaporation per pound of coal was at the rate of 9.69lb of water evaporated at 212 degrees, from a temperature of 100 degrees. The temperature in the chimney was in this case 700 degrees, and the proportion of ashes in the coal 4 per cent. The results obtained in this testing boiler certainly appear very high, considering that the water was being evaporated at the rate over 9lb per hour per square foot of heating surface. In the case of the trials of the torpedo boat boiler, the evaporation rose to as high as 17.54lb per square foot of heating surface per hour from a temperature of 56 degrees, and under a pressure of 115lb per square inch. Altogether, the experiments are of much interest and value.

Altogether Messrs John I Thornycroft and Co are decidedly to be congratulated on the results they have obtained with their high speed launches, and they deserve every credit for the ingenuity and skill which they have brought to bear upon the design of both the vessels and their machinery.

Following the relative success of the Thornycroft boats, the Admiralty provided details of *Lightning* to other shipbuilders, who then built similar craft to their own designs, with varying success.

TB13 was built by Maudslay, Sons and Field of Lambeth, and launched in 1879. She was 87ft long and displaced 28 tons. She had a brass hull but was a bad seaboat, rolling excessively, and had poor speed performance, her 450ihp being predicted to provide a speed of 20 knots, which was not achieved on trials. It is generally recorded that she was broken up in 1896, but notes of the late Oscar Parkes record she was sold in 1898/9 for £205.

TB14 was constructed by Yarrow (Yard No. 425), was 86ft long with a displacement of 33 tons. Her engines generated 550ihp to give a maximum speed of 21.9 knots (*Alfred Yarrow, His Life and Work*, compiled by Eleanor C Barnes, 1924). This biography states that the speed was 'approximately 3 knots ahead of the highest speed attained by any competitive vessel tested under the same conditions', and that 'she

The first torpedo boat to realise a speed of 21.9 knots an hour steaming past Greenwich Hospital. It should be observed there is no funnel, the smoke passing out of the sides, the object being to reduce its visibility. *(Alfred Yarrow, His Life and Work)*

had no funnel and was so low in the water that she was scarcely discernible at a distance'.

The biography continues:

> The abnormal speed of this special boat was mainly due to some interesting experiments, carried out by the firm, with screw propellers. At the time it was generally believed that for this size of vessel a propeller 5 feet 6 inches in diameter, with narrow blades, gave the highest efficiency. It was also thought that, within a certain limit, the larger the propeller and the greater the area of water acted upon, the less the slip and the better the result. With this in view, Yarrow constructed a propeller 12 inches larger in diameter than was at the time considered suitable. Contrary to expectation, it was found on trial that the boat lost in speed by the change. This led to the simple conclusion that an improved result might possibly be obtained by adopting the opposite course, and having a propeller smaller than the one considered the best. A very exhaustive series of experiments with propellers was carried out, perhaps the most valuable which had been attempted at that time. Twenty-five propellers were made, of various sizes, having different pitches and different areas, with two and with three blades. As a result of these experiments, a propeller of only 4 feet 4 inches in diameter, with three blades, was adopted, and although the slip of the screw was increased, the speed was greatly improved.

Accommodation was poor.

In a paper entitled 'Torpedo-Boats, Having Special Reference To Those Built By Messrs Yarrow And Co', given to the Royal United Services Institution on 9 May 1884, Yarrow quotes the speed as mentioned in the autobiography, but then goes on to describe some further trials:

> After this boat had been tried, with a view to improve its steering capabilities, we obtained permission to fit to it a forward rudder, and a set of experiments were tried

TB14. (© National Maritime Museum, Greenwich, London, Richard Perkins Collection)

> by the Admiralty to test the influence this bow rudder had on the manoeuvring capabilities of the boat. As the results obtained are instructive, I propose to give a brief description of them. The forward rudder was partially balanced, and arranged to slide within the boat in the same manner as a centreboard. Circles both to port and starboard at full speed and half speed were made first with the stern rudder only (the forward rudder being pulled up within the hull) and then with the two rudders worked in conjunction. The steering capabilities of the boat were improved by this system: the result has been the general adoption of it in all torpedo-boats, excepting only those of the smaller class. This forward rudder not only improves steering when going ahead, but enables the craft to be under control when going astern, which otherwise would be impracticable.

The diameters of the turning circles were 214yds when turning to port and 178yds when turning to starboard with one rudder, reducing to 94yds and 120yds, respectively, when operating with two rudders.

On 12 September 1901, whilst a tender to *Vernon*, she was undertaking searchlight operations off the Needles and struck Warden Ledge, resulting in a significant leak, and grounded in Totland Bay. Not seriously damaged, she was towed back to Portsmouth two days later. At the end of 1904 she was removed from the active list and put on the sales list, finally being broken up in March 1905.

The land-locked site of Hanna, David & Wilson of Paisley was used for the construction of *TB15*, a boat 87ft LOA and displacing 28 tons. Developing 450ihp, her nominal top speed was 21 knots. *TB16* was to have been built by Lewin of Poole but, because of delays in construction, the contract was cancelled.

Yarrow's *TB17* and *TB18* (Yard Nos 419 and 420) were originally built for Russia (see Chapter 1). They were 86ft long and displaced 33 tons, attaining speeds on trials of 20.6 and 20.8 knots. Although creating a good first impression they were described as 'notoriously shaky and weak in construction', their shell plating was only $\frac{1}{8}$in thick, and had to be virtually rebuilt. Unlike Thornycroft's *Lightning* where the rudder was split above and below the propeller shaft, on these two boats, the propeller shaft projected below the rudder. They had two funnels side by side and the conning tower was positioned aft. *TB17* was used for some spectacular 'boom jumping' trials during 1887, when stationed at Malta. Whilst still at Malta, she was sold in 1907, whilst *TB18* was sent to Gibraltar where she was sold in 1902 for £23.

TB19 was built by J S White and was 93ft long with a displacement of just 28 tons. Typical of other boats from White's, she had a heavily cut-away stern to improve manoeuvring – the 'turnabout' form. Plating was just 0.12in amidships with thinner ends and decks, down to $\frac{1}{16}$in. The decks were coated with Welsh's cement to improve the grip for the crew. The engine had two cylinders, 12.7 and 20.9in in diameter, with a 12in stroke and she carried 7 tons of coal. She was sold in 1900/1901 for £51.

TB14 on the River Thames.

TB17 or *TB18*, clearly showing the twin funnels side by side, typical of Yarrow's designs at that time.

TB20 was built by Rennie but their first boat was too slow, and was rejected and sold abroad. The replacement only produced 360ihp for a top speed of 16¾ knots and she had poor manoeuvrability. She spent much of her career in Hong Kong, but in August 1914 joined the Portsmouth Defence Flotilla.

The complement was the same for all these boats, eleven, comprising a lieutenant and a sub lieutenant or warrant officer; a chief engine room artificer, an engine room artificer, a leading stoker and two stokers; a petty officer and two able seamen; and a signalman.

TB13–TB20 all had their bow-mounted torpedo tube removed and replaced with dropping gear for two torpedoes during their careers, as did *Lightning*.

Following the building of *TB20*, there was a significant period of time when no first-class torpedo boats were built, primarily due to financial restrictions. During this period, other countries, particularly France and Russia, were adding to the number of torpedo boats in their fleets, a point mentioned by Yarrow in his paper of 9 May 1884 to RUSI, which also included a list of the number of torpedo boats owned by different countries and highlighted the number of miles of coastline to be patrolled by each boat – 197 miles for Great Britain or 800 miles if the colonies were included.

The lack of newly built boats was also highlighted in HMS *Vernon*'s annual report of 1882, which concentrated on the trials being undertaken with second-class boats. The report also included a list of first-class boats built by Yarrow since 1877, a total of forty-four, which included some noticeable records – 'the fastest boat in the navy' (Yard No. 425, *TB14*), 'the fastest boat in the French Navy' (Yard Nos 435/6), and 'the highest speed ever recorded' (Yard Nos 535/6 for Italy).

Four longer boats were ordered in 1884, two from Thornycroft (*TB21* and *TB22*, Yard Nos 201/2) which were launched in March and May

TB21. (© National Maritime Museum, Greenwich, London, Richard Perkins Collection)

1885, respectively, and two from Yarrow (*TB23* and *TB24,* Yard Nos 666–7). In his paper of 9 May 1884, Yarrow stated:

> At the present moment we are building for the English Government two first-class torpedo-boats. They are 113 feet long by 12½ feet beam. Our contract is that they shall maintain a speed of 18 knots fully equipped, conditions which no doubt can be easily complied with. The forward part of the boat is provided with two torpedo-guns, and they are to be provided with a revolving torpedo-gun aft.

Vernon's report records the dimensions of these boats to be 113ft long, 12ft 6in beam and displacement 61 tons. The Thornycroft boats are recorded as producing 736ihp, giving a speed of 19.82 knots but the Yarrow boats produced only 600ihp for a speed of 18¾ knots. The Yarrow boats could be distinguished by them having two funnels side by side, a feature typical of their designs at the time. Conway's *All The World's Fighting Ships 1860–1905* records these boats also carried two 3pdr guns, but no other evidence of this has been found. Five torpedoes were carried, the two not in the tubes being stored underneath the mess deck; 12 tons of coal were carried, giving a range of 1,600 miles at 10 knots.

TB22 photographed in 1904.

The complement of fourteen was made up of one lieutenant; one sub-lieutenant or warrant officer; two engine room artificers, one of whom was a chief artificer; four stokers, one of whom was a leading stoker; two petty officers and three able seamen; and a signalman.

TB21 and *TB22* took part in the manoeuvres of summer 1885, under Sir Geoffrey Hornby, and acquitted themselves well, but the six older boats that also accompanied the squadron performed poorly, particularly during bad weather. The two boats were fitted with water-tube boilers before being sent to Malta, where they remained until sold in 1907. In autumn 1887, while off the Ionian Islands, *TB21* collided with and sank the second-class boat *TB52* during the night. On 19 April 1893, while undertaking torpedo practice, she was also in collision with the old turret ship

TB21 and crew, 1887.

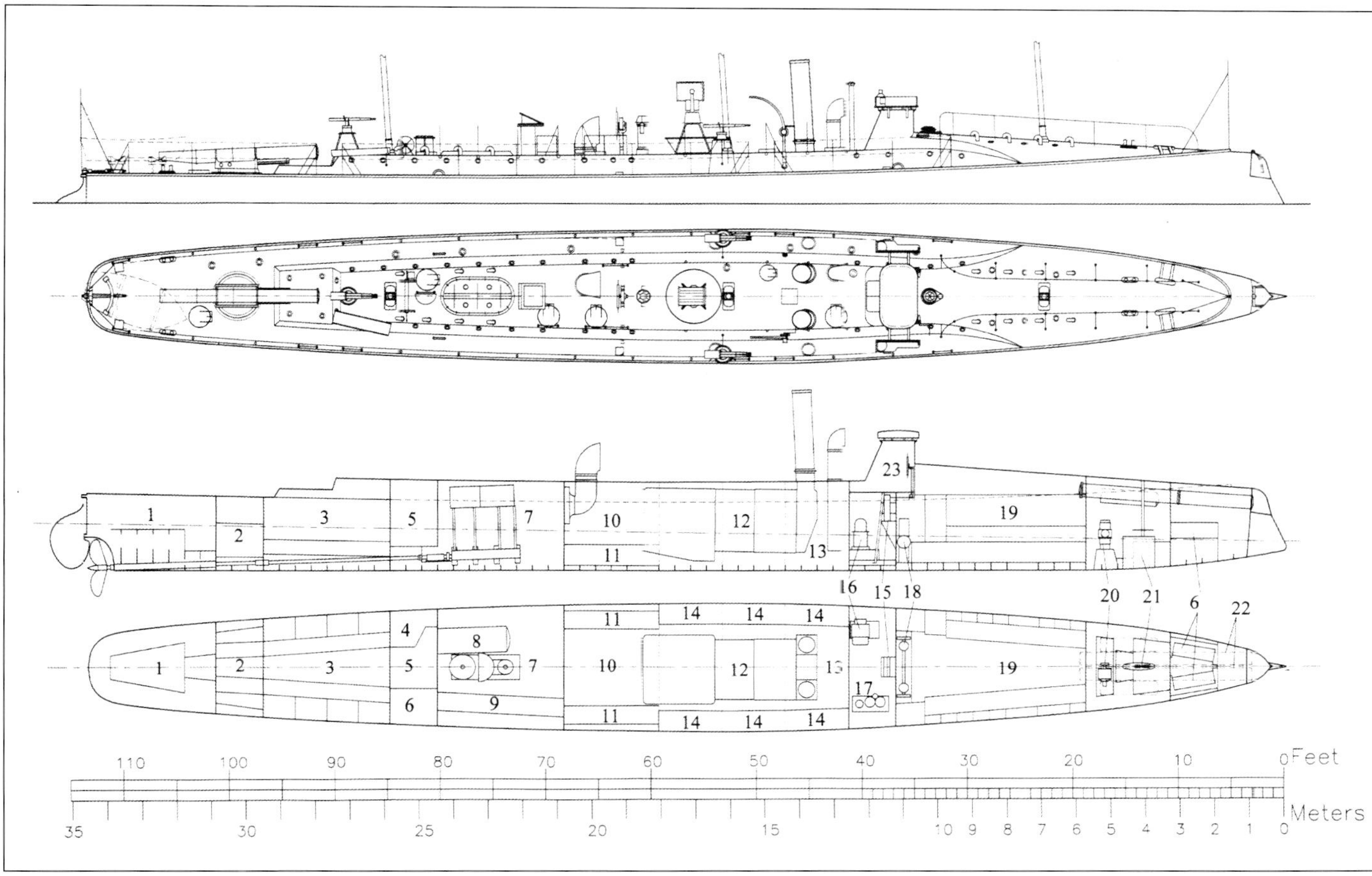

HM first-class torpedo boat No. 23. *(Warship 2005, Conway Maritime Press)*
***Key*: 1 store room; 2 pantry; 3 officer's cabin; 4 WC; 5 lavatory; 6 magazine; 7 engine room; 8 condenser; 9 feed water tank; 10 stokehold; 11 fire bar lockers; 12 boiler; 13 smoke box compartment; 14 coal bunkers; 15 steering engine; 16 galley; 17 Normandy condenser; 18 air compressors; 19 seamen's mess; 20 dynamo; 21 retractable bow rudder housing; 22 two torpedo tubes (over); 23 conning tower.**

Nile, which was moored in Malta Harbour, resulting in the fitting of a new bow.

TB23 and *TB24* joined the Channel Squadron in July 1886, *TB23* transferring to Portsmouth in 1889, at the same time as *TB24* transferred to Devonport. On 11 September 1893, whilst picking up ratings, *TB24* collided with the second-class boat *TB54*, creating a large hole in her port quarter. Neither of these two boats were considered worth reboilering and *TB24* was sold by auction in May 1904, *TB23* following the next year.

Following the war scare with Russia in 1885/6, the Admiralty ordered a large number of larger boats, their length nominally being 125ft. Initially intended as 'torpedo catchers', they were to be armed with more guns and only a single torpedo tube, but all were completed as torpedo boats. Complement was sixteen.

The report of a committee presided over by the captain of *Vernon*, recommended a fixed bow tube and two pairs of revolving tubes, one forward and one aft. No spare torpedoes were to be carried and the torpedoes were to be discharged by gunpowder, and not compressed air, as this was cheaper and lighter. It was originally intended that the turrets supporting the tubes should revolve but, as built, they were fixed, with the tubes rotating around them. Both the foremost and after conning towers were to be fitted for steering, and the boats were to carry 19 tons of coal for a range of approximately three thousand miles at 10 knots.

The first of these boats, *TB25* (Yard No. 212), was delivered by Thornycroft, *Vernon*'s 1885 report recording the length overall as 125ft with a beam of 12ft 6in and a speed of over 19 knots. Barnaby records LOA as 127ft 6in and power as 592hp, giving a speed of 19.38 knots. Conway's records a third LOA of 128¼ft, 700ihp and 20¾ knots. The various lengths quoted are probably due to the fact that when first constructed, *TB25* had a 'bull nose' ram bow which proved to be unseaworthy and she was returned to the dockyard, where the fixed bow torpedo tube was removed and she was rebuilt with a conventional

TB23. (© National Maritime Museum, Greenwich, London, Richard Perkins Collection)

TB23. Probably photographed during one of the naval reviews of Spithead, in 1887 or 1897. Note the civilian visitors on deck amidships. *(US Naval History and Heritage Command, NH54988)*

TB23; note the twin funnels.

TB23, a vessel built by Yarrow. *(Navypedia)*

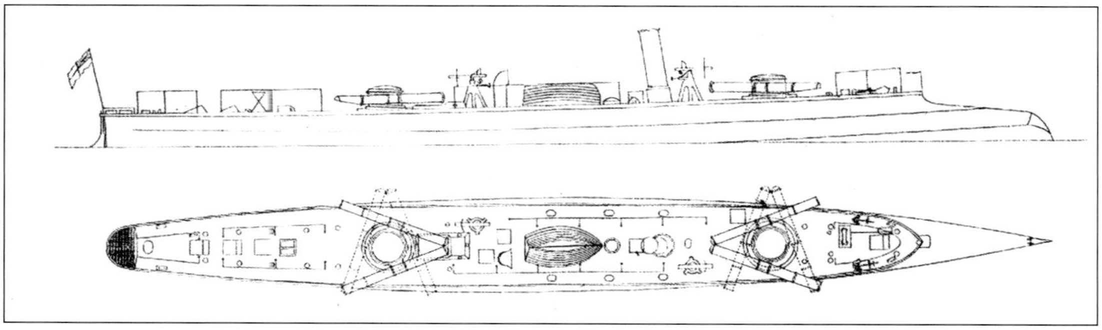

The committee's suggested arrangement. *(HMS Vernon Annual Report 1885)*

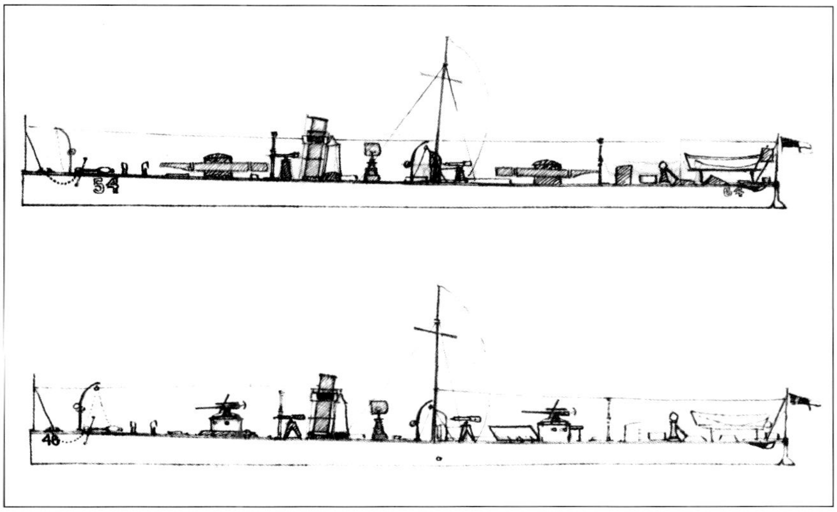

TB25–TB29 and *TB41–TB60* in two variants as originally envisaged. Top: as torpedo boat with four torpedo tubes; bottom: as gunboat with two 3pdr guns. *(© National Maritime Museum, Greenwich, London, Richard Perkins Collection)*

straight bow. *Vernon*'s report also states: 'The steering qualities of the boat are very good, Messrs Thorneycroft having fitted double rudders of peculiar construction, and having cut away the dead wood. It is now under trial; if found satisfactory all other boats of this class will be fitted in a similar manner.'

Fifty-four boats were ordered, twenty-five from Thornycroft, twenty-four from Yarrow and five from White of Cowes, Isle of Wight (IOW). The first four boats, *TB26–TB29*, were ordered from and constructed by Thornycroft (Yard Nos. 218–221) to the same design. A separate contract

TB25. (Navypedia)

was placed for the other twenty boats (*TB41–TB60*, Yard Nos. 222–241), but before all these were completed, the problem with *TB25*'s seakeeping had been identified during operations with the Channel Squadron summer manoeuvres 1886, and so some of the later boats were completed with straight bows, all the others being taken in hand and modified as soon as possible. Barnaby records a power of 672hp for a speed of 20.22 knots.

Having been launched on 10 October 1885, *TB25* arrived at Portsmouth in November. Whilst at Portsmouth, she took part in the annual manoeuvres during the summers of 1888, 1889, 1891 and 1892. *TB25* was reboilered in 1901 with water-tube boilers, and in the summers of 1903 and 1904 she took part in torpedo manoeuvres in the Irish Sea, became tender to *Vernon* in July 1904, and joined the Portsmouth Reserve in January 1905. She served as a patrol boat during the First World War, and was broken up soon afterwards.

TB26 and *TB27* were launched in the same month as *TB25*, just twelve and fourteen days later, respectively, and on 23 July 1887 *TB26* was present at the naval review at Spithead held to celebrate the Queen's Jubilee and afterwards she took part in the annual manoeuvres. During the 1892 manoeuvres she ran into *TB87* and was damaged, being replaced in the manoeuvres by *TB78*.

TB27 and *TB28* (launched 7 November 1885) also took part in the 1887 naval review; *TB27* then participated in the manoeuvres of 1892, 1894 and 1896. The Navy List shows her as a tender to *Vernon* in August 1901 and she was relieved by *TB77* in October. During the summer of 1904, *TB27* took part in torpedo manoeuvres in the Irish Sea, returning as tender to *Vernon* in December of that year, when she relieved *TB82*. *TB25*, *TB26* and *TB27* were all sold to Maden & McKee on 2 October 1919 for £500 each.

In July 1898 *TB28* struck a rock in Kalk Bay, Cape Town, and beached. She was refloated but not repaired, being expended as a target. *TB29*, launched 19 November, also went to Cape Town, having participated in the 1887 review, where she was sold to Runciman Walker & Co for £500 on 1 July 1919.

TB41–TB60 were all laid down and launched in 1885/6, all completing in 1886. *TB41* also attended the 1887 naval review and spent her career in home waters, taking part in many of the annual manoeuvres and in the torpedo manoeuvres in the Irish Sea. On 15 July 1890 *TB42* ran upon Bembridge Ledge, IOW, and sustained serious damage. On 31 January 1913 she collided with the submarine *A6*, whilst exercising off Spithead. She was holed below the waterline and was again towed to port for repair. *TB41* and *TB42* were both sold in 1919 for £500 each, *TB41* to Multilocular S Bkg Co and *TB42* to Maden & McKee.

On 9 May 1887 *TB43* was involved in a collision with *TB66* while operating off Portland. She was struck violently on the port bow, causing her forward compartment to fill. In 1888 she transferred to the Mediterranean, where she spent most of her career, being sold at Malta together with *TB44*, which had a similar career, in December 1919 for £624 each. On 14 July 1900 *TB45* was in collision with another torpedo boat when leaving Plymouth With her bows stove in, her place in the manoeuvres was taken by *TB51*. *TB45* was sold to T B Sales in August 1919 for £575.

TB46 attended the 1887 naval review and was also present at the Diamond Jubilee Review on 26 June 1897, when she was manned by the crew of *TB71*, which had been in a collision. She sank during heavy weather in the eastern Mediterranean in December 1915, but was raised and put back into service. In May 1887 a steam pipe on *TB47* burst, killing two men and burning and scalding three more, and leaving the boat disabled. The majority of her career was spent either at the Cape or in the Mediterranean, and she was sold in 1909/10 for £300. *TB48* attended the 1887 naval review, but little is known of her career, and she was sold circa 1915. Three other boats to attend this review were *TB49*, *TB50* and *TB51*. Subsequently, *TB49* collided with *TB52* in July 1899 and successfully jumped a boom, without damage, in Portchester Creek in January 1890. Sold to M Hayes & Son in August 1919 for £576 10s, *TB50* spent her career in home waters, being sold to R Longmate for £900 in February 1920, together with *TB55*.

In the autumn of 1877 *TB51* collided at night with a second-class boat which sank, two of her crew being drowned. In December 1913 her boilers were replaced, and she was sold for £400 to Multilocular S Bkg Co in December 1919, together with *TB58*. *TB53* collided with *TB49* prior to manoeuvres in 1899. In May 1904 *TB54* was damaged in a collision with a trawler whilst attempting to enter Plymouth Sound at night. Her boats and deck gear were carried away and she was sold in August 1919 to T R Sales for £575. *TB56* suffered the same fate as *TB40*, sinking during heavy weather in the eastern Mediterranean in December 1915 whilst returning to Malta.

TB57 was sold to Maclen & McKee in October 1919 for £500. On manoeuvres in August 1890, *TB59* was in collision with *TB81* at night in Falmouth Harbour whilst attempting to capture colliers. She managed to steam to Plymouth for repairs. *TB60* operated off the west coast of the Cape Colony during the Boer War when her main

TB25 after her refit in 1886 (top) and after receiving water-tube boilers (bottom). *(Navypedia)*

A 'coloured' postcard, printed in Germany, of *TB27* recovering a practice torpedo.

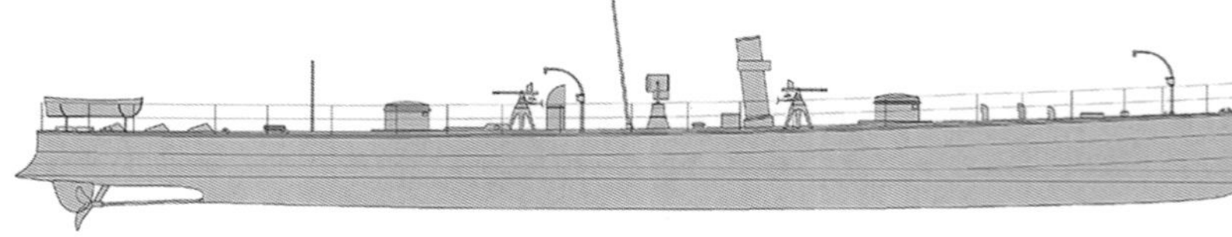

TB41 as a catcher, with no torpedoes. *(Navypedia)*

TB27 after receiving water-tube boilers – note the two funnels. *(Navypedia)*

TB42: note the 14in torpedo amidships about to be loaded into the after twin torpedo tube mount. *(US Naval History and Heritage Command, NH54993)*

TB48: note that light shields have been fitted to the two 3pdr guns and that torpedo tubes are not on board. *(US Naval History and Heritage Command, NH54995)*

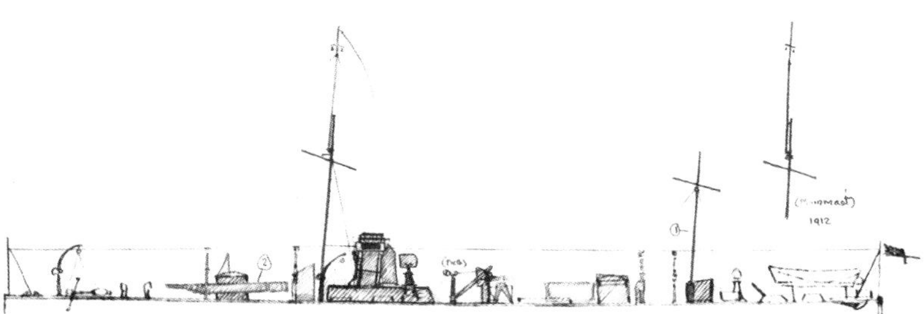

TB26 after reboilering. *(© National Maritime Museum, Greenwich, London, Richard Perkins Collection)*

shaft broke. Under sail she arrived safely in Saldanha Bay, finally being sold at the Cape to Runciman Walker & Co for £400 on 1 July 1919.

The surviving Thornycroft '125-footers' were reboilered with water-tube boilers, some receiving two funnels. *TB26*, *TB41*, *TB42*, *TB52*, *TB53*, *TB55*, *TB57* and *TB58* retained a single funnel, the area around the base of the funnel being raised. The raised areas varied in height, area and shape. For the boats with two funnels, the raised area also varied significantly, sometimes occupying the entire length between the funnels, and sometimes with separate raised areas at the base of each funnel. The funnels were circular in cross-section. *TB41* and *TB42* were reboilered in 1899/1900; *TB45* and *TB54* in 1900/1; *TB25*, *TB26*, *TB51*, *TB52*, *TB53* and *TB55* in 1902/3; *TB27*, *TB49*, *TB50*, *TB57*, *TB58* and *TB59* in 1904/5; *TB29* and *TB60* in 1905/6 and *TB43*, *TB44*, *TB46*, *TB47* and *TB48* in 1907/8.

During the First World War many were fitted with three twin 25mm/40 and a single 47mm/40 3pdr Hotchkiss Mk I mountings to be used for local patrols. Some were re-armed with the 3pdr fitted on an AA mounting, and most appear to have been given a depth charge armament.

Yarrow was awarded contracts for *TB30–TB33*, all completed in 1886, and *TB61–TB78*, all completed in 1887, to a very similar design, but the ram bow was more suitable for rough weather and was not rebuilt, therefore retaining the fixed bow tube. Unlike previous Yarrow boats, there was just a single funnel; 3pdr guns could be mounted on the turrets and twin-barrelled Nordenfeld machine guns were carried at deck level on the centreline, one just forward of the after torpedo tubes and one right aft. According to Conway's, the machinery produced 670ihp (compared to 700ihp for the Thornycroft boats) resulting in a decrease in top speed of 1¼ knots.

On 6 June 1887 *TB30* collided with *TB63* off the Nore and was slightly damaged. On 28 July 1889, together with *TB31*, *TB32* and *TB69*, she sailed from Portsmouth to Bermuda, escorted by HMS *Tyne*. Laid up in Bermuda, *TB30*, *TB31* and *TB32* were sold in 1905. In April 1905, whilst tender to *Osborne*, *TB32* collided with the barge *Vixen* at Cowes and her bows were badly damaged.

After attending the 1887 naval review, *TB61* and *TB62* sailed for Halifax, escorted by HMS *Tyne*, suffering bad weather which resulted in

A close view of *TB56* taken in 1896.

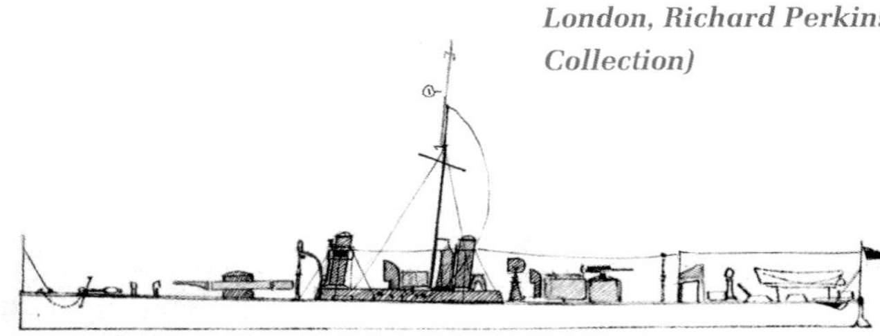

TB27 after reboilering. *(© National Maritime Museum, Greenwich, London, Richard Perkins Collection)*

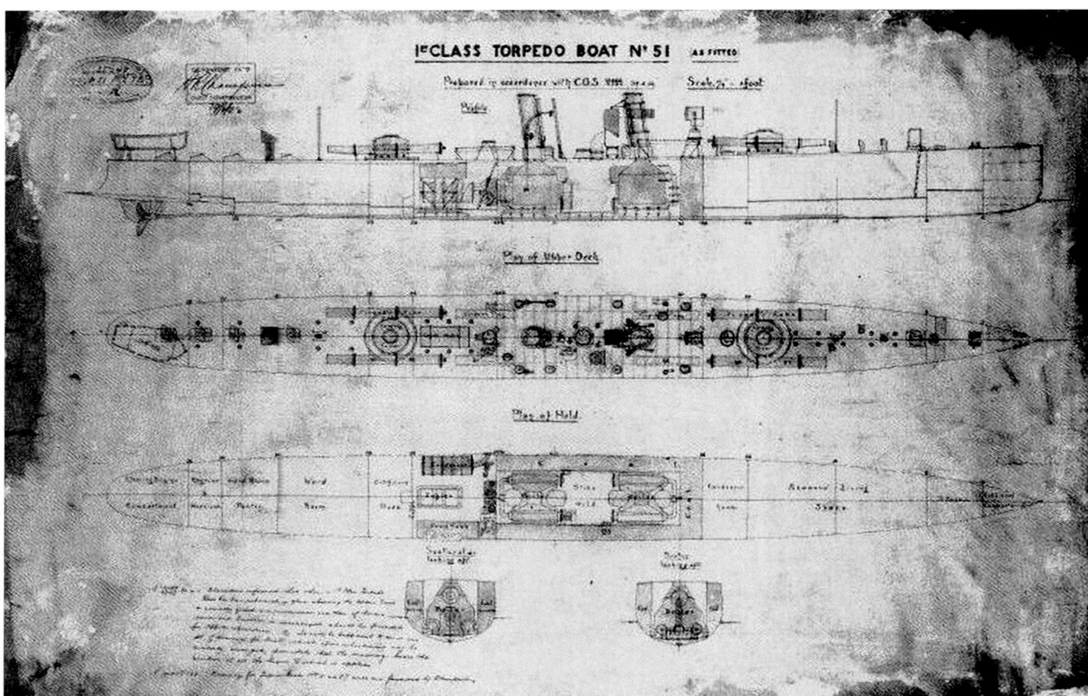

As fitted profile and plan of first-class torpedo boat No. 51, as reboilered at Devonport, 19 June 1902. *(© National Maritime Museum, Greenwich, London, DR25240)*

the torpedo boats being taken in tow for periods. They were stationed at St John's, Newfoundland. In October 1890 *TB62* sank during a gale while on tow to the West Indies, and in July 1905 *TB61* was convoyed to Bermuda by HMS *Latona*.

Having collided with *TB30* in June 1887, when she received little damage, *TB63* collided with *TB77* in July the following year, this time receiving much more damage, resulting in her crew transferring to *TB78* for the annual manoeuvres. Together with *TB64*, she sailed to Sheerness in September 1900, escorted by HMS *Vindictive*, soon returning to Portsmouth and then sailing to the Mediterranean with *TB83* and *TB84*. *TB64* was wrecked in the Aegean Sea during March 1915, the wreck being sold at Malta four years later for £625.

TB66 had an unfortunate career, colliding with *TB43* in May 1887 whilst on operations, stranding on West Barry Sands in December 1909

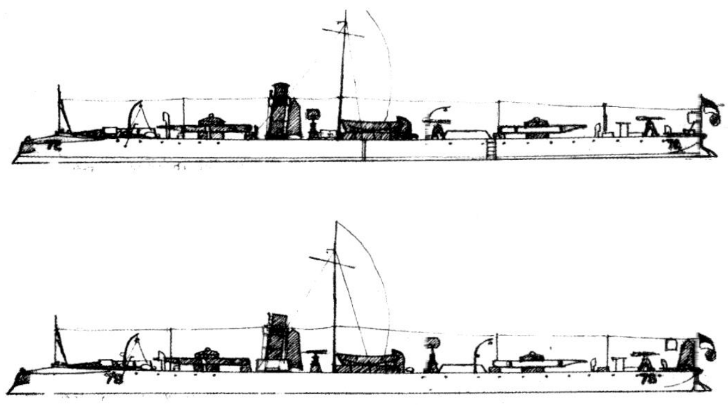

TB72 (top) and *TB78* (bottom). *(© National Maritime Museum, Greenwich, London, Richard Perkins Collection)*

TB75 built by Yarrow. *(US Naval History and Heritage Command, NH54803)*

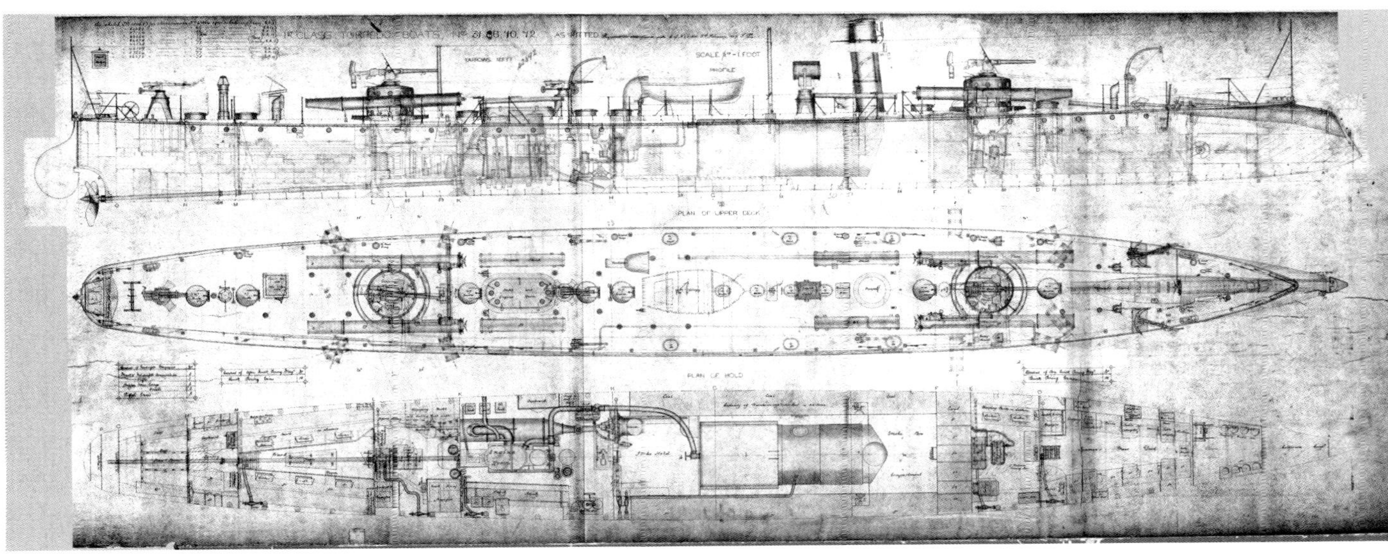

TB31, *TB66*, *TB70* and *TB72*. Although the title only references four boats, handwritten notes indicate that the drawing represents all boats in this series by Yarrow. *(© National Maritime Museum, Greenwich, London, M1046)*

TB63 as completed.

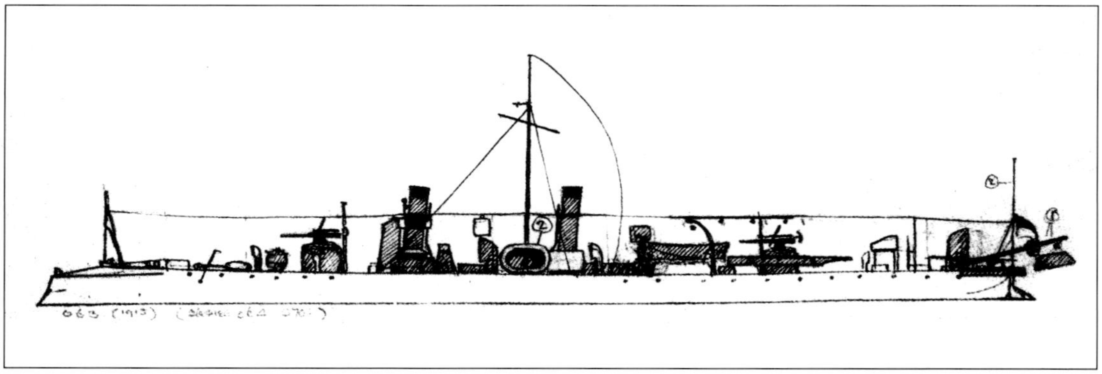

TB63, *TB64* and *TB70* after receiving water-tube boilers – note the tall, thin funnels. *(© National Maritime Museum, Greenwich, London, Richard Perkins Collection)*

TB65, *TB67*, *TB68* and *TB72* after receiving water-tube boilers: note the single funnel. *(© National Maritime Museum, Greenwich, London, Richard Perkins Collection)*

and being towed to Sheerness to receive a new propeller shaft, and then in February 1911 she collided with *TB76* near Herne Bay, receiving a large hole in her starboard side below water level. She was slung on a hawser between *TB76* and *TB113*, and towed to Sheerness by *TB114*. *TB66* was sold to T W Ward Ltd for £425 in June 1920.

TB67 and *TB68* both received Thornycroft water-tube boilers while at Chatham in 1901. In August 1904 *TB68* experienced problems with her steering gear whilst at Portsmouth and collided with *Zephyr*, and was struck by *TB67* in September 1910 whilst going alongside. Both boats were sold in 1920, *TB67* to Willoughby of Plymouth for £500 and *TB68* to T W Ward Ltd for £425. *TB69* was laid up at Bermuda in April 1905.

TB70 was sold at Malta for £625 in December 1909. *TB71* struck wreckage off Maplin Sands in December 1907, damaging her propeller, and was

TB76. *(US Naval History and Heritage Command, NH58404)*

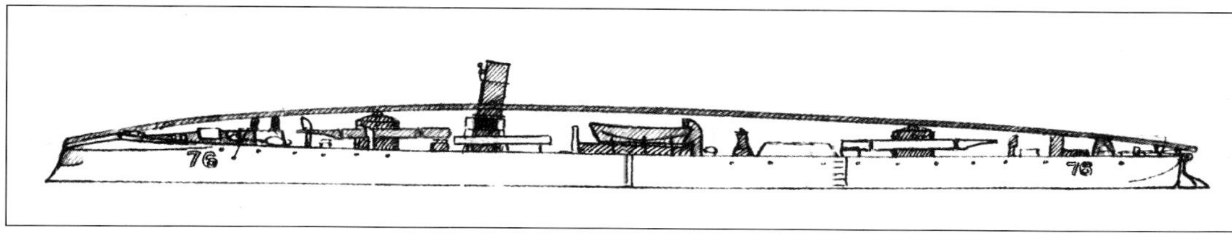

TB76 **as fitted for boom jumping trials at Portsmouth, October 1891.** ***(© National Maritime Museum, Greenwich, London, Richard Perkins Collection)***

towed to Sheerness. During the night of 25 October 1910, *TB72* collided with *TB66*, both boats being badly damaged. The bow of *TB72* was bent through ninety degrees, and she did not leave the dockyard until the middle of December. She was sold to T W Ward Ltd for £515 in December 1919 and broken up.

TB78. (US Naval History and Heritage Command, NH54807)

TB38 **built by White's.** ***(The National Archives, ADM176-728a)***

TB73 collided with *TB66* during the night of 15 July 1904 while on exercises, and in February the following year she was again in a collision while raising her anchor. *TB74* collided with a collier in August 1909, her fore compartment filling with water, but there were no casualties. She was sold to Willoughby of Plymouth for £450 in January 1920. *TB75* sank during the 1892 manoeuvres when she collided with *TB77* at Carrickfergus in Belfast Lough.

TB76 was undamaged in her collision with *TB66* near Herne Bay (February 1911) and was sold to T W Ward Ltd for £450 in June 1920. In July 1888 *TB77* collided with *TB63*, and on 8 August 1892 collided with *TB75*. *TB77* had her bows stove in, but no lives were lost. Prior to the 1903 manoeuvres, *TB77* was damaged when striking floating wreckage, but was repaired in time to take part. *TB78* ran aground on the sand banks near the Nore on 15 February 1910, and was refloated the next day.

As with the Thornycroft boats, the surviving Yarrow '125-footers' were reboilered, all having deck areas raised, *TB66*, *TB67*, *TB68* and *TB72* retaining one funnel, others receiving two. *TB78* was reboilered in 1901; *TB33*, *TB61*, *TB62*, *TB63*, *TB64*, *TB65*, *TB67*, *TB68* and *TB72* in 1902/3; *TB66*, *TB71*, *TB73*, *TB74*, *TB76* and *TB77* in 1904/5; and *TB30*, *TB31*, *TB32*, *TB61*, *TB69* and *TB70* in 1907/8.

Five boats, *TB34–TB38*, were awarded to White's. These employed the 'cut up' stern to improve manoeuvrability, but though developing more power (950ihp according to Conway's) had a lower top speed of 18–19 knots. They also had a greater beam than either the Thornycroft or Yarrow boats.

Originally built with two funnels side by side, when fitted with water tube boilers (*TB34* in 1902/3, *TB35* and *TB36* in 1904/5, *TB37* and *TB38* in 1907/8), two new funnels were fitted on the centreline.

All five of the torpedo boats built by White's, *TB34–TB38*, were present at the 1887 naval review. *TB34* spent her career in home waters,

TB34. (US Naval History and Heritage Command, NH54992)

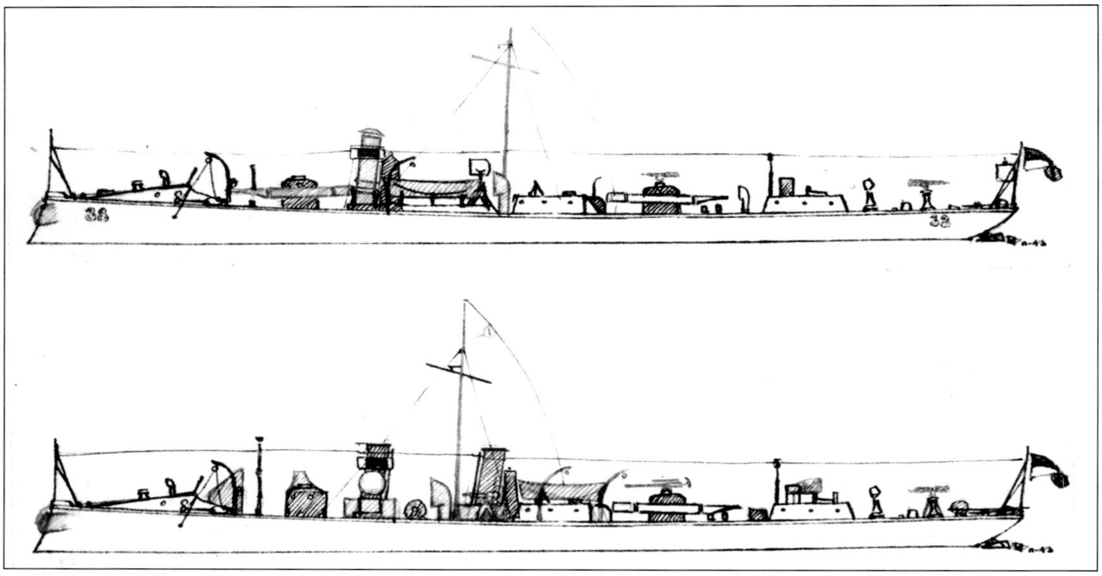

TB38 **as first built (top) and after being fitted with water-tube boilers (bottom).** ***(© National Maritime Museum, Greenwich, London, Richard Perkins Collection)***

being sold to Maden & McKee in 1919 for £500, but *TB35* and *TB36* sailed to Hong Kong in March 1888 for service on the China station, being sold in Hong Kong for £1,423 6s 8d in November 1919. *TB37* and *TB38* had similar careers, also being sold at Hong Kong in November 1919 for £1,321 12s 4d.

The last '125-footer', *TB79*, was also built by Yarrow to a similar design but had two funnels and a triple-expansion engine. Her hull form was also modified to improve steering, a problem that had been experienced with the earlier boats.

TB79

The Engineer, 10 December 1886

On Friday last an official trial was made of No. 79 torpedo boat, built by Messrs Yarrow and Company, Poplar, for the Government, when the speed realised was such as to surpass all previous records of similar craft in the service. The boat was loaded in accordance with the Admiralty conditions, and the trial took place below Gravesend. The test consisted of a continuous run of two hours' duration, during which time six runs were made on the measured mile at Lower Hope (three with and three against the tide), giving a speed during the entire run of 22.392 knots per hour, the highest recorded pair of miles being over 23 knots. After the above results had been obtained a series of trials were undertaken for manoeuvring power. When going ahead the boat turned in a circle the mean diameter of which was 85 yards in 58 seconds; when going astern the circle, of which the diameter was 65 yards, was completed in 65 seconds. One important feature of the boat was that when turning it had practically no heel whatever, a matter of great importance with respect to the efficient discharge of torpedoes from the side. It was also exceptionally free from vibration at all speeds, a glass of water full to the brim remaining unspilt on the table. The Admiralty authorities express themselves highly pleased with the working of the machinery, and with the performances of the boat, which possesses exceptional speed with remarkable turning powers. Instead of these first-class torpedo-boats being all completed for sea at Portsmouth, the Admiralty have ordered them to be distributed between Chatham, Portsmouth, and Devonport. Two will be sent to the western port on Saturday, and ten more are to be sent round on receipt at Portsmouth from the contractors. The complete particulars of the boat are as follows:

Length … 125ft
Beam … 13ft
Mean draught … 3ft 4in
Load carried … 10 tons
Turning circles – Going ahead: To port, 80 yards diameter, in 59 secs.
To starboard, 90 yards diameter, in 57 secs.
Going astern: Starboard, 70 yards diameter in 70 secs.
To port, 60 yards diameter in 60 secs.
Vibration – Practically none.

Steam (lbs)	Receiver	Vacuum (ins)	Revs per minute	Time (h m)	Speed (knots)	1st means	2nd means
139	59	26	411	2 42	22.22	23.13	
139	60	26	410	2 31	23.84		
140	60	26	400	2 32	23.63	22.18	22.26
140	60	26	398	2 54	20.63	22.34	22.40
140	60	26	404	2 30	24.00	22.46	22.46
140	62	26	403	2 52	20.93	22.46	22.43
140	62	26	401	2 30	24.60	22.40	
140	62	26	401	2 53	20.80		

Mean speed, 22.39 knots.

TB79. (US Naval History and Heritage Command, NH54809)

TB79 spent her career in home waters and in 1891 struck the Red Sands, near the Isle of Sheppey, damaging her propeller and so was unable to take part in the manoeuvres for that year. She received water-tube boilers in 1902/3.

TB39 and *TB40* were two boats originally ordered by Chile from Yarrow. They were only 100ft long, displaced 40 tons and produced 500ihp for a top speed of 20 knots. Armed with a single 14in torpedo tube and a twin-barrelled 25mm/40 Nordenfelt gun, they did not fit in with the general pattern of development, and were actually in Chile, in a disassembled state, when the 1885 Russian war scare caused the Admiralty to purchase them to reinforce the Pacific Squadron. They were assembled in Chile and then escorted north to Esquimalt, British Columbia, where they became tenders to HMS *Swiftsure*, being nicknamed *Swift* and *Sure*. They were later rearmed with two 14in torpedoes in dropping gear.

Torpedo boats were painted black in home waters, with their numbers painted in white, either on the bow, on both sides of the funnel or on boards placed both sides of the funnel. In 1907 torpedo boats *TB25–TB79* were renumbered, having a zero placed in front of the existing number.

TB79 after being fitted with water-tube boilers. *(© National Maritime Museum, Greenwich, London, Richard Perkins Collection)*

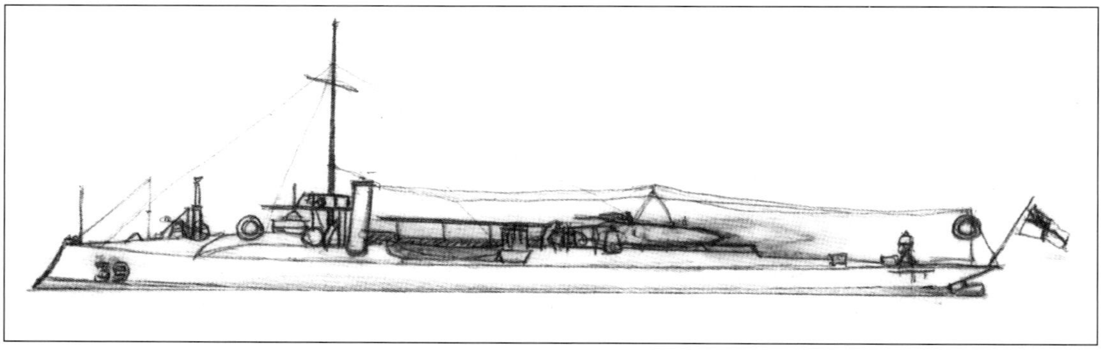

TB39. (© National Maritime Museum, Greenwich, London, Richard Perkins Collection)

TORPEDO BOAT CASUALTIES

***The Engineer*, 27 May 1887**

We told our readers in our last impression the story of the explosion of a boiler on board a torpedo boat. At the time we went to press our information was scant. Official, and, we may add prudent, reticence interfered to prevent anything like a detailed statement of the truth. Since we wrote the facts have become public; and they are far more serious and important than appeared at first sight. The Admiralty wisely determined to test a flotilla of torpedo boats purchased for the Navy at various times. The test was different from anything made before. Hitherto boats have been tried as weapons of attack and defence. Their sea-going qualities up to a certain point have been made the subject of experiment; but nothing was really known concerning their powers of endurance when steaming at full speed in charge of naval engineers. Now it is obvious that in case of actual war our torpedo boats might be called on to steam long distances in order to repel a threatened attack, and it is also clear that under such circumstances they would be called upon to go from place to place as fast as they could go. It was decided for these reasons that the boats of the flotilla should race over a distance of about 100 miles. The special correspondent of the *Army and Navy Gazette*, who accompanied the flotilla, thus describes what took place:

Thursday morning broke fine and clear, but owing to the northerly wind of the night previous, there was a heavy swell on until well into the afternoon. The flotilla formed in six divisions, and weighed by division, 10 min between each division, which, on getting under weigh, formed in single column line ahead, and made a preliminary canter at full speed. Each boat was four boats' lengths from the next ahead, and the strictest orders were given that under no circumstances whatever were the boats racing to close this distance. As they passed through the hole in the breakwater, time was taken for each boat by an officer belonging to the *Seahorse*, who was stationed there in a steam pinnace for the purpose. Our course lay between the Race and the Bill of Portland, and then W by N ¼N for the Orestone Rock. It at once became apparent that all our calculations as to the fastest type were at fault, for the Yarrow boats developed superior speeds to the rest, although from their bottle-nose snouts the way these boats took in water throwing the spray in a cloud over their stems, they must have been decidedly moist and unpleasant to their crews. The second division had barely started before No. 27 – Thornycroft – Lieut Coxon, returned with hot bearings. We were now struggling past the Bill, and the sensation crept over me – as I clung to the hand-rail, the speed of the boat and her motion rising over the swell and rolling from side to side, making it nasty work to hold on – that if anything happened to the box of boilers just behind me, the *Army and Navy Gazette* would be without 'copy' next week. Moreover, as the lieutenant in charge assured me, there was just a chance that we might break down and get swamped. As I was thinking of these things, we saw No. 41 Thornycroft – Lieut Colmore, rendered incapable, having broken something in her engines, and a moment later No. 50 – Thornycroft – Lieut Greville, drew out of the line for a similar reason. Leaving these boats tossing in the trough of the sea in very unenviable condition, we struggled on to the Rock, close to which the lamentable catastrophe occurred on board No. 47 – Thornycroft – Lieut Tower, the exact cause of which does not appear to be certain, although I expect that the crowns of her furnaces came down from lowness of water in her boilers. Such an accident nearly happened in No. 57 – Thornycroft – Lieut Harford, where the men rushed on deck, and I understand it was solely owing to the presence of mind of her artificer, that another disaster was prevented. No. 42 – Thornycroft – Lieut Armstrong, was put out of action by defects developing in the engine-room, and No. 55 – Thornycroft – Lieutenant Carey, also came to grief. Thus out of the twenty-two boats, seven, all of them Thornycrofts, came to grief, and another, No. 45, Lieutenant Thursby, lost a blade of her screw. The remaining boats finished the course, the first three being No. 31 – Yarrow – commanded by Mr Dawe, gunner, Lieutenant Hewitt not having turned up in time; No. 35 – White – Lieutenant Hamilton; and No. 46 – Thornycroft – Lieutenant Grant. The times were as follows: No. 31, 5 hours 10 min 15 sec; No. 35, 5 hours 10 min 20sec; No. 46, 5 hours 15 min. Thus there were only five seconds between the first and second boats. The *Rattlesnake*'s time was not taken, as no sooner did Captain Long hear of the accident to No. 47 than he transferred his flag to the *Seahorse*, and sent the 'catcher' to tow the disabled boat to Devonport. The *Seahorse* then cruised about picking up the disabled boats, and taking four of them in tow, started for Portland. However, somewhere off the Bill the hawser made fast to Nos 41 and 50 parted, and those craft went adrift. Very wisely, the captain left them to their fate, as the night was dark, and a collision might have resulted if attempts had been made to take them in tow again. I hear these two boats had a most unpleasant time of it, but they used their electric lights to show passing ships their position, and soon after 1am the *Seahorse* found them by this means, and skilfully passing a hawser to No. 41, towed them into harbour.

Opinions differ as to the value of torpedo boats, but it is certain that no maritime Power could be without them; and the fact that, out of twenty-four British boats, no fewer than eight were rendered *hors de combat* as soon as they were worked under conditions which might – and probably would – obtain any or every day if we were at war, is extremely serious. The failures we have recorded possess a national importance. It is a noteworthy fact that all the boats which broke down were by the same firm. There were four boats by Messrs Yarrow and Co, three boats by White, of Cowes, the remaining seventeen were by Thornycroft. If we refuse to class the failure of a propeller as a breakdown because the boat was still able to proceed, though at reduced speed, we find that the casualties to the boats of the Chiswick firm came to over 41 per cent. If out of 100 torpedo boats forty-one are to become unserviceable within an hour after they proceed to sea, confidence in the utility of such craft will be weakened. It may be urged – and has already been urged to some purpose – that the failures were due to the incompetence of the men in charge. If this were wholly true it would imply a very serious indictment of the Admiralty; we refuse, however, to believe it. While we admit that had more care been exercised in the stokeholes it is possible that no breakdown would have occurred, we hold that any system of design or construction which renders boilers and engines dependent for their safe working on exceptional skill and vigilance, must be defective. Whatever the probable shortcomings of the crews in charge could possibly have been, we think the main cause of the failures must be sought and found in the machinery of the boats, and even in the boats themselves, and we fancy, before we have done, that our readers will be of the same opinion. As we know nothing yet of the nature of the failures which took place in the engine or boiler rooms of Nos 27, 41, 50,

42, and 53, we can say little about them. No. 27 had hot bearings but they must have been very hot indeed to stop the boat. The bearings in a torpedo-boat engine are so comparatively small and light, and the appliances for cooling so perfect, that, as is known from experience, a very hot bearing can be cooled in a very few minutes; and in a long race, such as this under consideration, five minutes delay at the outset could not destroy the chances of a boat. Putting this on one side, however, we may confine ourselves to two casualties, namely, the failure of the boilers in No. 47 and No. 57. In both cases the crowns of the fire-boxes came down. In No. 47 the failure was sudden and complete; and, as we know, lives were lost. In the case of No. 57 the failure of the crown plate was not so sudden and complete, and no lives were lost; although the risk incurred was awful. Why did the furnace crowns come down? The first reply that will suggest itself to an engineer is that they came down because the boilers were short of water. On this point, however, there is a great deal to be said; and in order that our readers may comprehend the whole matter, we give here two sets of drawings showing the system of construction adopted by Messrs Yarrow and Co, and that used by Messrs Thornycroft and Co.

At first sight there does not seem to be much difference between them, but there is a difference – a most essential difference in detail. It will be seen that in neither boiler are bridge stays used. The tops of the inside and outside fire-boxes are secured to each other by stays. It will also be seen that the stays used by Messrs Yarrow have large heads jumped up out of the solid and forged to shape; that under these heads is a screw thread; that the opposite ends or points are also screwed. The stays are turned down between the threads, so that the threads stand up. These bolts are then screwed hard into place from the inside, and large square nuts are then screwed on the ends projecting on top of the fire-box shell. In locomotive work the crown stay bolts always have heads or nuts inside the fire-box on the crown stays.

Turning now to Mr Thornycroft's boiler, it will be seen that he dispenses with nuts and heads. His stays are screwed, just as Mr Yarrow's are, but there the resemblance ceases. The ends of the stays are rivetted over – the crown stays thus resembling the side stays. This we regard as an essentially weak system of construction, and to it we believe the failure of the boilers in 47 and 57 was partly due. The system of rivetting over cold answers well enough in a side stay which is not more than 6in or 7in long over all; but the crown stars are over 2ft long, and rivetting up cold has a very great tendency to do more harm to the screw thread in the 7⁄16in crown plate than anything else, for it is next to impossible properly to hold up a bar 2ft long to the rivetting hammer. It may be

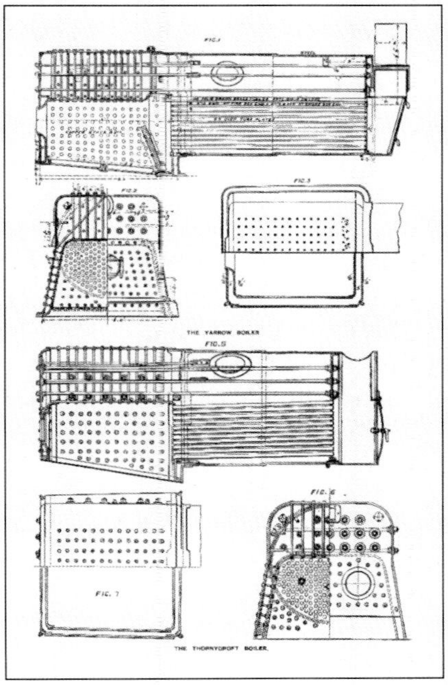

A comparison of Yarrow and Thornycroft boilers. ***(The Engineer, 27 May 1887)***

urged that; screwed and rivetted stay is just as strong as a screwed stay with head and nut. This we deny. That it may be quite strong enough under ordinary circumstances is one thing, that it is strong enough for torpedo boat boilers does not at all follow as a legitimate consequence. It will not do to assume that, because such a system of construction may give good results in a locomotive boiler, it must do so in a torpedo boat boiler. It has been urged that the crown plates came down in No. 47 and No. 57 because the plates were overheated from shortness of water. This we concede at once, but it does not follow that the men in charge were to blame. As a matter of fact, the crowns of the fire-boxes in torpedo boats are often left uncovered by water for some little time. When running before a sea, the boat will get on the back of a wave travelling at nearly her own pace and she will run with her head down and her stern up until she has outpaced the wave. During this time the crown of the fire-box may have no 'solid water' on it; but besides this, torpedo boats are so lively and jump about so much that in a heavy sea the crown plates are sure every now and then to get left dry, or nearly so, for a few seconds unless the water is kept high in the glass. If there are large nuts inside the box, these serve to keep cool considerable areas of metal just round the screw threads. It is well known that it is practically impossible to make a nut red hot if the stay remains cool, because the stay serves to convey away heat in a way very clearly set forth by Peclet, Wye Williams, and others. Every engineer will concede, we think, that if the top of a Yarrow box became overheated, it would be likely to come down between the stays in pockets; but it is evident that it must be made very hot indeed before the heads could be forced out of the stays or drawn right through the plate. It is, we think, incontestable that the Yarrow system must be stronger than the Thornycroft system. A leak might be started by the crown plate cracking, but its total disruption is to the last degree unlikely. It must not be forgotten, however, that these are the first failures of Thornycroft boilers that have taken place, and that the old *Lightning* has given no trouble and has been very hard worked. But the *Lightning* has been managed by men of great experience.

We have little doubt, that Messrs Thornycroft's other failures have been due to the desire to make the machinery of their boats as light as possible. It is a matter of interest to know that the Yarrow boats of the same dimensions weigh nearly seven tons more than the Thornycroft boats. Of this 3½ tons go to the hull and 3½ tons to the engines and boiler. For example, it will be seen by Fig I that Messrs Yarrow and Co raise the forward end of the internal fire-box. They thus get room for more tubes without raising the crown plate as a whole. The small portion actually raised being near the mid-length of the boiler, where the water level is not much affected by pitching, it is always covered. But the result of adopting this system of construction is that the boiler holds an extra half-ton of water. Messrs Thornycroft's engines are speeded higher than Messrs Yarrow's, the pitch of the screws being finer; and this we hold to be objectionable. Nothing can exceed the skill with which the Thornycroft engines have been designed and made; but facts are too strong for them and the advocates of high-speed engines. Those who hold that we may yet have 40-knot passenger steamers may draw an instructive lesson from the torpedo boat race of May 1887. The consolatory feature of the whole affair is that the boats of Messrs Yarrow and Mr White did their work without a hitch or difficulty of any kind, and it is not to be supposed that their engine-room staffs were better than those of the Thornycroft boats.

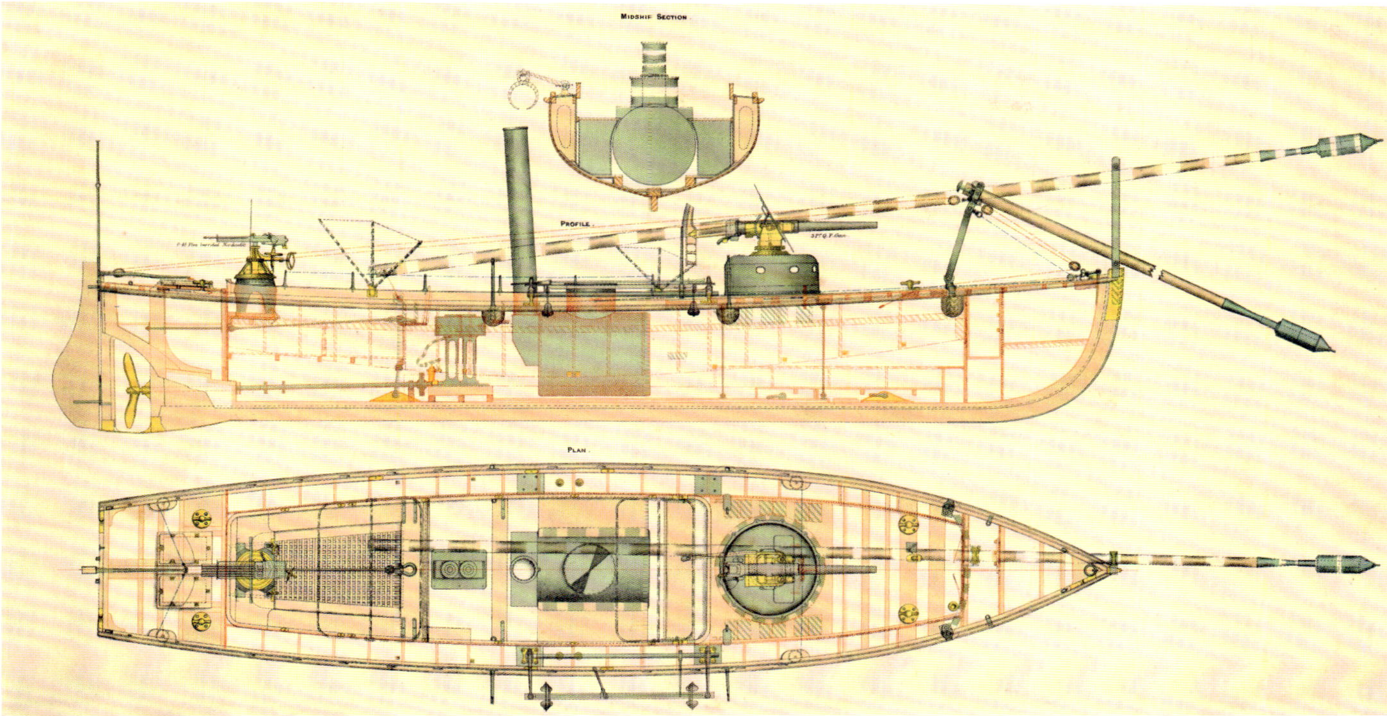

A 45ft steam pinnace fitted with a spar torpedo and two gun mountings. Produced by Portsmouth Yard, dated 18 January 1888; 3pdr QF gun forward, 0.45 five-barrelled Nordenfelt aft. *(© National Maritime Museum, Greenwich, London)*

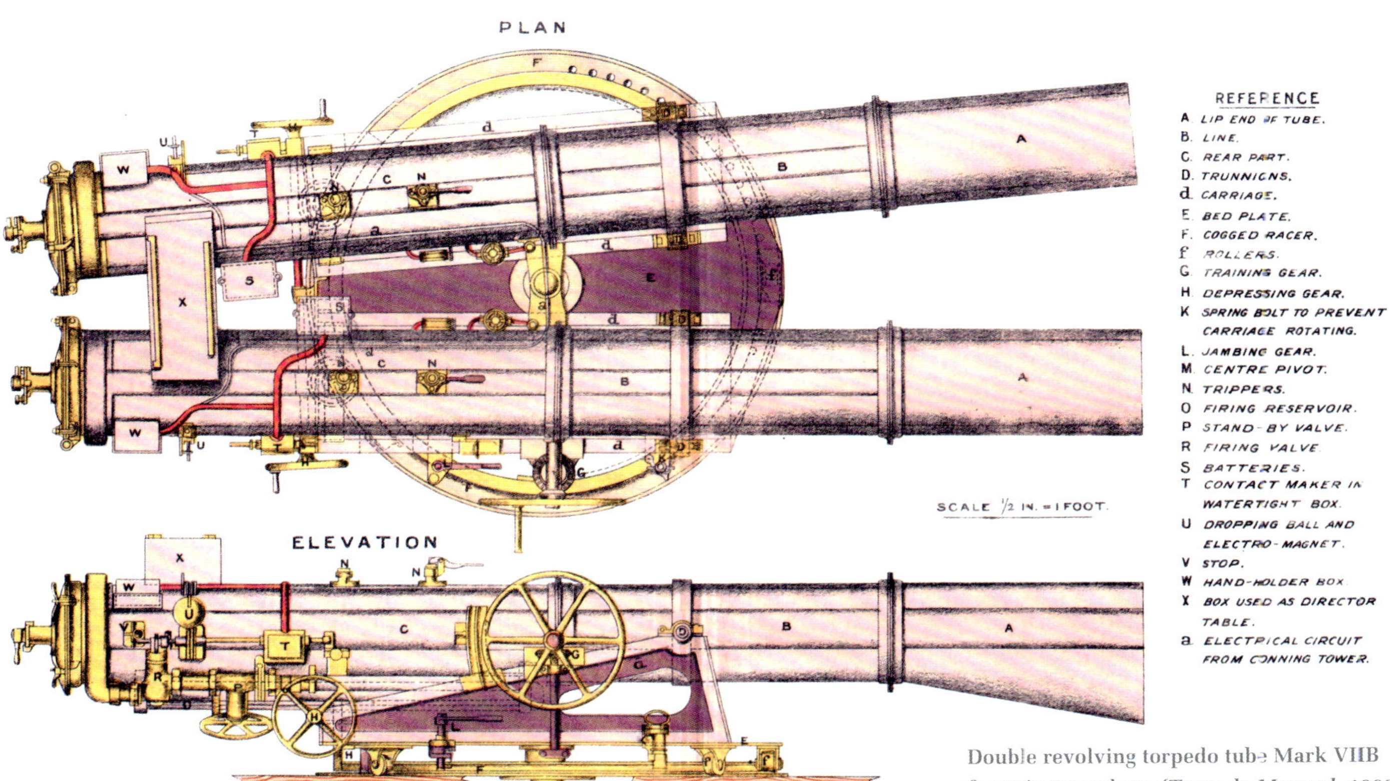

Double revolving torpedo tube Mark VIIB for 18in torpedoes. *(Torpedo Manual, 1909)*

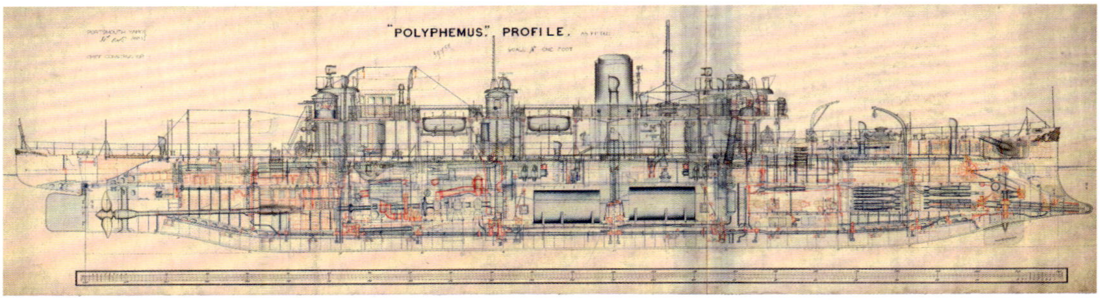

Profile of the torpedo ram HMS *Polyphemus*, 1885. *(© National Maritime Museum, Greenwich, London)*

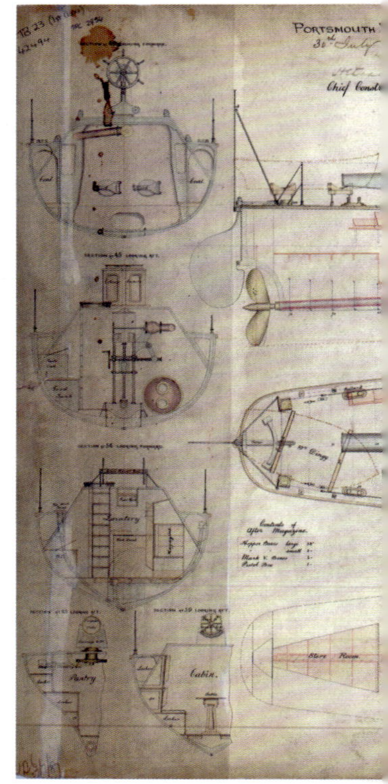

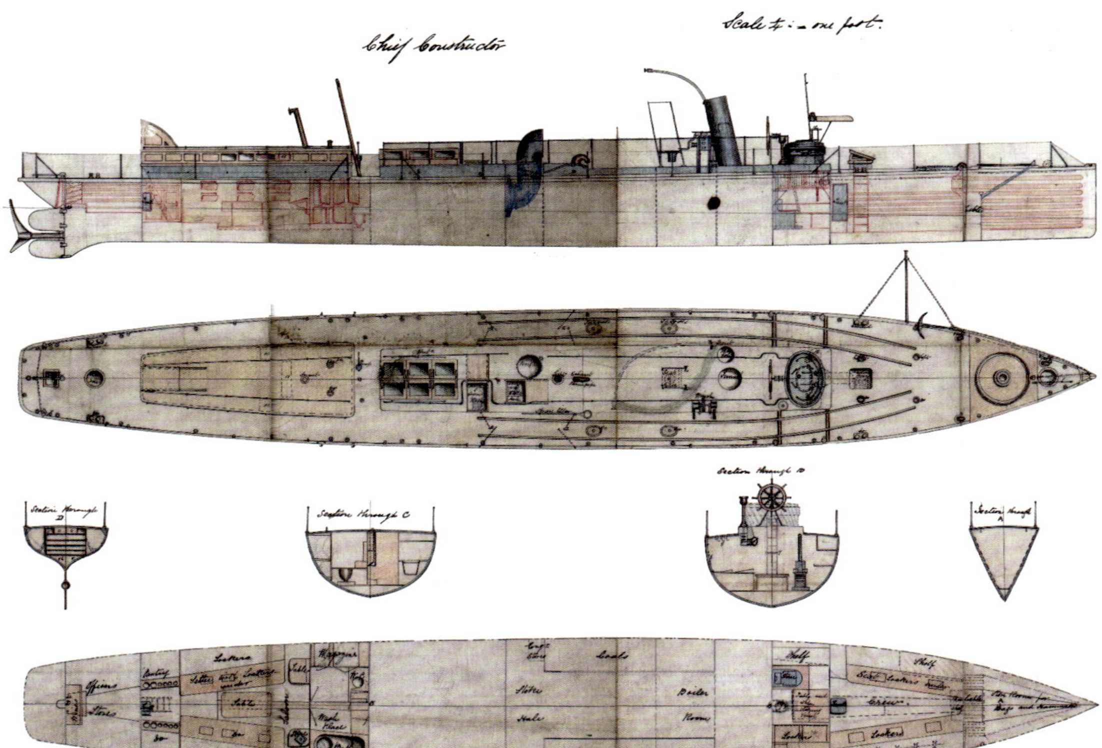

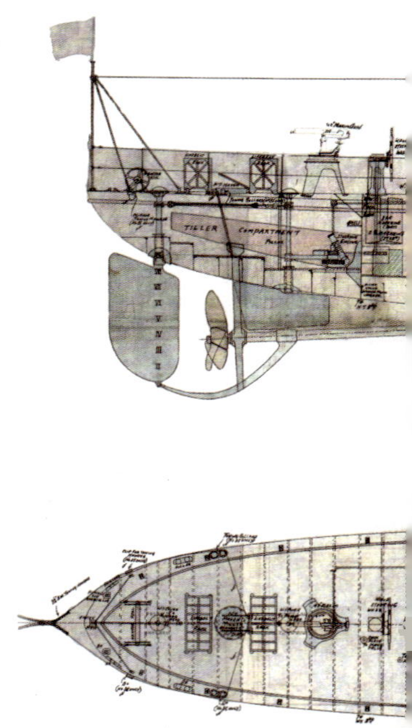

General arrangement of the first torpedo boat, *Lightning*, 1878. *(© National Maritime Museum, Greenwich, London)*

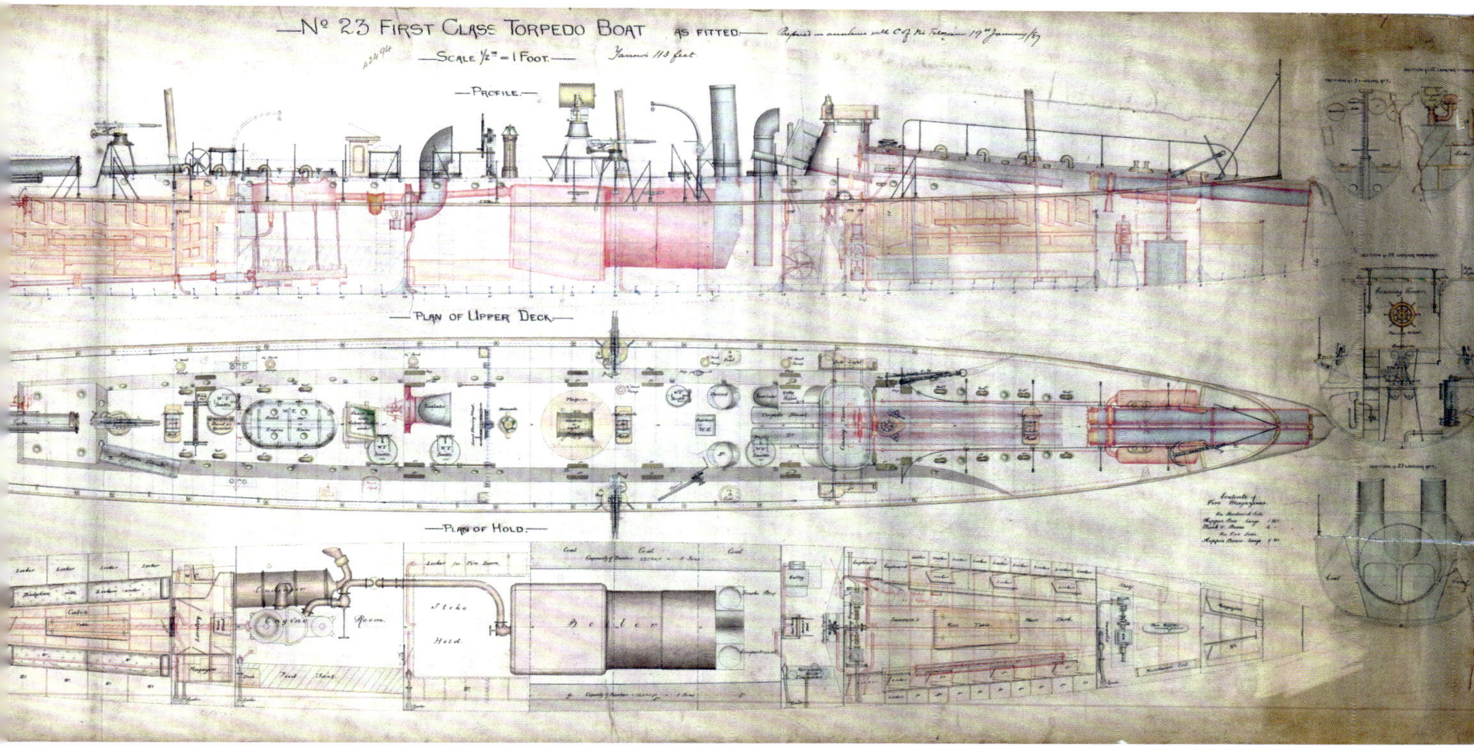

General arrangement of Yarrow's first-class torpedo boat No. 23, 1887. *(© National Maritime Museum, Greenwich, London)*

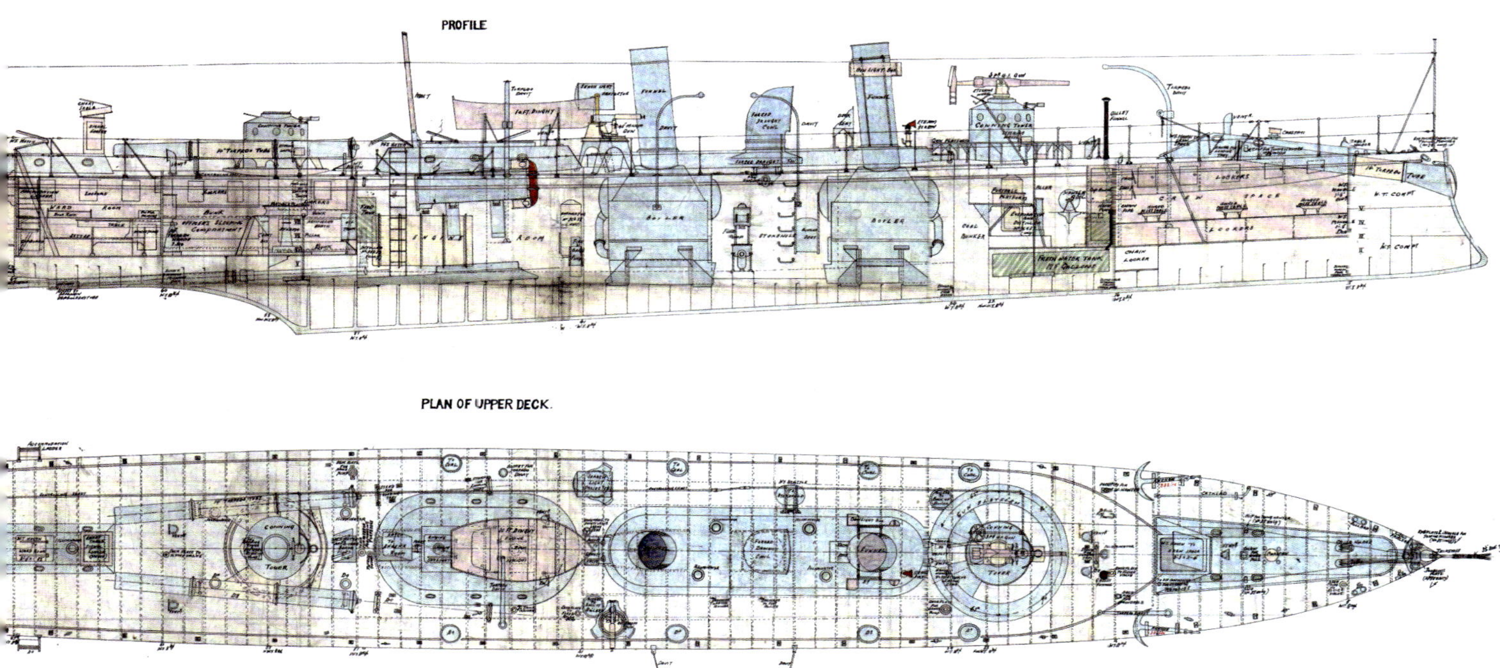

General arrangement of White's first-class torpedo boats Nos 35–38, after re-boilering in the early 1900s. *(© National Maritime Museum, Greenwich, London)*

General arrangement of Thornycroft's first-class torpedo boat No. 98, 1902.
(© National Maritime Museum, Greenwich, London)

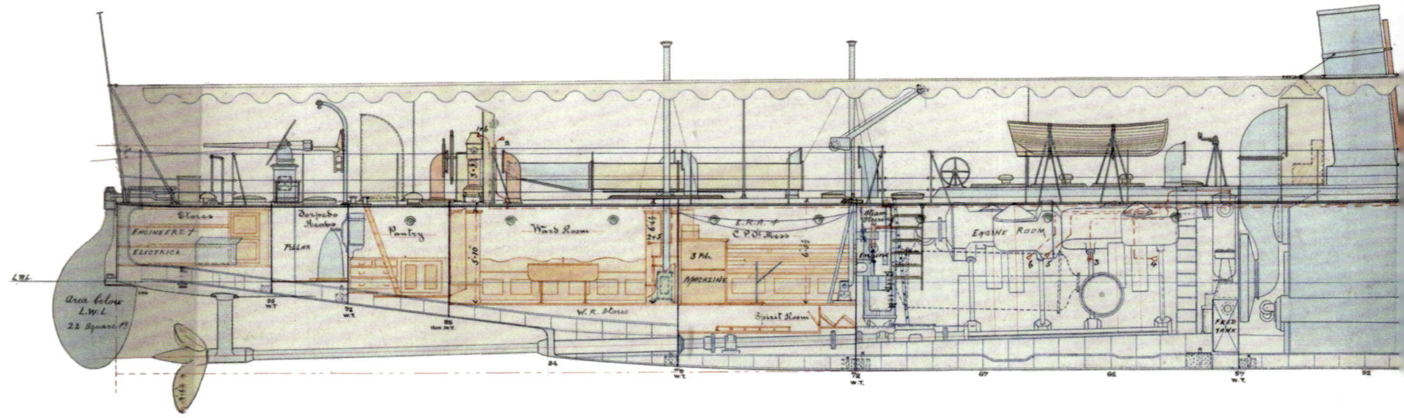

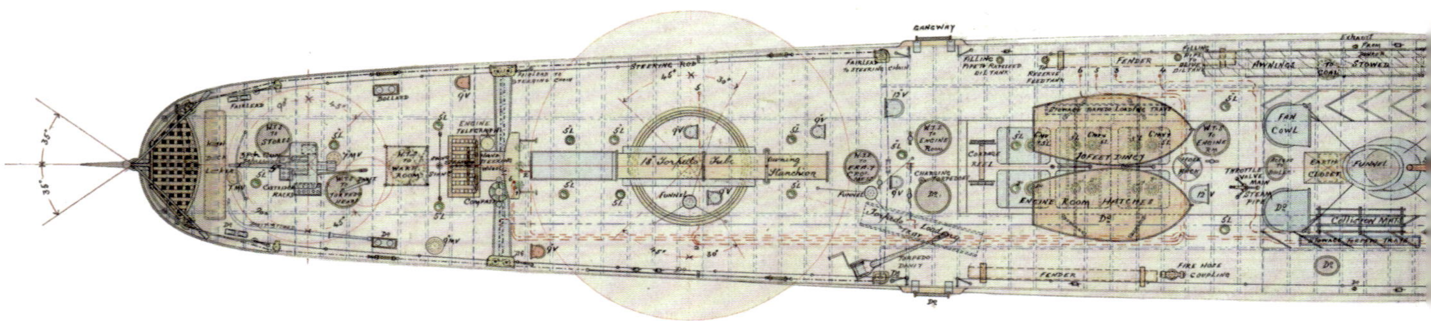

Sections and lower deck of Thornycroft's first-class torpedo boat No. 98, 1902. *(© National Maritime Museum, Greenwich, London)*

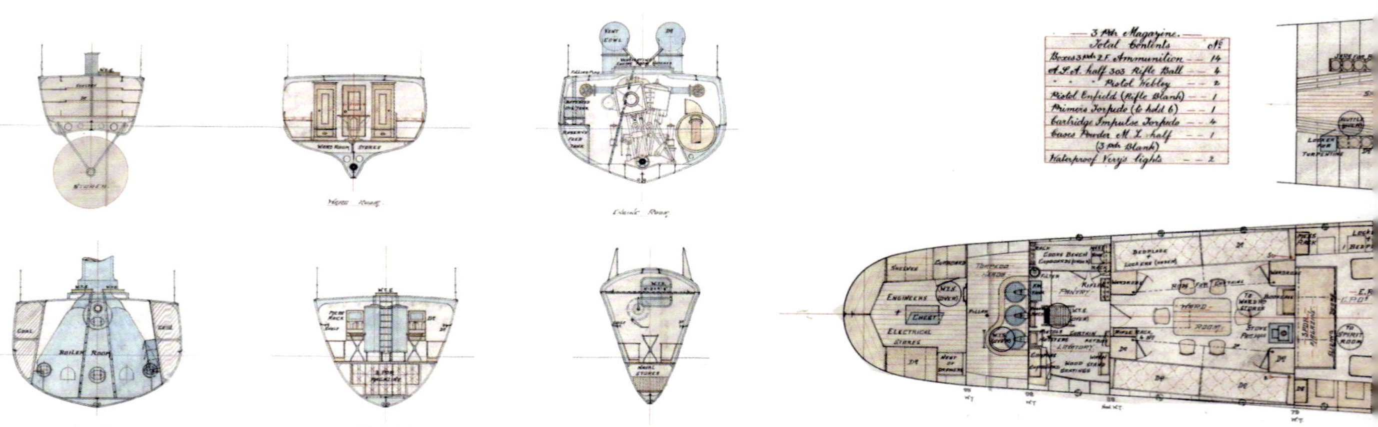

PLATE 5

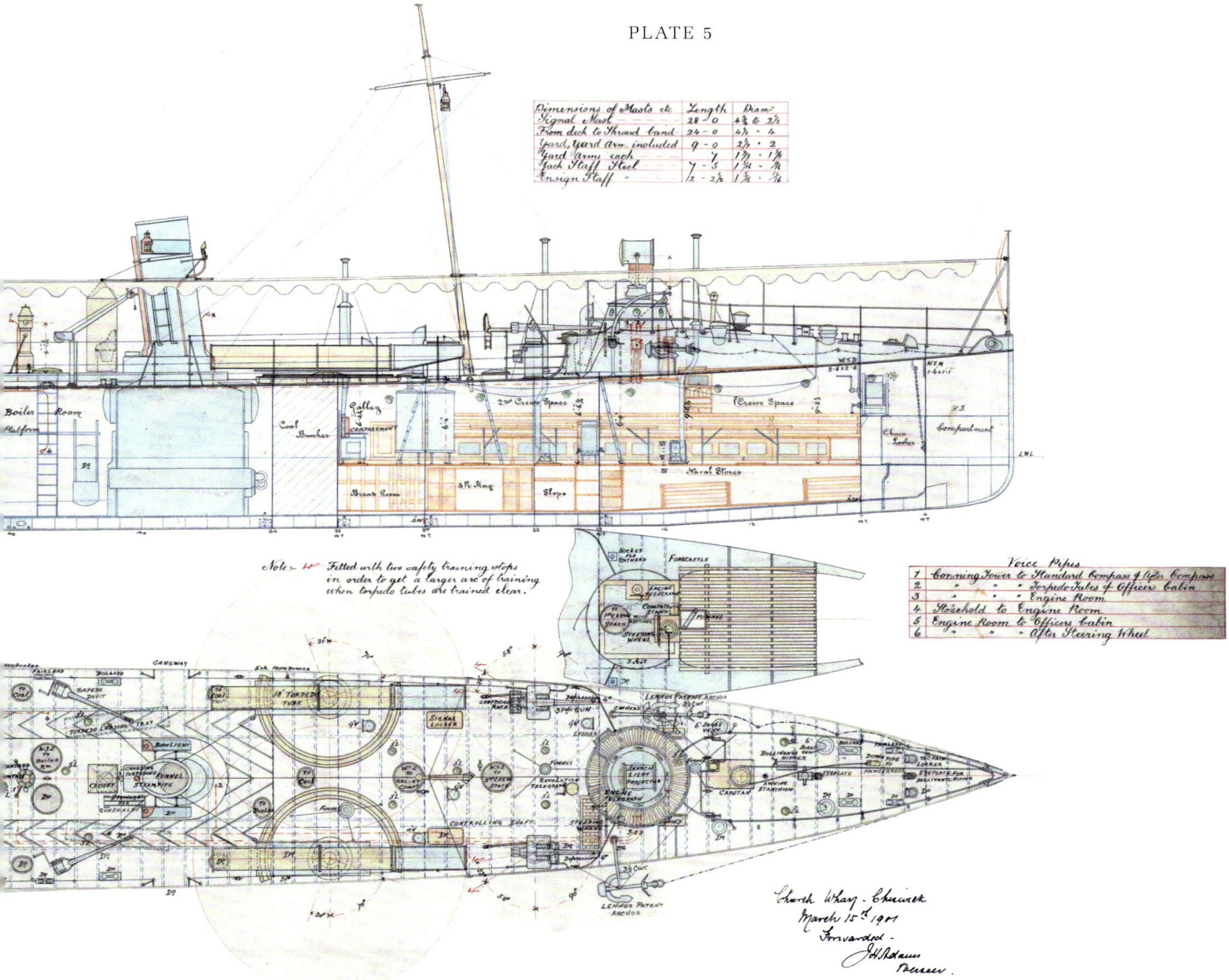

Dimensions of Masts etc Length Diam
Signal Mast 28 - 0 4½ to 2½
From deck to Shroud band 24 - 0 4½ - 4
Yard, Yard Arm included 9 - 0 2½ - 2
Ensign Staff 12 - 2½
Boiler Room
Platform
Coal Bunker
Galley
2nd Crews Space
1st Crews Space
Chain Locker
Compartment
Naval Stores
Slops
LWL
Note - Fitted with two safety training stops in order to get a larger arc of training when torpedo tubes are trained clear.
Voice Pipes
1 Conning Tower to Standard Compass & After Compass
2 " " " Torpedo Tubes & Officers Cabin
3 " " " Engine Room
4 Stokehold to Engine Room
5 Engine Room to Officers Cabin
6 " " " After Steering Wheel
FORECASTLE
GANGWAY
18" TORPEDO TUBE
FUNNEL
SIGNAL LOCKER
CONTROLLING SHAFT
CAPSTAN
LENNOX PATENT ANCHOR
Church Wharf - Chiswick
March 15th 1901
Forwarded -
J H Adams
Purser.

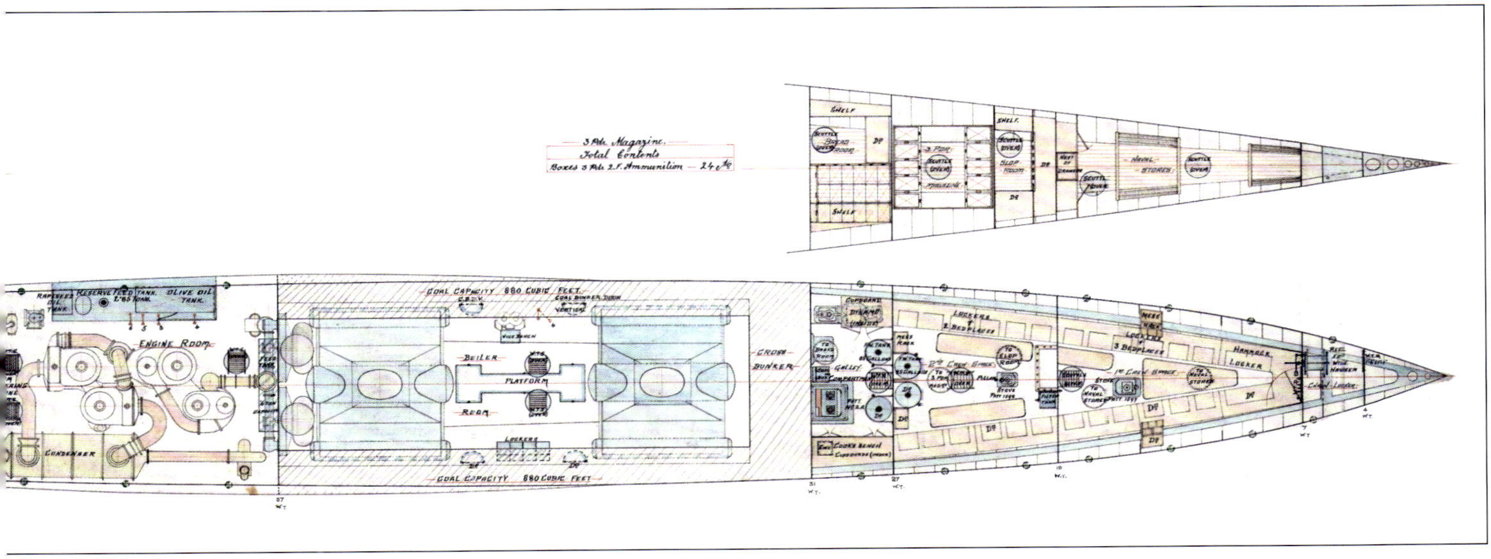

3 Pdr. Magazine.
Total Contents
NAVAL STORES
ENGINE ROOM
CONDENSER
COAL CAPACITY 880 CUBIC FEET
BOILER
PLATFORM
ROOM
CROSS BUNKER
GALLEY
COAL CAPACITY 880 CUBIC FEET

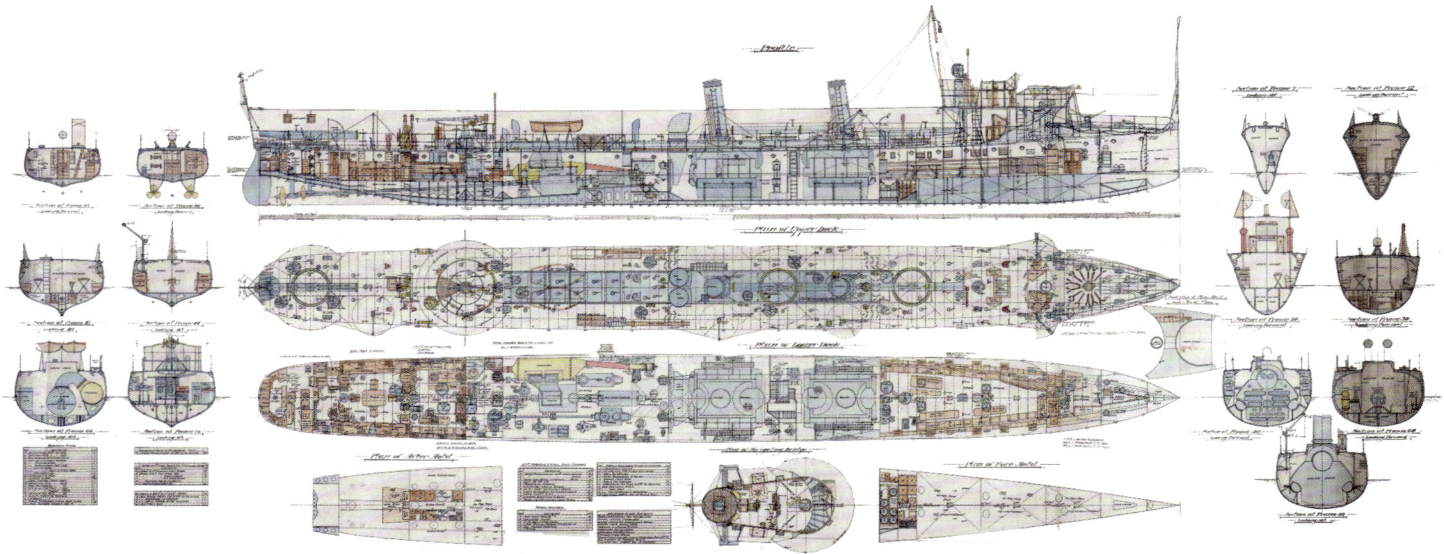

General arrangement of White's first-class torpedo boat No. 3, *Firefly*, 1907.
(© National Maritime Museum, Greenwich, London)

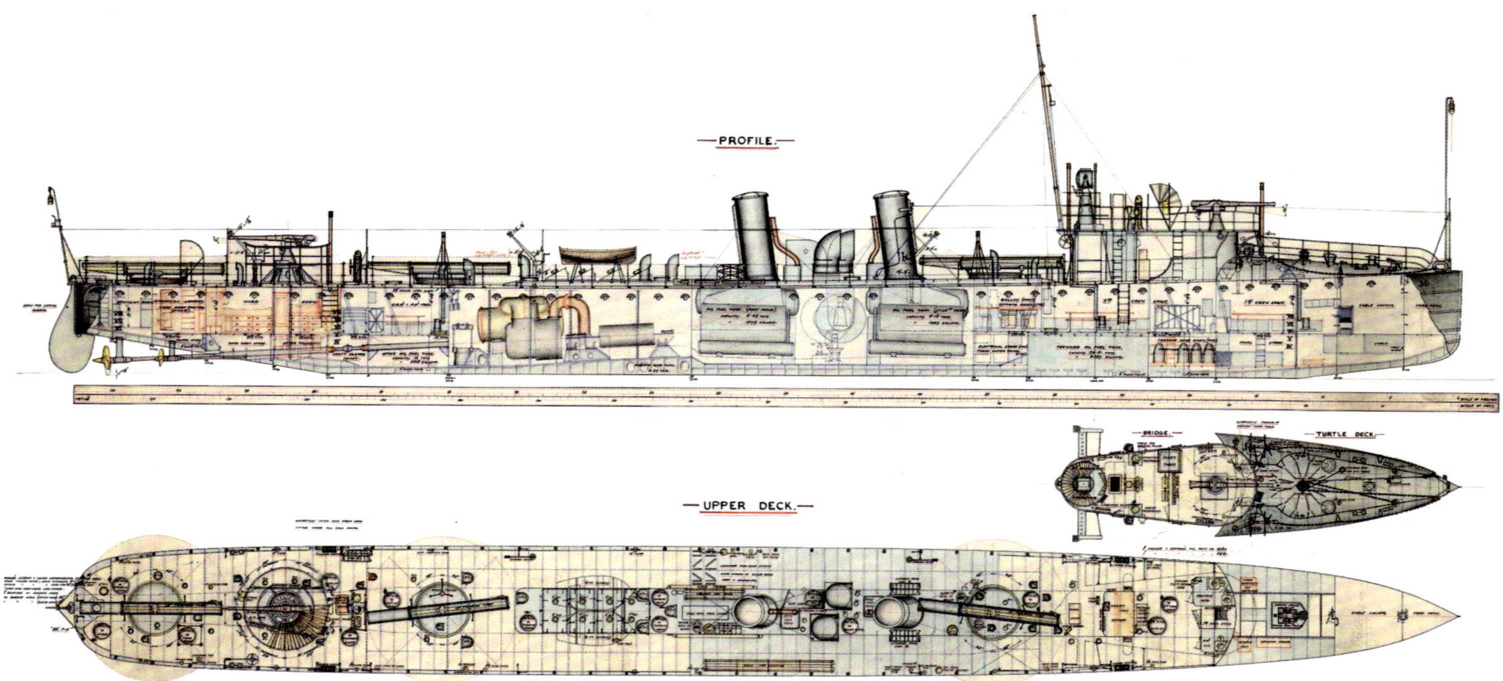

Denny's as-fitted drawing of *TB30*; length is shown as 179ft 11¾in, 1909.
(© National Maritime Museum, Greenwich, London)

PLATE 7

General arrangement of Hawthorn Leslie's first-class torpedo boat No. 33, 1909.
(© National Maritime Museum, Greenwich, London)

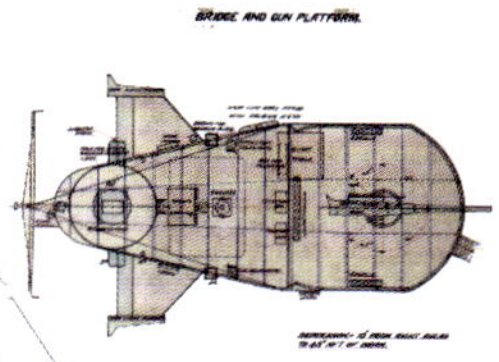

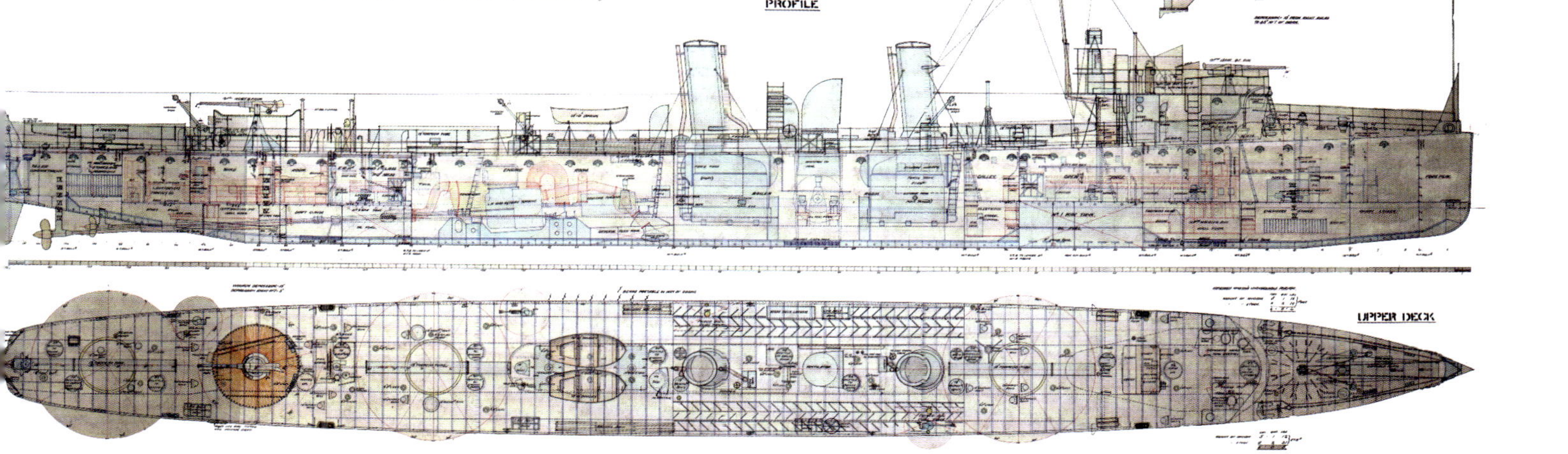

As-fitted profile of torpedo gunboat,
Halcyon, built by Devonport Dockyard, 1904.
(© National Maritime Museum,
Greenwich, London)

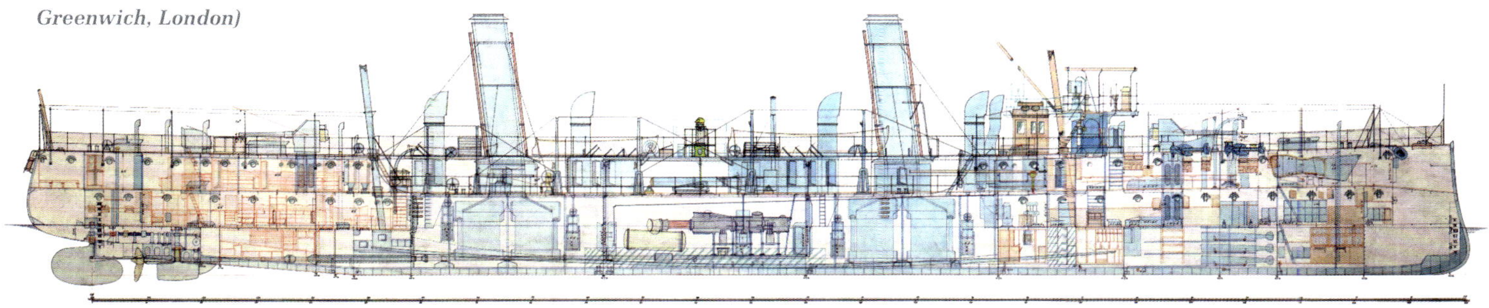

As-fitted deck plan of torpedo gunboat, *Halcyon*, built by Devonport Dockyard, 1904.
(© National Maritime Museum, Greenwich, London)

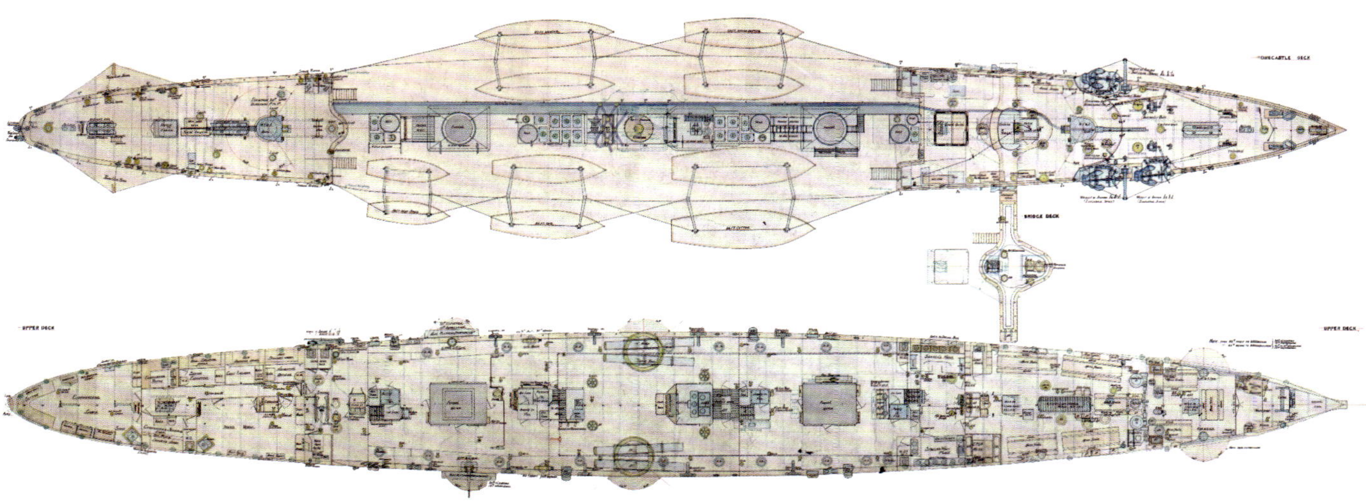

PLATE 8

Profile of the design for the torpedo depot ship, HMS *Vulcan*, 1888. General arrangement of Yarrow's second-class torpedo boats Nos 39–48, 1889. *(© National Maritime Museum, Greenwich, London)*

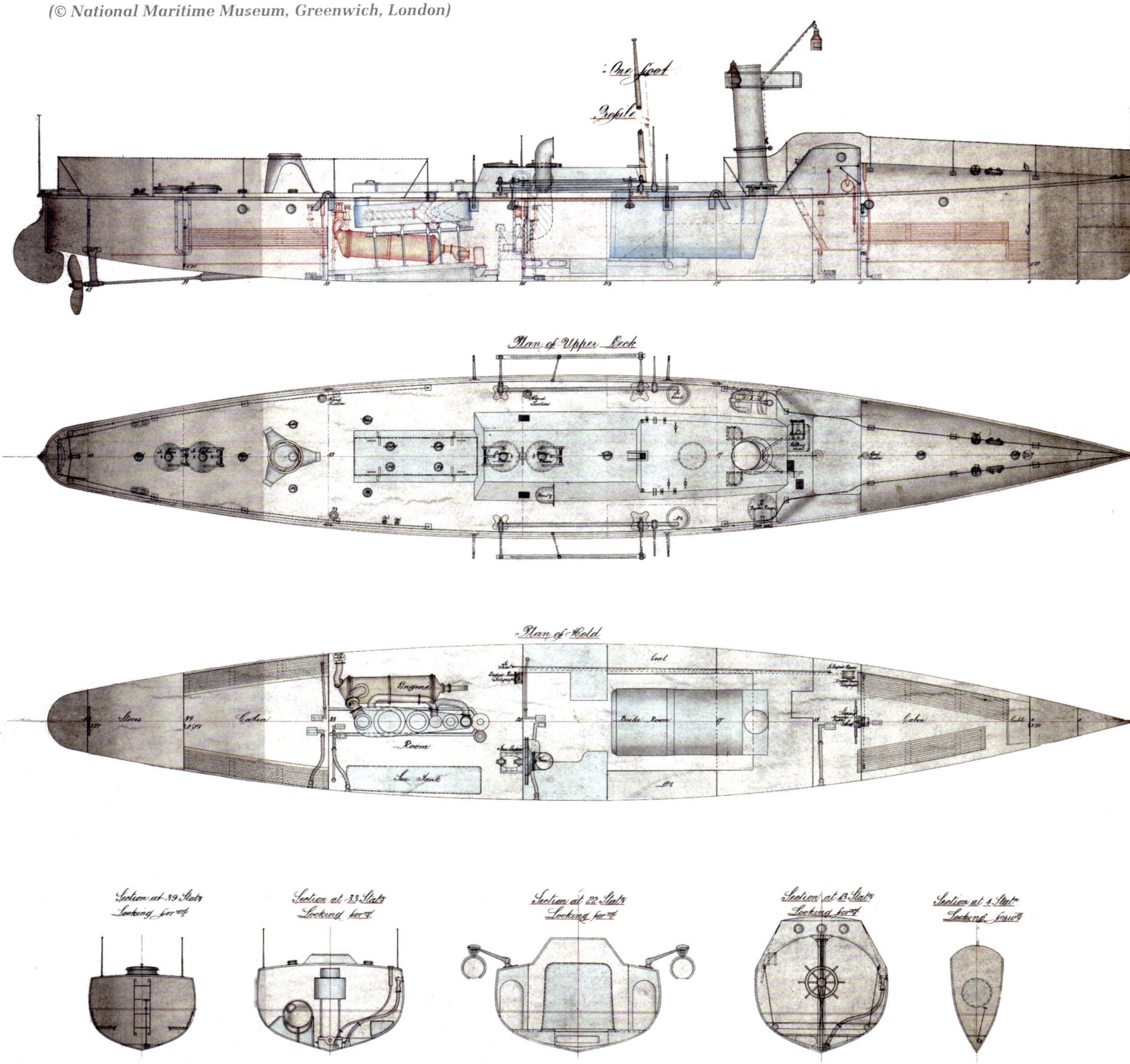

The Engineer of 16 December 1898 contained a report of the water-tube boilers fitted to *TB63* and *TB64*:

> The special type of water-tube boiler designed and constructed by Mr A G Mumford, of Colchester, for the first-class torpedo boats Nos 63 and 64, differs in several points from the boilers made by the same firm for the Sharpshooter Class torpedo gunboat *Salamander*. The main reason for the alteration in design was to accommodate the boiler to the smaller space allowed in the torpedo boats and the high efficiency required. The entire space occupied is – length 9ft; breadth, 7ft; and height, 6ft. The heating surface is 850 square feet, and the grate area is 22 square feet. It was designed for 400 indicated horse-power, but the results of the official evaporation trials proved that far greater power could be developed. Burning 25lb of coal, an evaporation of 9.88lb of water per pound of coal, from feed-water at a temperature of 58 degrees was obtained; burning 50lb, the evaporation was 9.05; 75lb, it was 7.4; and 100lb, 6.317, all from feed-water at a temperature of 58 degrees. These figures are unquestionably very good. Special attention has been given in this particular boiler to the reduction of the gases to a very low temperature, and by an ingenious arrangement this has been so far secured that the temperature at the base of the funnel never became excessive on the three-hours' trials. The boilers are fitted with Messrs Mumford and Anthony's patent feed apparatus.

The Mumford water-tube boiler fitted to *TB63* and *TB64* when reboilered.

CHAPTER FIVE

FIRST-CLASS TORPEDO BOATS, *TB80–TB117*

The Admiralty continued to press for higher speeds which resulted in larger boats. As part of the 1885/6 programme, *TB80* was ordered from Yarrow. The design was based on a design for Austria, often referred to as the *Falke* type.

TORPEDO BOAT *TB80* SPEED TRIALS

The Engineer, 13 and 20 May 1887

On Tuesday the largest, and, it is believed, the fastest of the new torpedo boats built for the British service underwent her first trial for speed in the waters of the Lower Hope. The No. 80 was built in the yard of Messrs Yarrow, of Millwall. There was a small company present to inspect the boat on her trial. Mr Smale and Mr Shapcott were present on behalf of the Admiralty authorities, and Mr Gowings and Mr Maystone on behalf of the Royal Dockyard at Portsmouth; Mr Crohn represented the builders.

The No. 80 is 135ft long, has 14ft beam, and is expected to make 23 knots an hour. She is of special build, and has powerful attributes, possessing a stem torpedo gun, two stern broadside torpedo guns – these guns, otherwise tubes, being the special means of launching torpedoes against the enemy – and five quick-firing Hotchkiss guns, together with all the means and appliances whereby she can carry on offensive and defensive action. The vessel is built throughout of mild steel, and has a cutaway stern and a balanced rudder. She has, too, a bow rudder, which can be taken up at will. The vessel is powerfully engined for her size, and in her engine-room are seven engines – namely, the triple-expansion engines of 1,500 horse power, a donkey engine, a circulating pump engine, a fan engine, a compressor engine, and an air engine to work Dr Normandy's distilling apparatus. The engine-room is protected by coal bunkers, and is fitted with the

TB80. (Navypedia)

Yarrow patent stokehole, a contrivance by which the boiler's fire will be maintained, even with a hole in the bottom of the boat, and she could steam under the circumstances of such a disaster some seventy or eighty miles. She is fitted below with a dynamo working an electric search light. The accommodation below provides for a crew of sixteen all told, a saloon for officers, not large, but sufficient, and a coal carrying capacity sufficient to carry the vessel at half-speed for six days. The deck gives the great outward features of the vessel. Her front torpedo tube, or the gun, as it is called, from which the torpedo is fired, is built in the boat; it is stationary, and is protected by a turtle back, surmounted by a conning tower, on which provision is made for a quick firing and powerful Hotchkiss. This conning tower is protected by plates of an extra thickness for from here the torpedo gun is worked and the boat steered. Behind the conning tower are two quick firing guns in echelon, that on the starboard being in advance of that on the port. There are two aft torpedo guns, which being intended for broadside use, are in revolving tubes. They are protected by a conning tower possessing the quick firing guns. This tower is of thicker steel than in other parts. The displacement of the vessel is 105 tons with a complete armament. The speed attained on the trial fully came up to expectations – namely, 23 knots per hour – and when the boat returned to Millwall the inventors and builders were congratulated upon their new success.

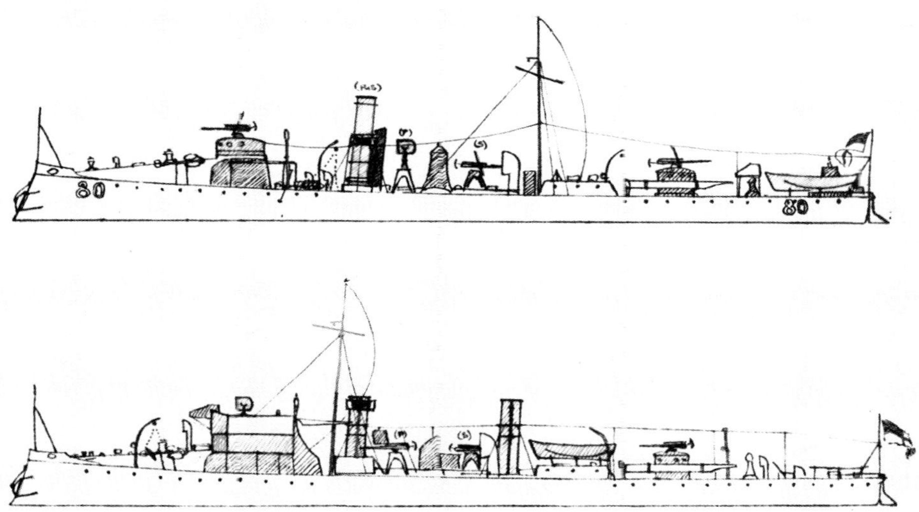

TB80 as built (top) and after receiving water-tube boilers (bottom). *(© National Maritime Museum, Greenwich, London, Richard Perkins Collection)*

	Steam (lbs)	Vacuum (in)	Revs per min	Time on knot	Speed (knots per hour)	Means (knots per hour)	2nd means (knots per hour)
1	160	26	380⅔	2-31	23.841	22.896	
2	160	26	383	2-44	21.951	22.896	22.896
3	160	26	381½	2-31	23.841	23.03	122.963
4	160	26	381¾	2-42	22.222	22.953	22.992
5	160	26	380½	2-32	22.953	23.162	23.057
6	160	26	384½	2-39	22.641		
Means	160	26	382½				22.977

TB80 could steer a complete circle of 100yds diameter in just over a minute. She had to be reboilered with a Thornycroft boiler in 1898, when her paired funnels (port and starboard) were replaced by two on the centreline. Her searchlight was moved from abaft the funnels to a much higher position on an enlarged bridge structure. In 1908 she had a topmast fitted and in 1909 minesweeping gear was added aft. In 1913 the bow torpedo tube was removed. She served at both Portsmouth and Portland, and was sold to Stanlee in 1921, being resold to J E Thomas on 22 October of the same year.

TB81 began life as *Swift*, a private venture built by White using the 'turnabout' feature of earlier vessels. She was flush-decked, with a strengthened ram bow for ramming hostile torpedo boats. *TB81* was 153ft 8½in long overall, 150ft between perpendiculars with a beam of 17ft 6in and a draught of 9ft 6in. Displacement was 139 tons normal and 169 tons full load. She was powered by a single three-cylinder compound steam engine, rated at 1,300 indicated horsepower, driving a single propeller shaft, which resulted in a speed of 23.79 knots during sea trials. Tandem rudders were fitted, allowing *TB81* to be the most manoeuvrable British torpedo boat of the time, despite being the largest, having a turning circle of 225ft. Two widely spaced funnels were fitted, side by side, ahead of the ship's conning tower.

She was designed to carry differing armament suites depending on the role she was employed in. For the anti-torpedo boat role, the ship could carry six 3pdr guns together with a 14in torpedo tube in the bow, while for the torpedo boat role, two more torpedo tubes could be carried at the expense of two of the guns. She had a crew of twenty-five. When reboilered early in the twentieth century, she was fitted with two tall, thin funnels on the centreline, with her mast forward of the fore funnel. The searchlight was moved forward to the enlarged bridge and a topmast was fitted in 1908, the lower yard being raised in 1911.

With the Russian war scare, the Admiralty purchased the boat before she had run her speed trials, but when the scare passed, *TB81* lay incomplete for some time while her future armament was discussed, whether she should carry more guns and act as a 'catcher'. Eventually she was completed as a torpedo boat.

TB80 after being fitted with water-tube boilers. *(Navypedia)*

On 3 August 1901, during the 1901 naval manoeuvres, *TB81* was trying to intercept the prototype turbine-powered destroyer *Viper* when both ships ran aground on the Renonquet Reef off Alderney. While *TB81* was refloated and repaired, *Viper* was wrecked. *TB81* was reboilered in 1905 and served as a patrol boat during the First World War, operating out of Portsmouth and Portland, and being fitted with hydrophones and depth charges. On 15 May 1917 *TB81* was directed by a seaplane towards a submarine which the aircraft had spotted and attacked in the English Channel. She detected a possible submarine contact on her hydrophone, and waited until the submarine surfaced. *TB81* gave chase, the submarine dived and she dropped a depth charge and brought up a patch

TB81 as built. *(Navypedia)*

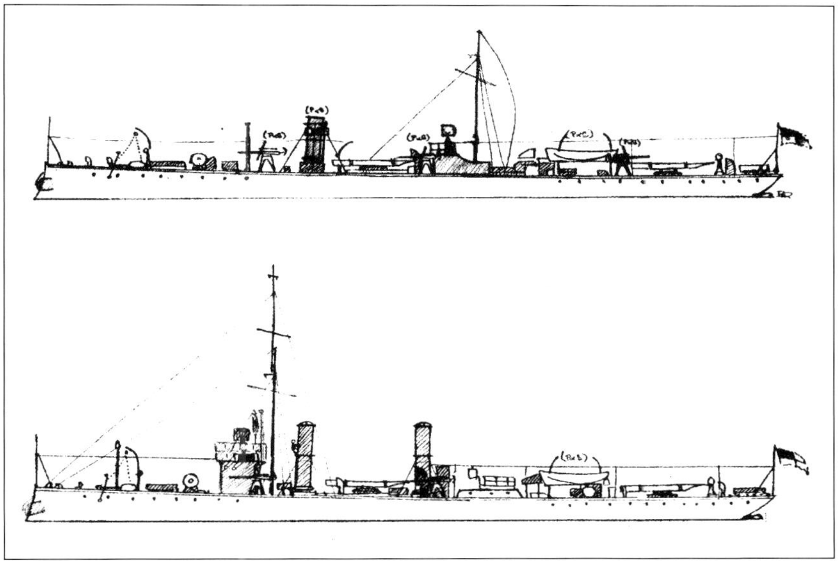

TB81 as completed (top) and after being reboilered (bottom). *(© National Maritime Museum, Greenwich, London, Richard Perkins Collection)*

of oil. *TB81* was paid off in 1919 and was sold for scrap to J E Thomas of Newport on 22 October 1921.

TB82 to *TB87* were the result of an invitation by the Admiralty authorities for six first-class torpedo boats, which was sent to a number of companies. The 1888 annual report from *Vernon* stated:

> Six 1st-class torpedo boats, 130 feet in length have been ordered to be built by Messrs Yarrow and Co. These boats will be on the lines of No. 30 torpedo boat, but 3ft shorter.
>
> They will be armed with a fixed stern tube with 3° depression, and a double revolving tube round a small firing tower aft. The tubes will be at an angle of 5° with each other, like the *Sharpshooter*'s tubes. Messrs Yarrow and *Vernon*, after consultation, proposed to do away with the firing tower, mounting the tubes on a revolving platform, on which the officer attending the director should be seated, with steam training gear, on the principle of a steam wheel, close to him, so that he could alter the training of the tubes with great rapidity. This, however, was not approved by the Admiralty, and the usual hand-training gear will be fitted inside the firing tower.
>
> The fittings of these boats have received very careful consideration, and it is confidently expected that great improvements will be made in the deck fittings over the other boats.
>
> In these boats the plan of an alternative armament has been abandoned and they will carry, simultaneously, three torpedoes and three QF 3pdr guns.

The propellers of these boats weighed 3cwt 3qtrs 6lbs.

TB81 after being fitted with water-tube boilers. *(Navypedia)*

THE NEW TORPEDO BOATS

***The Engineer*, 20 September 1889**

The designs submitted by Messrs Yarrow and Co, of Poplar, were those to which preference was given, partly in consequence of their guaranteeing a higher speed than any other firm. These boats are, as regards all leading particulars, similar to *TB79*, a sample boat, constructed three years earlier by the above firm, and which gave specially good results on account of her excellent speed, combined with exceptional manoeuvring powers. As is well known, she has become the favourite torpedo-boat in her Majesty's Navy, and it will be remembered by our readers that this one was selected to be placed under the command of Prince George of Wales during the Naval Review and recent manoeuvres.

TB82* as constructed. *(© National Maritime Museum, Greenwich, London, Richard Perkins Collection)

The new boats, which embody all the latest improvements, are 130ft in length by 13ft 6in beam. They are constructed of galvanised steel, and propelled by triple expansion engines indicating about 1,150 horse-power. All six boats have now been tested officially by the Admiralty authorities, the trial for speed consisting of a run of three hours' duration, without stoppage of any kind, carrying a load of 20 tons; and the speeds attained have varied from 22½ to 23 knots, the actual speeds being 22.53, 22.57, 22.64, 22.62, 22.59, 23.03, from which it will be seen how remarkably alike the results in all the boats have proved to be.

In comparing these boats with those constructed during the last Russian scare, four years since, it will be of interest to note that the former boats were stipulated, by the authorities then in power, to have a speed of 19 knots during two hours, carrying a load of 10 tons, whilst the present boats actually give from 3½ to 4 knots more during a run of three hours, with 10 tons greater load. These results represent the rapid advance which has been made in torpedo boat construction in this country during the last three years. The trials of these boats show that an equal advance has been made as regards steering efficiency and rapidity of manoeuvring, which is of almost equal importance to speed.

The forward part, extending from the bow to the conning tower, is devoted to the accommodation of the crew, and immediately aft of this compartment is a small space containing galley, electric light plant, and stores. Aft of this is placed the boiler, which is of the locomotive type, but of exceptional size and power, so as to avoid any forcing, which recent experience, both in the British and foreign navies, has shown to be so detrimental to the durability of a boiler, and to enable steam to be maintained by comparatively untrained men. We believe that a locomotive boiler, if properly designed and constructed of the best materials and workmanship, should be a thoroughly trustworthy, and probably the most advantageous steam generator, and in all those torpedo boats constructed by Messrs Yarrow and Co there has never, as far as we are aware, occurred any accident, although hundreds of these vessels are now afloat and in constant service. The great secret of construction to make a boiler trustworthy seems, as we recently pointed out, to be to design it so that the various parts can accommodate themselves, without strain, to meet the changes of form due to expansion and contraction, owing to variations in the rate of combustion and of pressure. If this main principle is kept always in view in the design there should be none of the troubles frequently experienced in working boilers under forced draught, which are mainly due to the rigidity of their construction, and under those circumstances when any part requires to change its form, however small, owing to the expansion and contraction due to changes of temperature, an overwhelming force is involved, and something must in consequence give way. Another special feature in these new boats, and one of great importance to fighting ships, is the adoption of Yarrow's system of enclosing the furnace or firebox of the boiler in a complete watertight casing. In this system all the air which is required for the purpose of combustion has to pass over the casing and then downward to the furnace. The effect of this is to prevent the extinction of the fire should a sudden inrush of water find its way into the stokehole or boiler compartment. The importance of securing immunity from this will be self-evident when the probability of damage to the thin steel plates of the hull, through shot or collision, is borne in mind. It has been found that when the boiler compartment is filled with water, the steaming power of the boat is sufficiently maintained to enable her to run fully fifty miles without a fireman entering the stokehole. Aft of the boiler compartment is the engine room, in which are placed triple-expansion engines capable of indicating about 1,150 horse power. Within the engine room, in addition to the propelling machinery, there are two engines for compressing air for the use of the torpedoes, an engine for driving the fan, which forces the air under pressure to the furnaces; also an engine for producing a current of water through the surface condenser, and an engine for steering the boat. Further aft we come to a cabin compartment, in which is provided sleeping accommodation for two engineers, also the magazine for the supply of armament for the machine guns. Aft of this we come to a neatly fitted-up cabin for the officers, and further aft a pantry for the officers' use.

TB82. (US Naval History and Heritage Command, NH54813)

The armament consists of one torpedo gun for direct ahead fire, placed forward below the turtle deck, and secured into the stem of the boat. Near the stern is provided a turntable on which are placed two torpedo guns for side fire. These two guns are placed at an angle of five degrees with one another, arranged on Yarrow's patent system; by which means, if the two torpedoes are fired simultaneously, by taking slightly divergent courses, they cover a much larger area, and consequently insure much more certainty of hitting the vessel aimed at, on the same principle that if firing at a bird on the wing a number of small shots are adopted, which disperse, in preference to firing one shot only. This system of arranging the torpedo guns is now becoming largely adopted, especially for side fire, where the difficulty of accurate aim is enhanced. The machine gun armament consists of three 3-pounder quick-firing guns; one amidships and one on each beam, in echelon. Steering gear is fitted at two points, one within the conning tower – which would mainly be used in time of war – and aft, on deck, in front of which a movable brass shield is placed for the protection of the steersman. As we have previously stated, the official trials of all six boats have already taken place. We append, however, the results of the last one, which gave the highest speed:

Steam (lbs)	1st recr (lbs)	2nd recr (lbs)	Vacuum (ins)	Air pressure (ins)	Rev (ins)	Speed means (knots)	1st means	2nd
166	65	17	23	2.56	402	26.000	23.043	
167	65	16½	23	2.46	410	26.086	23.098	23.070
166	65	17	23	2.50	403	20.111	23.005	23.051
164	64	16	23	2.23	407	25.899	23.005	23.005
165	65	16	23½	2.46	401	20.111	23.005	23.005
165	65	16	23½	2.60	408	25.899		

Mean speed during three hours loaded with 20 tons – 23.032 knots

As regards the manoeuvring power of these boats, it may be mentioned that they can turn to port or starboard within a circle the radius of which is only a trifle in excess of the length of the boat, and this result is obtained by means of only one rudder of the simplest construction. The times occupied in turning circles, when running full speed, averaged 75 sec. The rudder is designed in such a manner that when hard over it counteracts the natural heel of the boat, thus maintaining a steady platform and avoiding at the same time the risk of capsizing, to which torpedo boats, both in the French and Danish navies have lately shown themselves liable. The trials of all these boats took place below Gravesend, and the above speeds were obtained during runs over the measured mile at Lower Hope, at intervals determined by the Admiralty authorities during the run of three hours, and therefore represent the mean speed of the three hours' run. There is one point in the construction of these boats which should be noted, viz, the bulkheads are throughout intact, there being no opening or door of any kind in them, and which experience has shown to be so often open at the very time when the subdivision of the hull is most needed.

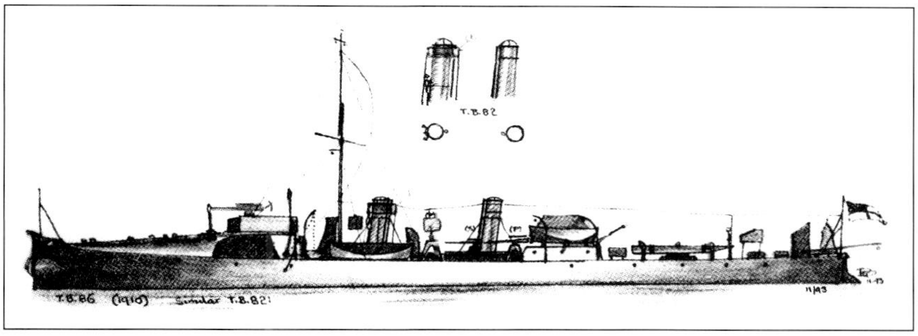

TB86 with two funnels on the centreline after receiving water-tube boilers. *(© National Maritime Museum, Greenwich, London, Richard Perkins Collection)*

During 1890, *TB82* was lent to *Vernon* for trial and experimental work. A considerable number of runs were made from the double tubes with very good results, the practice being much better than from the *Seagull*'s double tubes, probably due to the tubes being lower. All types of torpedoes with 14in tails were tried at speeds of 16, 18 and 20 knots.

A few runs were made from the stem tube, but they had to be discontinued on account of there being a projecting plate underneath the side strip, against which the tail took on discharge.

Following the 1889 manoeuvres a number of alterations were proposed for *TB*s *82–87*, and the following carried out:

Additional torpedo derrick supplied.
Tubes to be secured not exactly fore and aft.
Fire bridge of furnace made of ordinary fire bricks instead of slabs.
Metal screens for deck illuminators.
Casing over tiller head to be fitted so as to be easily removable.
A partial bulkhead fitted on lower deck to give increased strength – not fully implemented but boats were strengthened.
Increased sleeping accommodation for officers.
Supports of engine room hatch made of steel.

During 1892, *TB82* was again used for trials at *Vernon*, this time for the fitting of a Caird and Rayner's evaporator. The results were very satisfactory, inasmuch as the boat did not need to top up with water from the shore for more than ten days. *TB82* was also fitted with a new torpedo hoist from Messrs Morris and Bastert, which resulted in a recommendation that this hoist should be adopted in future boats.

When reboilered, *TB87* in 1900, *TB82* and *TB86* in 1902/3, *TB83* and *TB85* in 1905, and *TB84* in 1907, these six boats received two circular funnels on the centreline, the searchlight was moved forward to an enlarged bridge structure and the mast moved forward, ahead of the fore funnel. In 1910 *TB82* and *TB86* had the searchlight restored amidships and the gun mounting restored forward, although on a different structure.

During the 1891 naval manoeuvres, *TB82* ran aground on a sandbank near Kingston and

TB87, photographed c1910.

damaged her propeller blades, and during the 1904 torpedo manoeuvres, she collided with *TB86* off the Mull of Cantyre (Kintyre). In July 1895 *TB83* ran aground while entering Plymouth Sound, damaging her propeller. In April 1906, during a night operation off Malta, *TB84* collided with the destroyer *Ardent* and was sunk.

On 19 July 1893, whilst getting underway, *TB85* hit the pier at Falmouth, and a few days later, whilst trying to cut across the bows of a schooner, she was hit above water on the starboard quarter. In August 1908 she grounded during a night attack in defence of Plymouth. During the 1892 manoeuvres *TB87* collided with *TB26* on 25 July. The surviving boats were all sold to Stanlee in 1920/21, the first, *TB87*, being sold for £475.

The ten following torpedo boats had an increased length of approximately 140ft. *TB88* and *TB89* were built by Yarrow and, apart from the increased length and the increase in torpedo calibre from 14in to 18in, were very similar to the preceding six boats. The two deck tubes were to be parallel, but pointing in opposite directions. With slightly higher engine power and the increased length, they gained ½ knot in speed. *TB90* was also built by Yarrow to a similar design, being slightly smaller but fitted with four-cylinder, triple-expansion engines and water-tube boilers. With slightly lower power, her top speed dropped back to the 23 knots of *TB82*.

They were reboilered in 1905 but, apart from a new funnel, the appearance of *TB88* and *TB89* changed little. A topmast was fitted in 1907, minesweeping gear in 1908 and the bow tube was removed in 1910. Originally, *TB90* had a mast aft and in 1907 a topmast was fitted. In 1908, a second mast, also with a topmast, was fitted forward of the fore funnel. Minesweeping gear was fitted aft in 1908 and the bow tube removed in 1910.

In July 1895 *TB88* and *TB89* transferred from Sheerness to Gibraltar, being convoyed by the cruisers *Grafton* and *Theseus*. In May 1896, while cruising off Gibraltar, *TB88* struck one of the lightships anchored off the New Mole and sank her, but received no damage herself. They were both reboilered in 1904/5 and sold for breaking up in 1919. *TB90* was built at Poplar, but completed at Chatham and transferred to the Mediterranean in August 1896, along with *TB94*, *TB95* and *TB96*, being convoyed by *Charybdis*.

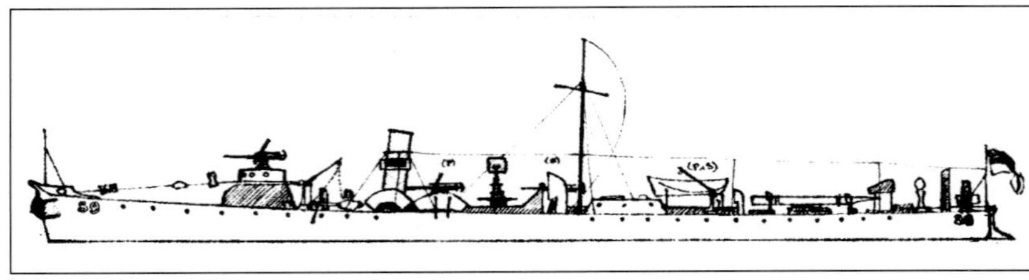

TB89. *(© National Maritime Museum, Greenwich, London, Richard Perkins Collection)*

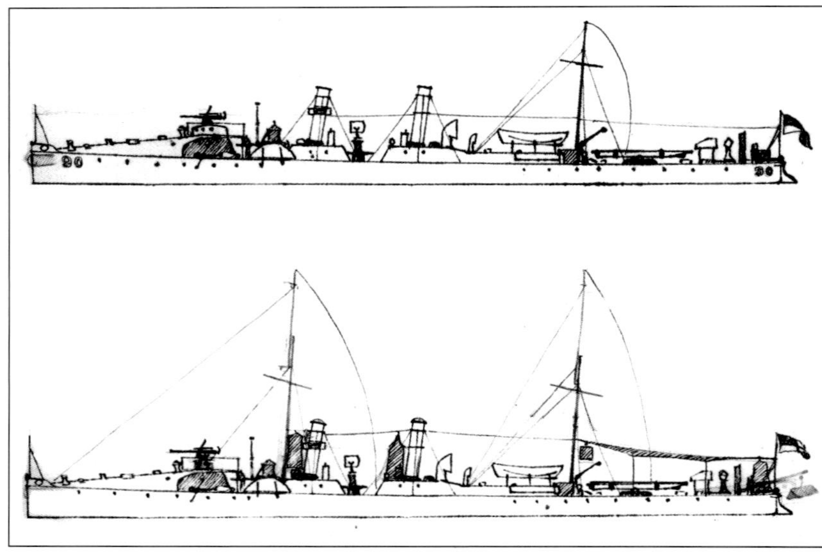

TB90, as constructed (top) and with two masts as in 1915 (bottom). *(© National Maritime Museum, Greenwich, London, Richard Perkins Collection)*

TB89, photographed in 1896. *(World Ship Society)*

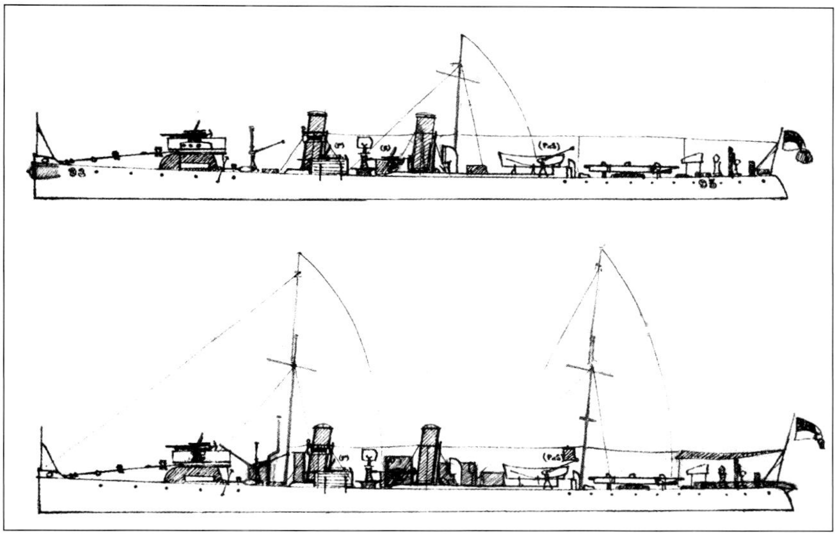

TB93, as constructed (top) and with two masts, as in 1917 (bottom). *(© National Maritime Museum, Greenwich, London, Richard Perkins Collection)*

TB91, photographed in 1895. *(The National Archives, ADM 176-732)*

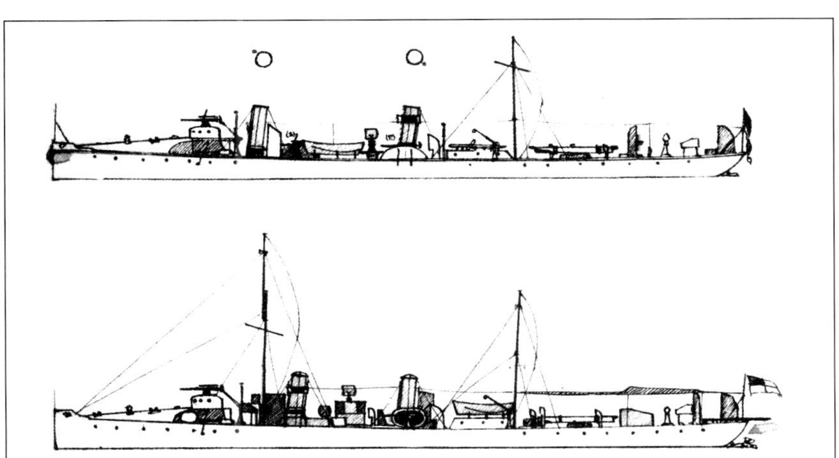

TB95 as built (top) and *TB94* with two masts as in 1918, after removal of bow tube. *(© National Maritime Museum, Greenwich, London, Richard Perkins Collection)*

In November 1898 she was in collision with *TB95* off Malta. The plates on the port quarter of *TB90* were badly stove in and the bow of *TB95* had to be replaced. *TB90* capsized off Gibraltar in 1918.

TB91, *TB92* and *TB93* were built by Thornycroft as Yard Nos 289–291. *TB91* had an overall length of 142ft 6in and, whilst producing 2,486 horsepower, achieved a speed of 23.71 knots. She had been built with a length 2ft longer than that of *TB92* and *TB93* so that the propeller could be positioned further aft. All three boats were built with four-cylinder engines and water-tube boilers, and *TB93* was the first torpedo boat to be fitted with twin screws.

As built, *TB93* had slightly wider funnels than *TB91* and *TB92*, but otherwise their appearances were very similar. In 1907 *TB93* had a second mast fitted forward of the fore funnel, and both masts received topmasts.

In May 1898 *TB91* went ashore in Tangier harbour and was refloated. In March 1899 *TB93* also went ashore on the breakwater at Gibraltar and in 1911 gave assistance to the P&O liner *Delhi* which had gone ashore off Cape Spartel, helping to rescue the passengers, who included the Princess Royal, her husband, the Duke of Fife, and their two daughters, who were on passage to Egypt. *TB91* and *TB93* were sold for breaking up in 1919, and *TB92* was sold at Gibraltar in 1920 for £1,000.

The next three boats, *TB94*, *TB95* and TB96, were built by White. They reverted to locomotive boilers and were subsequently reboilered. Their engines were built by Maudslay In 1909 a second mast was fitted forward of the fore funnel and topmasts were added to both, although that on the aftermast was only short. In 1908 minesweeping gear was fitted aft, and in 1909 the bow tube was removed and the funnels were fitted with cages.

TB94 underwent trials in August 1894 and was then stationed at Portsmouth. In July 1896 she sailed to Sheerness to become the commodore's boat in the Nore Division, but quickly returned after colliding with the three-masted schooner *Reaper*. Both vessels were

TB95 in dry dock with badly damaged bows. *(The National Archives, ADM176-734)*

badly damaged and *TB94* towed *Reaper* to Portsmouth. *TB49* replaced *TB94* in the Nore Division. In September 1896, together with *TB90*, *TB95* and *TB96* and escorted by *Charybdis*, she sailed to the Mediterranean, calling at Plymouth, Gibraltar and Malta. In April 1914 *TB94* collided with the quayside at Gibraltar, badly damaging her bows.

TB95 ran her trials in the month after *TB94*. In November 1898 she collided with *TB90* off Malta, damaging her bows. The plates on the port quarter of *TB90* were stove in. Both *TB94* and *TB95* were sold to Messrs Brand in October 1919. In April 1906 *TB96* ran aground near Algeciras while on exercises, and in November 1915 was sunk when in collision with SS *Tringa* in the straits of Gibraltar.

TB97, built at Birkenhead by Lairds, was launched on 16 September 1893 and was also fitted with locomotive boilers, being reboilered in 1909. She was sold at Gibraltar in 1920 for £1,000.

The nominal length of the next group of torpedo boats was increased to 160ft, but retained the same armament of three 18in torpedo tubes and three 3pdr gun mountings. The two forward guns and tubes were sided with the third gun and tube amidships aft.

TB98, *TB99*, *TB107* and *TB108* were all built at Chiswick by Thornycroft, with perpendicular bows. Barnaby records that *TB98* and *TB99* (Yard Nos 346/7) produced 3,071 horsepower for a maximum speed of 25.79 knots, but *TB107* and *TB108* (Yard Nos 351/2) only produced 2,947 horsepower, resulting in the slightly lower maximum speed of 25.41 knots. *TB98* was launched on 22 January and *TB99* on 6 March 1901. *TB98* arrived at Chatham on 9 March, in

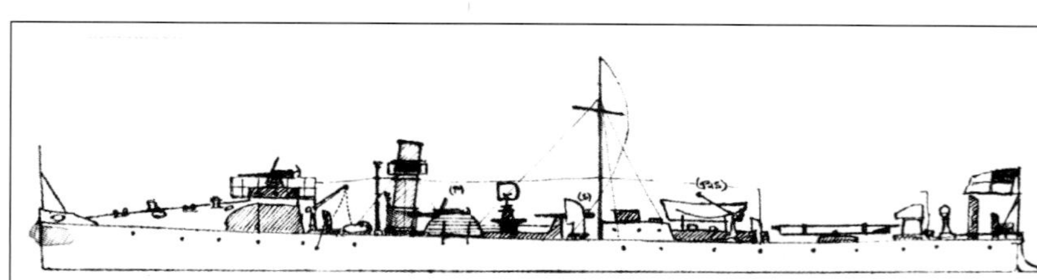

TB97. *(© National Maritime Museum, Greenwich, London, Richard Perkins Collection))*

TB98. (Courtesy Vosper Thornycroft)

time to participate in the annual manoeuvres. During these manoeuvres a proposal was made to move the torpedo tubes. *Vernon*'s annual report records it as follows:

> Attacking from right ahead, with its many advantages, is the method of torpedo boat attack most likely to be used in war time, the most favourable training of the tubes for this form of attack is from 20° to 40° before the beam, the object being to fire the torpedo as soon as possible, but not before the ship fired at subtends a large enough angle to present a large target to fire at.
>
> As it may not be known till the last minute on which side the enemy will pass, it would be convenient to have the two foremost tubes ready trained on the required bearing on either side.
>
> In their present position the foremost tubes cannot be trained together at a less angle than 55° before the beam, which is considered too far ahead.
>
> If the port tube were moved 4 feet forward, both tubes could be trained 30° before, or on any other bearing without fouling one another.
>
> The funnel prevents the tubes being placed further aft.

The report incorrectly records *TB98* as being built by Yarrow, rather than Thornycroft.

Both boats were sold to T W Ward in 1920, *TB98* for £1,025 and *TB99* for £900. *TB107* and *TB108* were both sold on the same day as *TB99* in July 1920, *TB107* to Ward for £900 and *TB108* to Willoughby (Plymouth) Ltd for £975.

TB109 to *TB113* were also built by Thornycroft (Yard Nos 359–363) but had curved, raked bows, hence were 2ft longer than their predecessors. They produced less power at 2,823 horsepower for a top speed of 25.14 knots. The Thornycroft boats all had their masts fitted in front of the funnels and their searchlights forward on the raised forecastle. *TB109* was used to test a new 18in lightweight tube in 1905.

In 1908 topmasts were fitted, and in 1910 canvas screens were fitted around the bridge, *TB109* having hers also extended aft. Subsequently the others also had their bridges enlarged and roofed in. Towards the end of the First World War, they received depth charges and some lost their after gun.

On 15 July 1904 *TB109* had her stern damaged when hit by *Hannibal*, which was being towed in Portsmouth Harbour. In March of the same year *TB110* collided with a torpedo boat destroyer during manoeuvres, damaging her bow, and in the same month ten years later collided with the railway steamer *Princess Margaret* in Portsmouth Harbour, once again damaging her bows. They were both sold to Stanlee in March 1920 for £900 each.

In July 1903 *TB112* went ashore on the east side of West Blockhouse Fort, Milford Haven. She got off the next day and was towed to Pembroke Docks. On 14 July 1904 *TB113* experienced problems with her steering gear whilst in Dover Harbour and the tide washed her against *Victorious*, damaging her plates. *TB113* was sold to Ward, Grays in December 1919, and

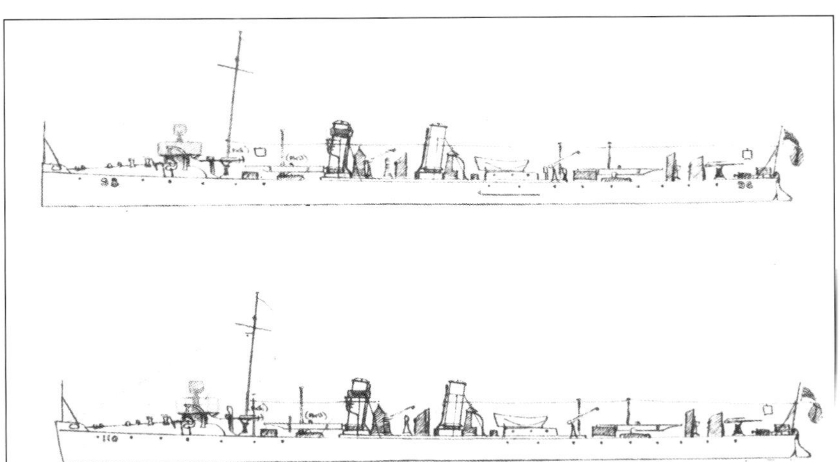

TB98 (top) and *TB110* (bottom) in the early years of the twentieth century. *(© National Maritime Museum, Greenwich, London, Richard Perkins Collection)*

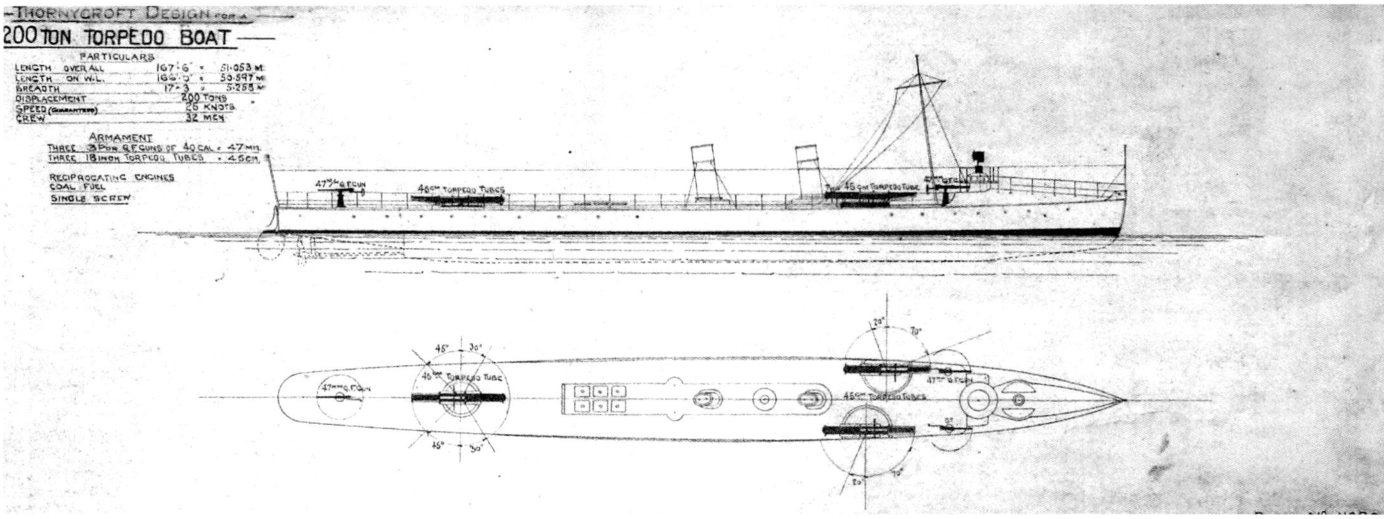

Shipbuilder's drawing of *TB103–TB109*.

TB110, photographed in 1901. *(Vosper Thornycroft)*

TB116, photographed in 1905.

TB111 and *TB112* followed in March 1920, each boat realising £1,035.

The last four 'first-class' torpedo boats, *TB114–TB117*, were built by White and were slightly longer. They were similar in appearance to the Thornycroft boats, and in 1908 had topmasts fitted. Their torpedo tubes were positioned as proposed for Thornycroft's *TB98*, following the 1901 annual manoeuvres. During the first years of the First World War their bridges were enlarged and roofed in. After the war, depth charges were added and the aft gun usually removed.

On the night of 1 April 1913 *TB114* collided with *TB18* in the Thames Estuary and was in danger of sinking. In October 1915 *TB116* sighted a submarine off Culver Cliff, IOW, at a range of

TB113 alongside, *c*1903.

TB117 as built (top) and *TB116* post-war (bottom). Note brackets on either side of funnel to support boards carrying identification number in white on black background. *(© National Maritime Museum, Greenwich, London, Richard Perkins Collection)*

1,200yds. The submarine dived before *TB116* could ram it, but she did fire at the submarine. *TB114* and *TB115* were both sold to T W Ward in 1919 for £1,035 each and *TB116* to J E Thomas in 1921. *TB117* was sunk in a collision with SS *Kamour-Aska* in the English Channel on 10 June 1917.

In 1887 the Indian Office ordered seven first-class torpedo boats for the Royal Indian Marine, but they were never delivered, being taken over by the Royal Navy in 1892. They were generally similar to the '125-footers', *TB25–TB38* and *TB41–TB79*, but their nominal length was 135ft, and in 1901 they were allocated the numbers *TB100–TB106*. The armament was five 14in torpedo tubes and two one-inch twin-barrelled Nordenfeld guns.

According to Conway's, *TB100*, *TB102* and *TB103* were constructed by Thornycroft, but they do not appear in Barnaby's listing. Originally to have been numbered *RIM 1–3*, their names were to have been *Baluchi*, *Karen* and *Pathan*. They were fitted with water-tube boilers when built and had a top speed of 23 knots.

TB102, originally to have been *RIM 7 Gurkha*, was built by Hanna, Donald & Wilson, and had a maximum speed of 21½ knots and was reboilered in 1905. *TB104–TB106*, originally to have been *RIM 4–6 Mahratta*, *Sikh* and *Rajput*, were built by White and had a maximum speed of 22 knots.

On the evening of 29 October 1909 *TB105* was undertaking a mock torpedo attack on *Hannibal*, off Berry Head, Torbay. She collided at full speed, badly damaging her bows and the area forward of the bridge. She was escorted into Torquay by *TB81*, *TB87* and *TB98*, and subsequently towed to Devonport by *TB81* and *TB87*. She was sold to Willoughby of Plymouth in January 1920 for £1,050. Six months later, Willoughby also purchased *TB104* for £650. *TB101* was also sold in 1920, to Stanlee for £425.

In 1907 the Admiralty decided that *TBs 98–107* were to carry RGF Mark III or FIISR torpedoes.

One significant advance in the search to increase speed was the introduction of water-tube boilers, which could produce higher steam pressures. Early use of the water-tube boiler within the Royal Navy was controversial. The first boilers were large-tube designs, with simple straight tubes of around 4in diameter, at a shallow angle to the horizontal. The tubes were jointed into cast-iron headers and gave much trouble with leakage at the joints. The boilers were also large, and although fitted to many pre-dreadnought battleships, could not be fitted to the small torpedo boats. To provide a lighter boiler for smaller vessels, smaller water tubes of around 2in diameter were necessary, giving a greater ratio of heating area to volume (and weight).

Both Thornycroft and Yarrow developed their own designs, Yarrow, in particular, spending a great deal of time, and money, experimenting with water circulation.

One day in 1877 William Crush, who was the head of the Yarrow boiler department, looked in at the cottage where Yarrow had lunch, and the conversation which then took place, although brief, led to somewhat important results for the firm.

> Yarrow: 'Well now, Crush, we must wake up about water-tube boilers.'
> Crush: 'Yes, we must.'
> Y: (putting his hands together with the fingers sloping on each side): 'Why not a boiler like this?'
> C: 'All right.'
> Y: 'Straight tubes?'
> C: 'Yes, we will go ahead and make one.'

A brief description of the Yarrow boiler, with reference to the three illustrations on page 113, will highlight those features which have contributed to its success.

The first illustration represents an end elevation, one half with the casing removed, and the other half showing it in position, the second represents an end elevation with the casing removed, and the third is a perspective view.

There are two nests of tubes which form the heating surface of the boiler. At the top end the tubes are secured into holes in the steam drum, and at the lower end into holes in what are called water-pockets. All the tubes are below the water level in the steam drum, so that they are under all conditions filled with water.

In cross-section the boiler is triangular, and the fire-grate forms the base of the triangle. Below the fire-grate is an ashpan. The smoke casing consists of sheet steel and asbestos, and the hot gases pass across the tubes, then on to the uptake and into the funnel. The steam drum consists of a thick tube plate for the lower half, the upper half being thinner, because it is not perforated with holes for the tubes. The water-pockets, whenever possible, are made large enough to admit of a man getting inside.

The special feature of the Yarrow boiler which distinguishes it from all others of its class, is that the tubes are straight. In all other small tube boilers the tubes are bent into more or less fantastic shapes. Previous to the assured success of the Yarrow boiler, engineers thought it necessary to bend the tubes in order to allow them to expand and contract freely when exposed to variations of temperature. Yarrow's experiments, however, conclusively proved that the tubes nearest the fire did not increase appreciably more in length than those farther from the fire, even when the rate of evaporation was much higher than ordinary practice demanded. The reason for this is that the temperature of the tube is practically the temperature of the water inside it, irrespective of the intensity of the heat outside. Consequently, as Yarrow often said, to bend the tubes to allow for variation of length was to guard against a difficulty which did not exist. Under certain conditions, however, the tubes nearest the fire may bend slightly, probably owing to the internal surface not being perfectly clean, which would mean that the metal of the tube might attain a temperature slightly higher than the water contained in it. Yarrow often contended that after use such slight bending of the tubes should not be looked upon as a defect, saying: 'If the tube wishes to bend, let it do what it wishes, for if we oppose the forces of nature we shall certainly come to grief.'

It is self-evident that the cleaning of the tubes internally is of the utmost importance, and one reason for general adoption of the Yarrow boiler is that each tube, being straight, can be examined internally. A man in the steam drum can look through each tube, while another man holds a light at the lower end. Any obstruction in a tube is liable to cause it to overheat and burst, and if the tubes are bent, it is impossible to examine or clean them efficiently. Obtaining tubes capable of withstanding the increasing boiler pressures was difficult and most makers had already

End elevation (half casing removed).

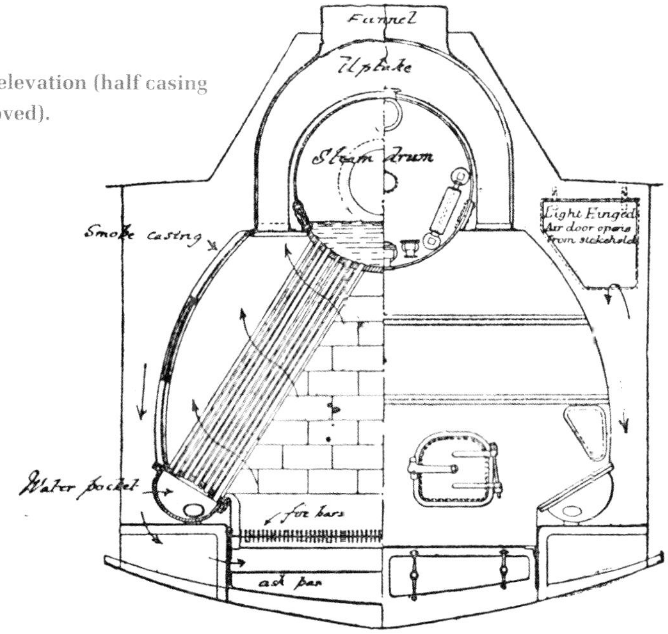

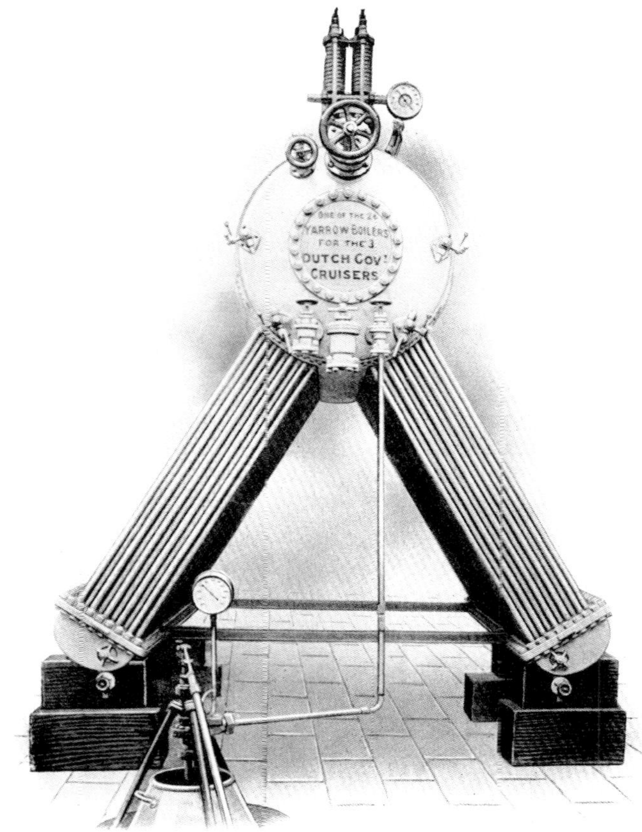

Boiler for a cruiser.

Perspective view.

experienced problems with the welds in the tubes. A less obvious benefit of straight tubes was that they could make use of the newly developed seamless-drawn tubes then being produced.

In every class of boiler there must be proper provision for the circulation of the water, and in a boiler working at a high rate of evaporation this becomes more essential. In the Yarrow boiler the circulation is allowed to adjust itself in accordance with the laws of gravitation, and the design is so satisfactory, and the circulation so active, that the rate of evaporation may amount to as much as 25lb of water per square foot of heating surface per hour, without risk of overheating the tubes.

The first Yarrow water drums or 'troughs' were 'D'-shaped with a flat tubeplate, so as to provide an easy mounting for the tubes. The tubeplate was bolted to the trough and could be dismantled for maintenance and tube cleaning. This 'D' shape was not ideal for a pressure drum, though, as pressure will tend to distort it into a more circular section. Experience of boiler explosions had shown that sharp internal corners inside boilers were also prone to erosion by grooving. Later boilers used a more rounded section, despite the difficulty of inserting and sealing the tube ends when they were no longer perpendicular. These later drums had a manhole in the ends for access.

The advantages of the Yarrow boiler may be briefly summarised as follows:

> It is simple to construct, and easy to maintain.
> The tubes can be thoroughly cleaned internally, and the inside surface of each tube can be easily examined.
> The very rapid circulation enables the boiler to stand excessive forcing without damage, so that, if two or three boilers in a big installation are thrown out of action by shot or otherwise, it is perfectly safe to work the remaining boilers to an extent considerably in excess of that for which they were designed.
>
> The large furnace capacity enables the combustion to be carried out very completely, far more than in boilers of many other types, where the combustion has to take place in a space of restricted size. A small combustion chamber is specially objectionable in cases where the tubes approach the horizontal, because when the gases in the act of uniting with the oxygen of the air come in contact with the cold surface of the tubes, their combination is stopped in the same way that the gauze screen of the Davy lamp prevents the flame inside from passing to the explosive gases outside.

The first Yarrow boilers tried in war vessels were supplied for second-class torpedo-boats in 1887. Among other early vessels fitted with these boilers were some torpedo boats built in 1890 for the Argentine government and, owing to the highly successful results obtained, this boiler was selected for the British destroyer *Hornet*. In 1893, when *Havock* and *Hornet* were built, it was decided, in order to test the relative merits of locomotive and water-tube boilers, that both vessels should be alike in every respect, except that *Havock* was to be fitted with locomotive and *Hornet* with Yarrow boilers. On trial, the displacement of *Havock* was 11 tons more than *Hornet*, owing to the greater weight of the boilers. *Havock* attained a speed of 26.1 knots, and *Hornet* a speed of 27.3 knots. The coal consumption for the same speed was found to be about 5 per cent less in *Hornet* than in *Havock*. This comparative trial formed a conclusive proof of the advantages of the water-tube boiler.

Thornycroft also recognised that the locomotive boiler was no longer good enough for the increased powers and pressures that were now required. Between 1888 and 1890 a considerable number of torpedo gunboats were built, commencing with *Sharpshooter*, which had the designed speed 21 knots. The engines were intended to develop 4,500ihp, but difficulties were experienced with the grouped locomotive boilers and it was found impossible to obtain more than about 3,700ihp and a speed that did not exceed 20 knots. Even this power was not developed without great difficulty, and in 1892, when eleven new vessels of the type were built, the displacement was increased to 810 tons, chiefly to provide more machinery space. All but one were fitted with locomotive boilers developing about 3,700ihp and giving a speed of 19.2 knots.

This one exception was *Speedy*, which was also the only torpedo gunboat built at Chiswick. A new type of water-tube boiler was designed for

Speedy. This provided sufficient steam for an increase of about 1,000ihp as compared with other vessels of the class, and gave about a knot additional speed. This boiler was entirely different from the horizontal-coil type used in *Peace*, but was similar in principle to a small experimental boiler that Thornycroft had designed and fitted to the second-class torpedo boat No. 100 in 1886. This was a three-drum type, with vertical tubes steeply curved in over the fire space and then diverging, so as to enter the upper drum in directions normal to the drum plating and thus facilitate proper expansion of the tube ends. The tubes all entered the upper drum above the water level, a point that aroused acute controversy, as most boilermakers favoured 'drowned' tubes, ie, with their entry below the normal water level of halfway up the drum.

The Thornycroft boiler split the usual central furnace into two. There were four drums: two main drums vertically in the centre – a steam and a water drum – also two wing drums at the outside edges of the furnace. The design was notable for its early use of the water-wall furnace. The outer bank of tubes was shallow, consisting of only two rows of tubes. These rows were spaced closely, so that the tubes formed a solid wall, without gasflow between them. The inner bank of tubes was similar: the two rows of tubes closest to the furnace formed a similar water wall. These tubes were splayed apart at their base, so as to provide space for gas flow between them. Within the tube bank, gas flow was mostly parallel to the tubes, similar to some early designs, but contrary to the crossflow design of later three-drum boilers. The exhaust gas emerged into the heart-shaped space below the upper central drum, exiting to the funnel through the rear wall. The steam drum was circular, with perpendicular tube entry. The tube ends spanned a considerable circumference of the drum, so that the upper tubes entered above the water level.

The upper and lower central drums were linked by downcomers. Unusually these were internal to the boiler and heated, although not strongly, by the exhaust gases. They were formed as several (eight or nine) 4in vertical tubes on the centreline of the boiler. They were formed into a shallow 'S'-shape to give a little flexibility against thermal expansion. The small wing drums were connected to the lower central drum alone, by large external pipes outside the rear casing of the boiler.

The first torpedo boats were all fitted with locomotive boilers, the surviving boats generally having them replaced by water-tube boilers in the early years of the twentieth century, provided their hulls and engines were still in a satisfactory condition. Yarrow's *TB90* was the first boat to be constructed with water-tube boilers, but this approach was not universally followed in later boats, many of them reverting to locomotive boilers.

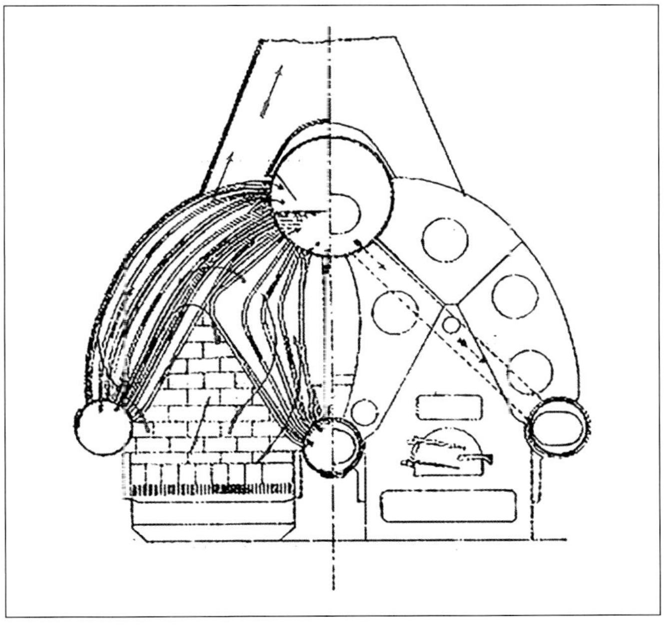

Thornycroft boiler.
(Stokers' Manual 1912)

TURBINE PROPULSION

HMS *Vernon* Annual Report, 1887

The Turbine system of propulsion has been under trial during the year by a private company, and has given remarkable results.

The *Turbinia*, the vessel in which the system has been fitted, is 100ft long by 9ft beam, displaces 441 tons, and draws 3ft of water. She is fitted with three separate turbine motors, one high pressure, one intermediate, and one low pressure, each being coupled direct to its own shaft, each shaft carrying three propellers.

It was found necessary to fit three propellers on each shaft to overcome the loss due to cavitation (that is the vacuum formed abaft the screw) consequent on the very high speed of revolution, at full speed about 2,100 per minute.

The maximum boiler pressure is 210lbs per square inch, pressure at engines 157lbs per square inch, ratio of expansion nearly two hundred fold, and highest speed attained 34½ knots estimated from the curve of steam pressure and speed obtained when running on the mile at 32.76 knots. This speed is far in advance of anything previously obtained from a boat of this size.

A higher speed is expected from the *Turbinia* after alterations have been made in the boiler feed, which is the only limit at present, and a design for a larger vessel has been got out from which a speed of 36–40 knots is anticipated.

A drawback is that the engines, as now arranged, will not go astern more than 3 knots. A separate motor is being fitted to the centre shaft to give a speed astern of 10 knots.

Among the advantages claimed for the compound steam turbine over the ordinary engine are the following:

– Increased speed.
– Shallow draught.
– Safety to machinery for war purposes.
– Reduced weight and space.
– Largely reduced vibration.

No foreign Governments have, up to the present, ordered any vessels fitted on this principle.

In 1898 the regulations for preventing collision at sea were updated, and resulted in torpedo boats of less than 150ft carrying just bow lights and a masthead light, and those over 150ft receiving an additional signal lantern for use as a stern anchor light.

CHAPTER SIX

THE *CRICKET/GADFLY/MAYFLY* CLASS (*TB1–TB36*)

The new First Sea Lord, Jacky Fisher, appointed in 1904, wasted little time in implementing his desire for fast warships with the Tribal group destroyers being supplemented by some smaller coastal destroyers. The Director of Naval Construction (DNC) issued the requirements for the latter in December 1904 – length not to exceed 165ft, armament to be three 18in torpedo tubes and two 12pdr guns, capacity of fuel oil sufficient for eight hours at full speed or 1,000 miles at economical speed. They were to be turbine powered with a full-load trial speed of 26 knots. Originally the 12pdr guns were to be of the 18cwt variety, but this was reduced to the lower velocity 12cwt models and all three torpedo tubes were to be on the centreline.

Thornycroft, Yarrow and White were invited to bid and all three offered the same machinery arrangement of three shafts with an astern turbine on the centre shaft. Parsons proposed that half the total power would be on the centreline shaft. All versions were longer than the original requirement, according to Conway's, varying between 175 and 180ft with a beam of 17ft 6in to 18ft. Barnaby records that *TB6* to *TB10* were 168ft LOA, and that *TB19*, *TB20*, *TB31* and *TB32* were 180ft LOA. Dittmar and Colledge record that *TB1–TB12* were 175ft (OA), 167ft (PP) by 17½ft and *TB13–TB36* were 185ft (OA), 177ft (PP) by 18 ft.

Vernon records *TB1–12* as having an average length of 170ft; beam, 17ft 6in; draught of water, 6ft 6in; tonnage, 260 tons. Fitted with turbine engines, they carried 43¾ tons of oil. With a full speed 27.5 knots and an economical speed 12.2 knots, they could steam for eighteen hours at full speed. They were fitted with three 'light pattern' 18in torpedo tubes on raised racers, fired by powder impulse. The forward tube was before the foremost funnel, the second tube between the funnels and the third tube right aft. The training of the after tubes was limited to 60° abaft the beam, as trials showed that a torpedo fired directly astern whilst the boat was steaming full speed ahead would dive to the bottom, because when entering the water it had about 9 knots of stern way on.

Two 12pdr guns were carried, one on the fore conning tower and the other abaft the engine room. A searchlight was mounted on the fore bridge, which was also fitted with firing gear for the two forward tubes, the aft tube being fitted with telephonic communications.

The modified proposals were accepted in May 1905.

For the 1905/6 programme, in late 1905 five boats were ordered from White (*Cricket*, *Dragonfly*, *Firefly* (see Plate 6), *Sandfly* and *Spider*), five from Thornycroft (*Gadfly*, *Glowworm*, *Gnat*, *Grasshopper* and *Greenfly*) and

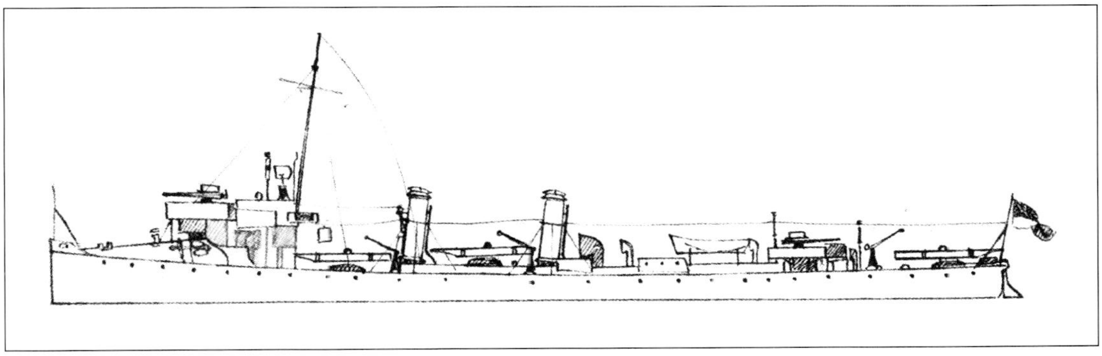

TB1–TB5 built by Samuel J White & Co Ltd, Cowes. (© National Maritime Museum, Greenwich, London, Richard Perkins Collection)

two from Yarrow (*Mayfly* and *Moth*). The first boats ran trials in October 1906, and shortly after all were re-rated as first-class torpedo boats, receiving the designations *TB1* to *TB12* respectively, the earlier boats carrying these numbers having all been decommissioned. The trials of *TB12* on 2 March 1907 resulted in a speed of 27.306 knots at 1,173rpm. Barnaby records *TB6* to *TB10* achieved a speed of 27.505 knots when producing 5,650 horsepower, *TB19* and *TB20* achieved 26.339 knots with 5,360hp, and *TB31* and *TB32* achieved 26.55 knots with 5,730hp. When fully fuelled, the boats trimmed by the bow and they did not steer well when going astern at any time.

In November 1906 four more boats were ordered from White (*TB13–TB16*), two from Denny (*TB17* and *TB18*), two from Thornycroft (*TB19* and *TB20*), two from Hawthorn Leslie (*TB21* and *TB22*), one from Yarrow (*TB23*) and one from Palmers (*TB24*) in the 1906/7 programme. The DNC did provide a sketch general arrangement drawing, dated June 1906, but details were left to individual shipbuilders.

The last twelve boats were ordered in September 1907 under the 1907/8 programme, four from White (*TB25–TB28*), two from Denny (*TB29* and *TB30*), two from Thornycroft (*TB31* and *TB32*), two from Hawthorn Leslie (*TB33* and *TB34*) and two from Palmers (*TB35* and *TB36*).

They all had two circular funnels but there were numerous variations in arrangement of the mast and yards. *TB1–TB5* had the three torpedo tubes sighted between the fore funnel and the raised turtle-back deck, between the funnels and right aft, whereas *TB6–TB10* had them between the funnels, midships immediately forward of the aft gun and right aft. The remainder had them sighted between the fore funnel and the raised turtle-back deck, midships immediately forward of the aft gun and right aft.

Some were painted light grey while undergoing trials, but all were painted black when first in service. Many were painted grey part way through the First World War. It was common for canvas screens to be fitted around the bridge to provide protection for the personnel.

TB1 (*Cricket*) was launched at Cowes, IOW, on 23 January 1906. At the end of 1906 she was commissioned with a full crew and became tender to *Victory* in the Portsmouth Torpedo Boat Flotilla. Two months later she became tender to *Sapphire* at Portsmouth as part of the Home Fleet. In July 1907 her crew was reduced to a nucleus and she became tender to *Hecla* as part of the Portsmouth Reserve Flotilla. She was present on 3 August 1907 when the Home Fleet was reviewed by King Edward VII at Cowes. She took part in the 1908 fleet manoeuvres during

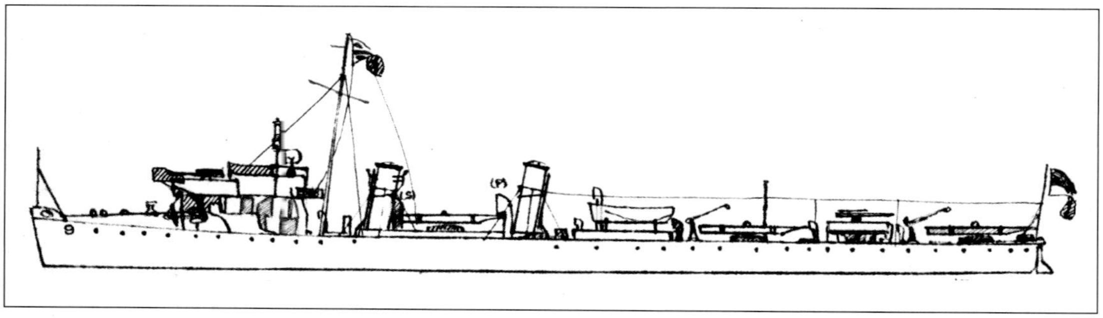

TB6–TB10*, built by J I Thornycroft & Co Ltd, Chiswick. *(© National Maritime Museum, Greenwich, London, Richard Perkins Collection)

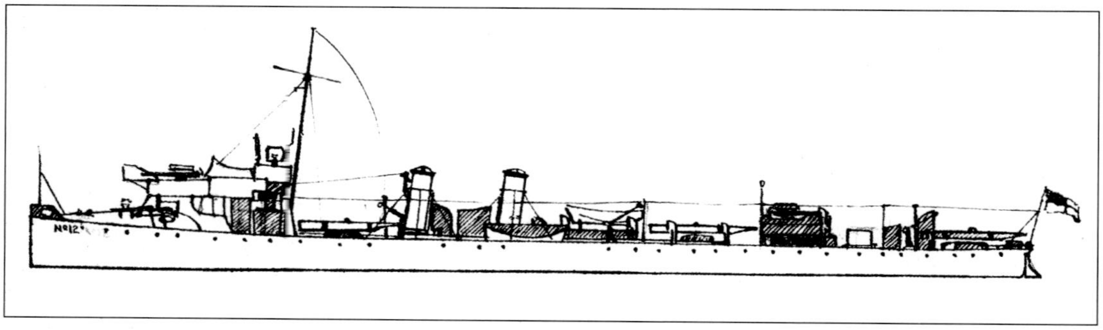

TB11* and *TB12*, built by Yarrow & Co, Poplar. *(© National Maritime Museum, Greenwich, London, Richard Perkins Collection)

July of that year. On 1 March 1909 the Home Fleet was reorganised, and *TB1* became part of the 3rd Division of the Home Fleet. In June and July 1909 she was involved in further manoeuvres, and on 10 August *Topaz* replaced *Hecla* as mother-ship, *Hecla* resuming this position in March 1910, the flotilla then being designated the 4th Destroyer Flotilla. Present at the Spithead Review to celebrate the coronation of King George V on 24 June 1911, *TB1* then took part in the annual manoeuvres. Reorganisation of the flotillas in April 1912 resulted in *TB1* recommissioning on 1 May with a nucleus crew as tender to *Tyne*, part of the 8th Flotilla based at Harwich. In July and August 1913 she took part in annual manoeuvres and in January 1914 paid off at Devonport. She later recommissioned for service with the 7th Flotilla, as tender to *Leander*. On the outbreak of war on 4 August 1914, the crews of the patrol flotillas were brought up to strength, and *TB1* was based on the Humber. The laying of minefields by the Germans off the east coast caused the patrol flotillas to extend operations to cover the entire coast from the Firth of Forth to Harwich. *TB1* was allocated to the Humber Estuary. In the middle of September, *TB1* collided with *TB5*. On 19 February 1915 *TB1*, *TB2*, *TB3* and *TB5* left the 7th Flotilla and moved to Newhaven where they were used for escort work. On 26 July 1917 *TB1* was present at the sinking of the cruiser HMS *Ariadne* off Beachy Head by the German submarine *UC65*. She was sold to the Fowey Coaling & Ship Co for £2,300 on 7 October 1920.

The career of *TB1* was similar to that of many of the others in this class. *TB2* (*Dragonfly*), *TB3* (*Firefly*), *TB4* (*Sandfly*) and *TB5* (*Spider*) were also launched at Cowes in 1906, on 11 March, 1 September, 30 October and 15 December, respectively. On 14 October 1914 *TB3* was damaged in a collision. *TB4* participated in the Dover Patrol during February 1915. Prior to her collision with *TB1*, *TB5* had also been in a collision with *TB34* in April 1913 at Harwich. *TB2*, *TB3*, *TB4* and *TB5* were all sold to T W Ward Ltd for £1,104 each on the same day as *TB1* was sold.

TB6 (*Gadfly*), *TB7* (*Glowworm*) and *TB8* (*Gnat*) were launched at Chiswick in 1906, on 24 June, 20 December and 1 December respectively, and *TB9* (*Grasshopper*) and *TB10* (*Greenfly*) were launched at the same location in 1907 on 18

TB1, ex-*Cricket*, was launched in January 1906.

TB4, ex-*Sandfly*, built by J S White.

March and 15 February, being allocated Yard Nos 415 to 419. On 31 May 1912 *TB6* damaged her stern in a collision with the tug *Marmion* and on 22 October 1920 was sold to Stanlee SB Company. For part of their careers, *TB7*, *TB8* and *TB9* acted as tender to HMS *Actaeon*, the torpedo school ship at Sheerness, and *TB7* and *TB8* were finally sold to T W Ward on 9 May 1921, but *TB9* was sunk in a collision in the North Sea on 26 July 1916. *TB10* was mined in the Thames Estuary, near the South Goodwin Light, on 10 June 1915, the mine having been laid by *UC11*. At the time, *TB10* was rescuing survivors from *TB12*.

TB11 (*Mayfly*) and *TB12* (*Moth*) were both launched at Poplar in 1907 on 29 January and 15 March respectively. The names of both vessels were taken away prior to launch. *TB11* spent her time at Devonport, and early in October 1912, whilst going alongside a coal lighter in the River Medway, was caught by a strong tide, causing her to collide with the lighter resulting in a 7ft gash, 10–12in wide, in her starboard side. She was repaired in Sheerness Dockyard. *TB11* was mined off the east coast on 7 March 1916. During a gale on 8 August 1907 *TB12* dragged her anchors in Portland Roads and went ashore on the breakwater, receiving little damage. *TB12* was mined in the Thames Estuary, near the South Goodwin Light, on 10 June 1915, the mine having been laid by *UC11*.

TB13–TB16 were launched at Cowes in 1907 on 10 July, 26 September 19 November and 23 December respectively. On 23 July 1909 *TB13* was badly damaged on the starboard side in a collision in the Solent, her stokehold and engine room flooding. She was docked at Portsmouth for repairs. She later served with the Dover Patrol and was sunk in a collision in the North Sea on 26 January 1916. *TB14* was sold to Philip of Dartmouth on 7 October 1920 for £1,257 10s for use as a jetty. In February 1915 *TB15* and *TB16*

TB6, ex-*Gadfly*. (Vosper Thornycroft)

TB12*, ex-*Moth*, the last to receive a name.** ***(US Naval History and Heritage Command, NH54815)

***TB15*, one of the second batch of three vessels to be built by J S White.**

TB20 was built by Thornycroft and launched in January 1908.

both joined the Dover Patrol and were sold to T W Ward on 7 October 1920 for £1,105 and £1,104 respectively.

TB17 and *TB18* were launched at Dumbarton on 21 December 1907 and 15 February 1908 respectively. On 25 April 1912 *TB17* collided with *Lightning* in Stangate Creek on the River Medway. *TB18* encountered rough weather off Start Point in February 1910 and was taken in tow by *Albacore*, but the tow ropes parted and, after drifting for some time, she was towed to Plymouth by *Sharpshooter*. At the beginning of April 1914, whilst exercising at night in the Thames Estuary, she collided with *TB114*, both vessels being badly damaged and in danger of sinking. Both vessels were sold at Gibraltar in 1920, *TB17* for £3,000 and *TB18* for £5,000.

TB19 and *TB20* were built at Woolston, Thornycroft having relocated from Chiswick to Southampton. *TB19* was launched on 7 December 1907 and *TB20* on 21 January 1908. Both boats were sold to T W Ward in May 1921. *TB21* and *TB22* were launched at Hebburn on the River Tyne on 20 December 1907 and 1 February 1908 respectively. *TB21* ended her wartime career on patrol duties at Portsmouth, being sold to Maden and McKee on 7 October 1920 for £1,500, along with *TB22*, which was sold for the same price. Both boats were resold in 1924 to Hayes of Porthcawl.

TB23 was the last vessel to be built at Polar before Yarrow relocated to Scotstoun, Glasgow, her launch taking place on 5 December 1907. In May 1913 she was detailed for service under the

TB21, built by Hawthorn Leslie.

TB24, the first of three vessels built by Palmer, was sunk in a collision in January 1917.

commanding officer of *Hermes*, the parent ship of the Naval Air Service. She was sold to T W Ward in May 1921. *TB24* was launched at Jarrow on 19 March 1908, and it was some fifteen months before she commissioned at Chatham with a nucleus crew. She was wrecked off the Dover breakwater on 28 January 1917.

TB25, *TB26*, *TB27* and *TB28* were launched at Cowes in 1908, the first two on the same day, 28 August, with *TB27* following a month later and *TB28* another month after that. They were all sold on the same day, 9 May 1921, to T W Ward, *TB25* going to Grays and the others to Rainham. *TB29* and *TB30* were launched at Dumbarton on

TB25 in December 1908. Built by J S White, she had been launched in August 1908.

TB26 in 1910. Another vessel from White, launched on the same day as *TB25*.

the same day, 29 September 1908, the trials of the first boat taking ten days, 13 to 23 October. On 30 August 1914 *TB30* grounded and was docked at Leith for repairs. Both boats were sold at Malta on 28 November 1919 for £2,252 10s each.

TB31 and *TB32* were launched at Woolston on 10 October and 23 November 1908. On 25 December 1914 *TB31* was attacked by a submarine in the Firth of Forth, but the torpedo missed its target. They were both sold to T W Ward, Rainham, on 9 May 1921. *TB33* and *TB34* were both launched at Hebburn on 22 February 1909. *TB33* was attacked by a submarine at the same time as *TB31*. *TB34* was sold to T W Ward at the same time as *TB31* and *TB32*, but *TB33* was not sold until 24 August 1922, to Cashmore.

The last two boats, *TB35* and *TB36*, were launched at Jarrow on 19 April and 6 May 1909. *TB35* was sold to Cashmore with *TB33*, and *TB36* to Ward, together with *TB31* and *TB34*.

With the arrival of the first 'torpedo boat destroyer', HMS *Havock*, in 1894, emphasis quickly changed to these large vessels.

TB30, the last of four vessels built by Denny.

CHAPTER SEVEN

SECOND-CLASS TORPEDO BOATS

TB51–TB62, showing different heights for the aft conning tower. *(© National Maritime Museum, Greenwich, London, Richard Perkins Collection)*

TB63, built by the American Herreshoff Manufacturing Company.

Many small craft were fitted with temporary arrangements to enable them to launch torpedoes. They were often the larger ship's boats normally fitted for lifesaving purposes or to transfer men to and from the shore when anchored. These boats were not normally given a formal torpedo boat designation.

The concept of carrying boats on larger ships, such as cruisers, led to the development of the second-class torpedo boat, the first twelve to be designated as such being built by Thornycroft in 1878/9. The Thornycroft yard numbers were 82–93 and the Admiralty designations *TB51–TB62*. They were 60ft 4in long overall, had a displacement of approximately 10½ tons, and with a 108hp vertical engine and a locomotive boiler, achieved a maximum speed of 16.51 knots. They were armed with two 14in torpedoes, originally launched from lowering cages, and later using dropping gear. The first six were completed in 1878, and the others in 1879.

TB63, built by the American Herreshoff Manufacturing Company.

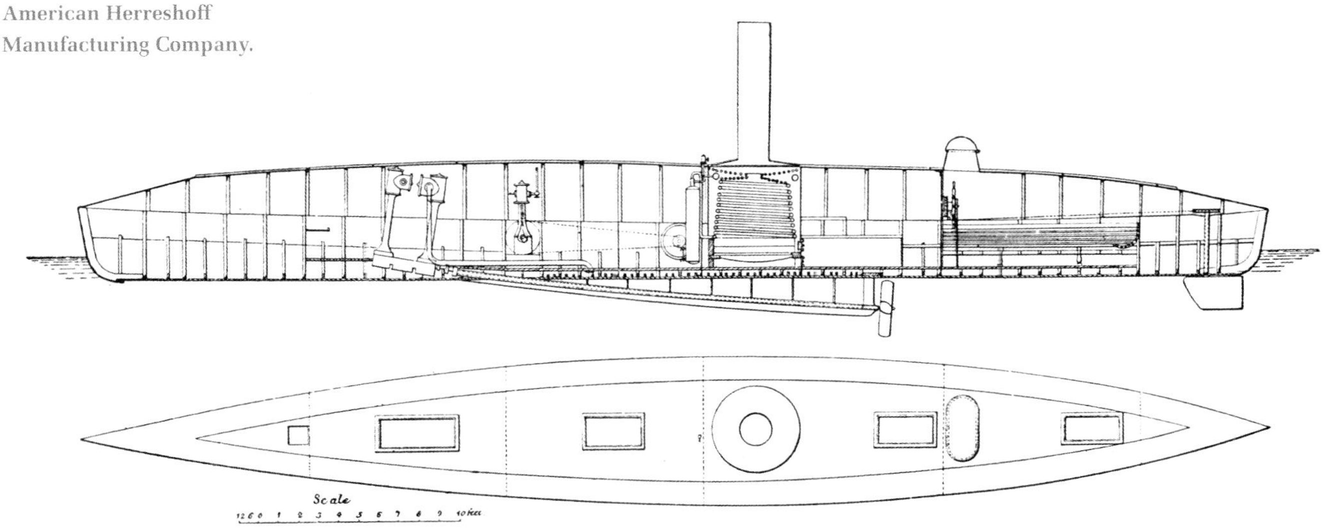

The next boat, *TB63*, was the only torpedo boat built overseas. It was constructed by the Herreshoff Manufacturing Company, of Bristol, Rhode Island, US, being completed in 1878. The boat was 59ft 6in long with 7ft 6in beam, and had a composite hull with timber planking below the waterline, and a steel skin above, while there was also a steel superstructure covering the machinery and men. The form of this superstructure is shown right, which also shows the manner in which the junction was made between the steel upper skin and timber planking. The planking of the lower hull was of white pine, one inch thick, and the skin of the upper part was of the best homogeneous steel plates 1/16in thick.

The composite system of construction was adopted because a wooden covering below water could be made and kept more smooth than a steel one, while it was, at the same time, more durable on account of the very small thickness of steel which would be admissible in order to keep down the weight. It was proposed to cover the bottom with copper or Muntz metal when desirable. The lines of the hull were nearly alike at the bow and stern.

The boat was propelled by a compound engine of the intermediate receiver type and having a 6in and a 10½in cylinder, each with 10in stroke. The air pump was 3in in diameter and the feed pump one inch in diameter, both having 5in stroke and both being double-acting. These pumps were driven by a small independent horizontal engine. There was also another independent engine for driving the fan blower, this engine being a small vertical of 21hp. The fan supplied air at a pressure of about 4in of water to the closed compartment in which the boiler was placed.

The boiler was of a special type patented by Messrs Herreshoff, which consisted of a coil of wrought-iron pipe 2in in diameter and about 300ft long, this coil forming a kind of combustion chamber above the grate, which was 4ft in diameter. The feed was supplied to the upper end of the coil and the mixed steam and water escaping from the lower end passed into a separator, where the water was deposited, the steam being then led through a short super-heating coil on its way to the engine. The separating chamber of the boiler was placed in the engine room, where the blowing-off valve could be managed by the man who attended to the feed pump and fan engine.

The engine was placed well forward in the vessel and the shaft ran at an inclination through the bottom of the boat. In order to counteract the effect of running a screw with a steeply inclined shaft, the latter was curved throughout its length, so that the after end was brought nearly horizontal. The shaft was of steel and was kept to the curve by being run in a brass tube which was bent to the desired curve, and which formed a kind of continuous bearing from end to end. The tube extended to within about a foot of the engine, and the stuffing-box was fitted to its inner end.

The curved tube forming the shaft bearing was securely fixed inside a double-walled copper chamber, which projected below the bottom of the boat, and served the triple purpose of a support to the shaft, a fixed centreboard or false keel, and a surface condenser. The keel formed by the condenser, being at the centre of the length of the vessel, formed a kind of pivot on which the boat could be turned. The exhaust steam from the engine entered the condenser near the forward end, and the suction pipe to the air pump drew from the after end.

The screw was 38in in diameter, with 5ft pitch, and was situated more than one-third the length of the vessel from the stern. Owing to its position, the screw was always working in solid water, and its power to suddenly start or stop the boat was thus greatly increased. By reversing the engine, the boat could be stopped in three-quarters of its own length.

The rudder, like the screw, was placed in an unusual position, below the bottom of the boat, but close to the stern. The rudder was partly balanced, and mounted so that it was free to turn in any direction, either forward or backward. The steering wheel was situated below a small conning tower, and the motion was communicated from it to the rudder head by means of a chain and rag wheel. When the boat was going ahead, the preponderating side of the rudder was towards the stern, but when going astern the rudder was allowed to swing completely round, so as to bring the preponderating part towards the bow. Under these circumstances the steering when going astern was as easy as when going ahead. The boat, when going either backwards or forwards,

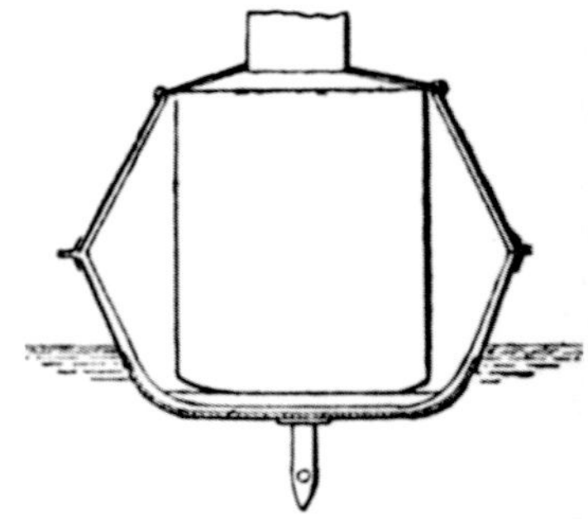

A cross-section of *TB63*. *(Engineering, 31 January 1879)*

TB64–73. (© *National Maritime Museum, Greenwich, London, Richard Perkins Collection)*

TB74 and *75.* (© *National Maritime Museum, Greenwich, London, Richard Perkins Collection)*

could be turned in a circle, the diameter of which was about three times her own length, or about 180ft.

The weight of the boat with fixtures was 6 tons, or with torpedoes and stores, 8 tons. The strength required for hoisting was given by the steel skin and the steel superstructure, while when running at full speed the boat was remarkably free from vibration, owing partly to the screw running in solid water, and partly to the curved form of the superstructure, which gave great stiffness to the ends of the vessel.

On Monday, 20 October 1879 the boat was examined by the First Lord of the Admiralty, who was accompanied by admirals Hood, Wellesley and Sir Houston Stewart, and Mr Barnaby, the chief constructor, who witnessed some experiments made with it at the Royal Victualling Yard. On this occasion the boat was hoisted by a crane with all stores and the crew on board. It did not show any signs of springing, and it was then lowered into the river, and steam got up to blow off at the safety valves in five minutes after lighting the fire.

TB74 was the first to be built by Yarrow.

On 11 December of the same year, a race was held between the Herreshoff *TB63* and the Thornycroft *TB56*, over a course of 2⅔ miles long. From a cold water start from the tug *Manly*, the boats ran to Spit Buoy. *TB56* recorded a time of 22 minutes 21 seconds and *TB63* a time of 24 minutes 30 seconds. Despite recording a longer time, the Admiralty liked the rapid starting capacity of the Herreshoff boat, who supplied Thornycroft with their boilers until 1882.

Thornycroft built nine more boats, *TB64–TB73* (Yard Nos 104–113) in 1880/81. These were of a similar design to the previous ones, but had a ram bow and the longer overall length of 62ft 10in. They produced 159hp, giving a maximum speed of 17.64 knots. They also carried two 14in torpedoes in dropping gear and had a crew of seven.

The next two boats, *TB74* and *TB75*, were built by Yarrow in 1883, and were swiftly followed by two more, *TB96* and *TB97*. *TB74* and *TB75* were 60ft 8in long, and *TB96* and *TB97* were 3ft longer. In other aspects they were similar to the preceding Thornycroft boats but their armament was two 14in bow torpedo tubes and a machine gun. The torpedoes were launched using steam power. Although their machinery produced nearly twice as much power as that of the Thornycroft boats, their top speeds were similar.

Thornycroft built *TB76–TB95* (Yard Nos 117–136) between 1880 and 1883. They were 62ft 10in overall and produced 150hp, for a top speed of 17.64 knots. They also carried two bow torpedo tubes and had a complement of seven. The bow torpedo tubes were more accurately described as troughs on the forecastle, and a description of their operation is included in Chapter 2. At first the firing valves gave some trouble, but *Vernon*'s report of 1883 stated that after some modifications, they 'now work very well'. The first two boats were fitted with Herreshoff boilers, but these were soon replaced with locomotive boilers, the engines in both cases being two-cylinder vertical engines.

The annual report from *Vernon* for 1885 included the following statement:

> It has been decided to abolish the use of the steam impulse in second-class boats, to remove the troughs, to deck over the bows of the boats and to fit dropping gear; this has already been done in some of the boats with very satisfactory results, for they have been thus rendered more seaworthy, and better practice is made with the dropping gear than was done with the steam impulse.

TB76–95. (© National Maritime Museum, Greenwich, London, Richard Perkins Collection)

TB85. (Joe Hinds)

TB98. (© National Maritime Museum, Greenwich, London, Richard Perkins Collection)

TB98 was built by Thornycroft, Yard No. 141, completing in 1883, as an experiment to test the Ruthven 'turbine' in a hull as similar as possible to the other second-class boats. To maintain trim and accommodate the 'turbine', the boiler had to be placed aft. With this form of water jet propulsion by centrifugal pump, her speed compared badly with her sisters (just 12.6 knots, *Vernon*'s report of 1883 states a mean of 11.872 knots; when running light, without her torpedoes), manoeuvrability was 'disappointing', she had difficulty in going astern, and the propulsion system made a noise that could be heard ten miles away on a calm day. She was armed with two 14in bow torpedo tubes.

TB98
HMS *Vernon* Annual Report, 1884

No. 98, second class hydraulic torpedo boat, has been for some time attached to the *Vernon* with a view of ascertaining her fitness for torpedo service. She was built by Messrs J and I Thorneycroft, of Chiswick, as an experimental boat.

The principle of the boat is as follows:

Water is drawn in through a large suction underneath, and by means of a turbine is pumped out through pipes on each side, the ends of which are capable of being reversed at will. When these pipes are turned aft the boat goes ahead, and when turned forward the boat goes astern; to stop the boat, the pipes are put central, without stopping the main engines. The mouth of the pipes is above water.

The principal, and, perhaps, most important defect in this boat for torpedo purposes, is her want of speed, which is much below the requirements of a torpedo boat, her greatest speed being 11.87 knots; in other respects she compares very favourably with other 2nd class boats. An experiment was made so as to compare the merits of this boat with No. 97 (a 2nd class boat fitted with screw propeller) when attacking a ship at night, both with and without the electric light; the results showed:

1st. That when approaching a ship with the electric light, the hydraulic boat was not more easily discernible than a boat with screw propellers.

2nd. That when running away from a ship with the electric light she was seen for a greater distance than No. 97.

3rd. That when approaching a ship without the electric light, No. 97 was first heard, owing to the beating of the propellers, while the noise of the discharge of water from the hydraulic boat, was mistaken for the breaking of the waves.

Another experiment was also tried, namely, endeavouring to choke the suction by seaweed. A number of bags of seaweed were emptied over the bows, and the boat was steamed through it several times, without, however, being affected by it in any way.

The turning powers of this particular boat are somewhat disappointing, for though she will turn in a small space, yet the time occupied in turning is very great. Our experience showed that the best way to turn, is to go full speed ahead with both discharges, and put the helm hard over.

The 1884 *Vernon* annual report also included the extensive results of numerous trials that had been carried out, comparing the second-class steel torpedo boat, *TB97*, which fired torpedoes from troughs using steam impulse, and the wooden boat, *TB6*, with torpedoes fired from dropping gear. When launching in smooth water, the starboard torpedo of *TB6* was deflected 5° outwards, but the port torpedo not at all. The dropping gear was not fitted parallel to the boat's centreline. There was no deflection for *TB97*, but problems were experienced with varying discharge velocity, despite the condenser vacuum remaining constant.

Further trials were carried out by *TB6*, in rough water. Allowing for the deflections measured in still water, five torpedoes were fired at a target at 400yds range. The results were that the torpedo generally came within 20yds of the target, although one did miss by 50yds. Similar trials were carried out, with the target at a range of 240yds, but this time the helm was put hard over immediately the torpedo was dropped. The results showed an error of just a few yards. Similar trials were not carried out with *TB97*.

A comparative trial was then carried out, in which the two boats ran a distance of 3.15 miles, turned through 540°, and returned to the starting point. *TB6* achieved this in 33 minutes 45 seconds and *TB97* took three minutes less. However, *TB97* experienced significant problems with her torpedoes, the covers working lose and the troughs creating great quantities of spray. Her steering was wild and erratic when steaming with the wind aft.

TORPEDO BOAT TRIALS

The conclusions derived from the 1884 trials were as follows:

1. That the steel boat has a decided advantage in speed over the wooden boat.
2. That boats fitted with troughs for the torpedoes in the bows cannot carry the torpedoes without incurring the risk of damaging them in anything but smooth water.
3. That in troubled water the wood boat fitted with dropping gear, made very successful running with her torpedoes.
4. That in troubled water the steel boat could not have fired her torpedoes with any prospect of success without reducing speed.
5. That in anything but smooth water the wooden boat is more suitable for torpedo purposes than the steel boat of the same type as No. 97.

In support of the second conclusion, it is as well to point out, that although the stop for holding the torpedo in its place, and the bolts for securing the covers may be improved, yet there must always be a certain amount of play for the torpedo in the trough, and since the torpedo (which is buoyant) is constantly water borne and then left dry, this fact alone must tend to injure it more or less.

As regards the fifth conclusion, although the steel boat undoubtedly possesses a greater speed, yet the higher freeboard of the wooden boat causes her to carry her torpedoes in much greater safety, and also enables her to fire them when it would be impossible for the steel boat to do so with any moderate degree of accuracy.

During the whole of the runs in smooth and rough water, the admirable steering qualities of the wooden boat were very noticeable; the slightest movement of the helm readily directed the course as necessary, and the helm could be moved as required with perfect ease.

The respective advantages of the two boats may be summed up as follows:

Steel boat	Greater speed.
	Smaller target.
Wooden boat	Better sea boat.
	Better manoeuvring powers.
	Greater safety for torpedoes.
	More reliable discharge.

It was considered that the trough system would never answer in rough water, but that dropping apparatus would hold out the best chance of success, and it was recommended that it should be fitted to a boat of this type for more exhaustive trials as soon as possible.

The following is a list of the defects developed during the trial in No. 97 Steel Boat:

1. Stop for retaining the torpedo in the trough very unsatisfactory.
2. Bolts for securing the lids to the troughs unsatisfactory.
3. No communication to engine room or stokehold, which is necessary before firing torpedo, so that orders to open the 'stand by' valve and various cocks may be given.
4. Atmospheric valve of port impulse was broken.
5. Cylinder cover of impulse was bent, 3 studs broken, studs broken on several occasions.
6. Impulse tube was bent.
7. Impulse very uncertain.

TB99 and *100*. (© National Maritime Museum, Greenwich, London, Richard Perkins Collection)

The last two second-class boats built by Thornycroft, *TB99* and *TB100* (Yard Nos 207 and 208), introduced a new arrangement of rudders and propeller, with twin rudders virtually 'enclosing' the propeller. Completed in 1885 and 1886 respectively, *TB100* used Thornycroft's patent tubulous water-tube boiler, while *TB99* retained a locomotive boiler. The arrangement of propeller and rudders gave them improved manoeuvrability, and speed was 16.1 knots from 181hp. At 64ft long, their twin torpedo tubes were fired by a powder impulse mechanism. They had a displacement of 9 tons and carried a load of 3 tons. In 1889, while attached to *Defiance* in Devonport, *TB100* was fitted with dropping gear, in order to assist with training crews. Whilst serving with *Defiance*, her Thornycroft boiler worked well, with high evaporative power and no problems experienced in keeping steam, but concern was expressed about accessibility to the tubes for cleaning.

TB1–TB12 were ordered from Whites of Cowes in three batches. They were built of wood and were sturdier than the other lighter second-class boats, but were slightly slower. They were completed between 1883 and 1883. They were approximately 56ft long, with a 9¼ft beam, but the dimensions did vary somewhat. Propulsion was similar to the other boats, with a two-cylinder engine and locomotive boiler. Armament also varied, being one or two machine guns with either a single 14in bow torpedo tube or dropping gear for two 14in torpedoes. Some were fitted with a spar torpedo as an alternative. Complement was higher at nine. These boats were built with the White's 'cut away' stern to improve their manoeuvrability.

Before the contract for these boats was placed, a number of trials had been carried out on a similar 48ft long boat in the Mediterranean. Subsequently, Mr White built a boat on the same principle 55ft long.

The Admiralty ordered the captains of *Excellent* and *Vernon* to try this boat and report on the following points:

– What speed a boat having this turning power should have, in order to enable her to steam from outside machine gun range to within Whitehead torpedo range, turn and steam again outside machine gun range in the same time as a second-class boat can perform this evolution.
– Qualities boat has for gun and torpedo service as compared with second-class boats.

TB1–12. (© National Maritime Museum, Greenwich, London, Richard Perkins Collection)

TORPEDO BOAT TRIALS: REPORT FROM CAPTAIN W E GORDON OF *VERNON*

On Saturday, 16 September, in compliance with the conditions laid down in paragraph 2 of Admiralty letter, Nordenfeldt range being taken as about 2,000 yards, and torpedo range from 200 to 300 yards, the distance to be passed over is roughly a mile, so that the measured mile in Stokes Bay was taken for the experiment.

Mr White's 55ft boat and my second-class *TB69* ran at full speed, from the eastern end of the mile, putting their helm over in passing the western marks, with the following result – time taken to run mile up, turn and run back was 11 min 1 sec (11.6 knts) for *TB69* and 8 min 40 sec (14.66 knts) for the White boat.

It will be seen from this that no speed was got out of the second-class boat on account of priming, and the circle of turning in Mr White's boat was not very small or quick as he preferred to put his helm only partly over in order not to check the speed more than necessary. The slow speed of the second-class boat rendered the actual trial of little value, but I did not think it necessary to repeat. The conclusions were that Mr White's boat was equal to a 15 knt boat when running one mile, and a 16 knt boat when running half a mile, turning and returning on the same track.

This test of a boat's efficiency does not appear to me of any superlative importance, as in making an attack it is very improbable that a boat would return on her tracks, but would rather pass on, or sheer off at some much greater angle.

In answer to paragraph 3 of Admiralty letter, ordering me to report on the boat's qualities for gun and torpedo purposes, I may state that the advantages of the boat do not rest on her turning power, as exemplified in the foregoing experiment, so much as on the following points:

1st. Her superior manoeuvring power, both in turning and going astern, would be most valuable for eluding guard boats, either in approaching an enemy, or in escaping, after having discharged a torpedo. It might also be valuable in enabling the boat to successfully place a spar torpedo when advancing from right ahead or right astern, and escaping afterwards.

2nd. She appears to possess greater stability and strength; but on this point, ie, that of her build, the dockyard officers can give a more valuable opinion.

3rd. Mr White claims greater unsinkability from his double bottom and air chambers, but in this I should think the compartment of the second-class torpedo boats would give as good, if not better, results, *vide* the accidents to the second-class boats that ran into one another at torpedo defence experiments in *Hecla*, February 1880. In Mr White's boat I should advise the addition of a small steam ejector.

4th. The protection from rifle or machine gun fire is, I should think, in favour of the wooden boat, and her arrangement lends itself more easily to the adoption of shields, such as are carried in other service steam launches.

5th. Mr White's boat is in my opinion, capable of carrying and discharging Whitehead torpedoes satisfactorily, and the apparatus for this purpose may be portable, so that it can be entirely removed when the boat is required for other purposes.

6th. She is, I presume, capable of carrying service fittings for spar torpedo without detriment from weakness in her speciality of build, but this should, perhaps, be tested.

> 7th. She appears to me to be more capable of fulfilling the ordinary requirements of a ship's boat, and in almost all kinds of boat expeditions, landing of troops &c she would be the most fit to nurse other boats and render general service.
>
> 8th. So far as weight and size are concerned, Mr White claims a small advantage for his boat, and if the engine and boiler could be portable, as in other steam launches, much weight might be saved for hoisting in.
>
> Finally, the proposed new arrangement of the stokehold being placed abaft the boilers will, in my opinion, be equally good with the present, as far as torpedo fittings are concerned.
>
> Captain Gordon also wrote a subsequent letter in November 1882:
>
> With reference to Admiralty letter, directing another comparative trial to be made between Mr White's 55 foot steam launch and an efficient torpedo boat with speed of 15 knots.
>
> I have the honour to point out that though second-class torpedo boats, on their original trial under the management of the makers, made over 15 knots speed, they do not often reach that speed when in the hands of ordinary engineers and stokers, not even when the engineer is so practised and skilful a one as Mr Minhinick, in charge of *Vernon*'s torpedo boats.
>
> I submit that when a further trial takes place, either both boats should be under the management of our service engineers and stokers, or both boats under the management of their own builders.
>
> It was decided that the boats were to be under the management of naval engineers and stokers, but the builders were to be afforded an opportunity of being present.
>
> The result of this trial; at which neither of the builders was present, was a total time of 9 min 28 sec, including turning time of 24 sec (13.2 knt), for White's boat and 8 min 57 sec, including turning time of 1 min (15 knt), for *TB69*.
>
> This was a very severe trial for Mr White's boat as the engineers and stokers were put into the boat for the first time, on the morning of the trial, while *TB69*'s engineers and stokers were well used to their boat.
>
> In order to have brought the times of both boats equal, Mr White's boat would have to run at 13.9 knots, and it is probable that with a little more knowledge and practice in the boat this speed would have easily been attained by the naval engineers.
>
> At the same time *TB69* would, on actual service, not have lost so much time in turning, as she would in that case probably not make a complete half circle. Fifteen knots is about the ordinary speed that, with great care and practice, can be got out of second-class boats, but to get this speed the boats must be constantly practised.

In 1883 *Vernon* reported that:

> the trials with the dropping gear have hitherto proved satisfactory when the centre of the frame is placed 3 feet abaft the centre of the boat, any position further forward gives a decided deflection outwards to the torpedo; so that the apparatus for firing Whiteheads from these boats, will consist of one set of dropping gear of the service pattern, on each side.

The last second-class torpedo boats to be built for the Royal Navy were constructed by Yarrow and were of two different designs. *TB49* and *TB50* were completed in 1888, the year before *TB39–TB48* were built.

In the issue dated 27 April 1888, the weekly publication *Engineering* described *TB49* and *TB50* as a new type of second-class torpedo boat. The boat was 60ft long overall and 8ft 6in wide, 3ft shorter, and from a foot to 13in wider than the old type of second-class boats. She attained a speed of rather more than 17 knots on her official trial with 4 tons on board. The speed, when light, for six runs on the measured mile was 18½ knots. The latter was considered a very high speed for so small a vessel, but the speed of 17.031 knots on a four-hour trial with 4 tons on board was considered more remarkable still.

The boat differed from ordinary second-class boats in the manner of ejecting the torpedo. The more ordinary method of firing the torpedo was from a tube or tubes, built into the hull and pointing forward through the bow, but in these two boats the bow fire was abandoned, and a swivelling gun placed aft.

Observers commented:

> It is certainly a remarkable sight to see the manner in which this little vessel winds amongst craft or round buoys, or turns circles of surprisingly small diameter. She seems to pivot on a point very near the bow, chiefly accounted for by the way the deadwood is cut away aft. This allows the stream of water diverted by the unusually large rudder to swing the after part round with facility.

She also had a comparatively small bow wave, achieved by placing the greatest cross-section further aft than would have been done had speed alone been the priority.

On one occasion in early 1888 *TB50* made the run from the Thames to Portsmouth and, the weather being bad, was taken through the somewhat intricate, but more sheltered fairways and channels of what is known as the 'overland passage'. Off Margate she managed to run aground, and as the sands there are very hard, she smashed her propeller. After a time, she was got off and beached, when a new propeller was fitted.

TB39–TB48 were of a similar size and performance, but returned to launching their two 14in torpedoes by dropping gear.

At the end of the section on second-class torpedo boats in Conway's *All The World's Fighting Ships 1860–1905*, there is the comment: 'The last class was built on the lines of the aluminium boat Yarrow had built for the French Navy. Larger than their predecessors, six were intended to be carried on the torpedo boat carrier

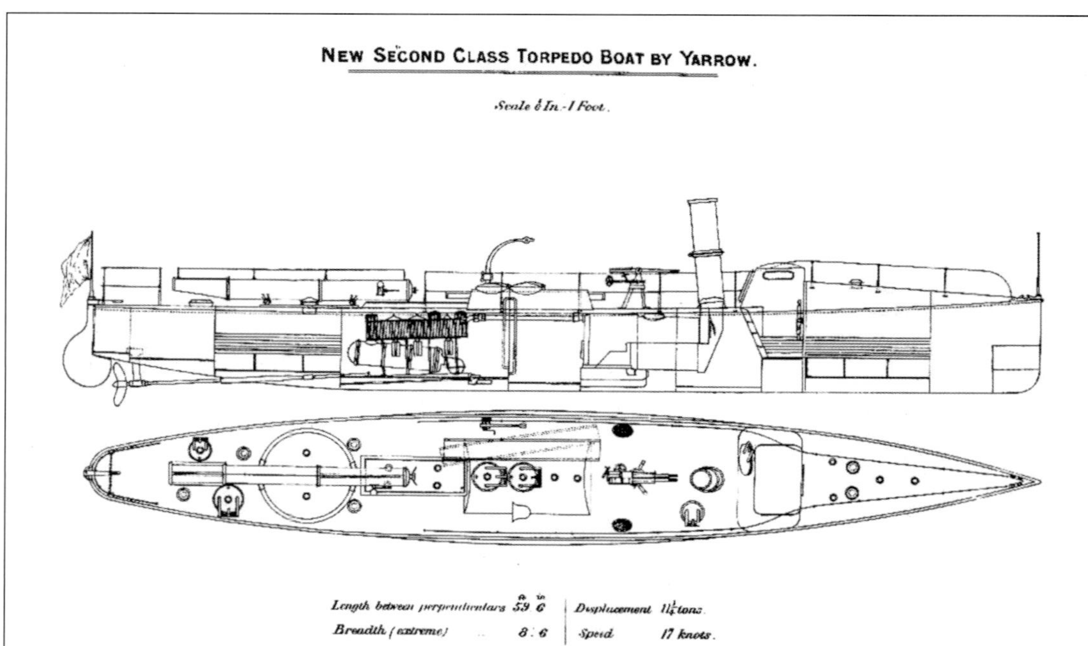

Shipbuilder's drawing of *TB49* and *50*.

An illustration of *TB49*. (*Engineering*, 27 April 1888)

Vulcan.' Likewise, in his article in *Warship 2005*, D K Brown states: 'The latter group (ie *TB39–TB48*) were based on their aluminium boat for France but were of steel construction. Six of this group were carried in *Vulcan*.' However, a feature in *The Engineer* of October 1894, describing the French boat, includes an illustration showing its appearance to be very similar to that of *TB50*, with a trainable torpedo tube aft.

The 1884 annual report from *Vernon* recorded that there were forty-eight boats in service distributed as follows: *TB51–TB54*, *TB56* and *TB57* with torpedo depot ship *Hecla*; *TB55* and *TB59* onboard second-class cruiser *Iris*; *TB61* and *TB62* onboard armoured cruiser *Northampton*; *TB65* and *TB73* onboard sister-ship *Nelson*; *TB64* and *TB67* onboard turret ship *Wivern*; *TB68* with the training ship *Indus*; *TB69* and *TB97* at *Vernon*; *TB70* onboard turret ship *Inflexible*; *TB71* and *TB80* onboard ironclad ram *Hotspur* at Devonport; *TB72* with torpedo school ship *Defiance*; *TB74* onboard turret ship *Colossus*; *TB78* and *TB79* onboard second-class cruiser *Phaeton*; *TB83* and *TB85* onboard sister-ship *Leander*, and *TB84* and *TB86* onboard her other sister *Arethusa*, both at Chatham; *TB82* onboard turret ship *Agamemnon*; *TB87* onboard sister-ship *Ajax*, also at Chatham; *TB88* onboard *Dreadnought* in Malta; *TB89* onboard turret ram *Conqueror* at Chatham. *TB93* was at Sheerness, and *TB63*, *TB66* and *TB98* were at Portsmouth, as Steam Reserve. The others were 'unappropriated', mainly at Portsmouth, but with two in Malta, both landed from battery ironclad *Superb*.

TRIALS OF SECOND-CLASS TORPEDO BOATS *TB69* AND *100*

HMS *Vernon* Annual Report, 1887

With a view of determining the best type and armament of Second Class steel torpedo boats capable of being carried and hoisted out by sea-going ships, comparative trials were carried out by *Vernon* between No. 69 and No. 100 Second Class boats.

The former, built by Thorneycroft [*sic*], is of the ordinary type now in the Service, with low ram bow and conning tower forward, and carrying two torpedoes in dropping gear. The latter, also by Thorneycroft, is, except in armament of somewhat similar lines to his 125ft boat, with the twin rudders each side of the screw; she has, however, open bow and stern sheets, with water escape tubes to prevent them remaining filled in a seaway, and has a high conning tower and turtle-decked bows in which she carries two fixed stem tubes fitted for powder impulse.

The boats were tried for accuracy of practice in smooth and rough water, and also for general behaviour in a seaway. As regards the practice, it was found that the stem tubes gave excellent results with efficiently-controlled torpedoes in both smooth and rough water, and decidedly better than is obtained from dropping-gear.

The bluffness of the bows necessary for carrying the two torpedoes in stem tubes caused the boat's seaworthiness to be injuriously affected, throwing up immense quantities of spray, and causing heavy pitching in a moderate sea, whilst with the dropping gear this was not experienced to any such extent, though the small stability possessed by No. 69 caused her to heel over much more than No 100. The open bow and stern sheets, though affording good standing room for the crew, and tending to keep the weights in the boat lower, afford no shelter for any lengthened cruising. The twin rudder showed a marked superiority over the ordinary rudder in 69, in giving the boat exceptionally good manoeuvring powers. It was, however, considered that the two stem tubes affected the boat's seaworthiness to such an extent as to condemn that form of armament in any boats in which a revolving tube could be carried, and experiments were therefore carried out in No. 69 to ascertain if that form of armament could be used from that class of boat.

A tube from No. 25 First Class boat was therefore mounted amidships, so as to be capable of being fired 50° before and abaft the beam, and very satisfactory practice was made in smooth and rough water, with the boat heeling and rolling as the torpedoes were discharged, the absence of any heel when the torpedo was fired being most marked, and the boat's seaworthiness unaffected by it. The weight of the tube and mountings was about 13cwt, and its height above the water-line 3ft, with the boat on even keel.

A design of a light tube and mounting was then prepared by Vernon, and in consultation with Messrs Yarrow and Co, was submitted as being the most suitable type of boat for further experiments.

One of the principal points in the armament of these boats is that the torpedo armament should be easily removed for hoisting the boat in and out, if she is required as a guard boat only, and this is feasible with the revolving tube, but not with the stem tube.

Two boats of this design, involving all the latest improvements in design, have been constructed. They possess remarkable stability and steering power,

Dimensions, armament, etc, of new second-class torpedo boats

No.of boat	Builder's name	Extreme length	Extreme beam
		feet	ft in
12 wood	White	56	9 6
49 steel	Yarrow	56	8 3
50 steel	Yarrow	60	8 6
99 steel	Thornycroft	65	8 0
69 steel	Thornycroft	63	7 6

and have triple expansion engines which have given a speed of 17.1 knots.

The following table shows the details of the different types of boats:

No. of boat	Date of building	Builder's name	Speed (knots)	Length extreme (feet)	Beam (feet)	Displacement (tons)	Height of conning tower (ft in)	Distance of conning tower from stem	Armament
69	1880	Thorneycroft	16.8	63	7½	10.5	4 1	14½	Dropping gear
100	1886	Thorneycroft	16.1	63	8	11	5 2	21½	2 stem tubes
49	1887	Yarrow	17.1	63	8½	11¼	5 0	16	1 revolving tube

Further trials were carried out the following year, including *TB12* (wooden boat built by Whites), *TB49* and *TB50* (built by Yarrow), and *TB69* and *TB99* (built by Thornycroft). The results are summarised in the table below.

During 1891 *Vernon* experimented with dropping gear fitted to smaller boats – a 32ft steam cutter (No. *328*) and a 40ft steam pinnace (No. *19*). Trials showed that the 32ft boat was unsuitable; after launching the torpedo from one side, the boat listed so much that the other torpedo became submerged and could not be fired. The 40ft boat was found to be more suitable and it was recommended that the centreline of the dropping gear should be inclined at an angle of 6° across the keel line of the boat in order to reduce the deflection from 8° to 2°.

The following year, further trials were carried out to compare No. *19* 40ft steam pinnace with a smaller 37ft steam pinnace from *Alexandra*. The 37ft pinnace was found to be more stable, and so a ton of lead ballast was added to the 40ft pinnace. This improved stability and so a short 18in torpedo was tried, replacing the previous 14in torpedoes. It was decided that the pinnace was not suitable for the larger 18in torpedo.

Draught of water		Speed		Displacement		Metacentric height, fully equipped	Armament					Coal carried	Remarks
Forward	Aft	On measured mile	Actual at sea complete	Without armament and crew	Complete for service		Discharging apparatus	No. of torpedoes carried	Total weight	Height above water†	Gun armament proposed as torpedo boat*		
ft in	ft in	knots	knots	tons	tons	feet			cwt	ft in		cwt	
1 11	4 6	16.0	11.3	11.25	16.75	Not known – considerable	Dropping gear	2	19.0	4 6	1 two-barrel 1in Nordenfelt	36*	Gun armament, originally proposed to be alternative only in these boats. † Height of torpedoes above water when turned inboard.
2 1	4 0	16.1	12.3	10.5	14.25	0.8	One revolving tube	1	16.5	4 5	Nil	26	
2 0	4 0	17.1	12.6	11.25	15.0	0.9	One revolving tube	1	16.5	4 4	Nil	28	
1 0	3 5	16.0	11.8	10.5	13.5	Not known tubes	2 fixed stem	2	33.0	2 10	Nil	30	
1 3	3 6	16.8	?	10.5	14.0	Not known	Dropping gear	2	16.5	4 3	Nil	30	

CHAPTER EIGHT

TORPEDO GUNBOATS

The primary purpose of the torpedo gunboat, like that of the torpedo boat destroyer, was defensive – smaller and faster than traditional cruisers, they were intended to protect the fleet from attacks by torpedo boats. Sometimes called torpedo catchers, they were powerfully armed with guns, but carried torpedoes as well, so that they could also fulfil the role of torpedo boats. They were larger and more seaworthy than torpedo boats, but were constructed using conventional techniques and powered by conventional machinery hence were not able to achieve the speeds of the smaller torpedo boats. Although the Admiralty persisted with the design of these vessels for some years, they were not a great success, primarily because of their lack of speed.

In the 1884 report from *Vernon*, there is the following statement:

> Mr White, of Cowes, is now building a vessel, at his own risk, for the purpose of chasing torpedo boats and destroying them, either by ramming or with machine, or quick-firing, guns, of which it is proposed she should have a large supply. Armament to the weight of 10 tons is being allowed for.
>
> This vessel is 150ft in length, 17ft 6in in beam, and will have a draught of water of about 7ft 6in. She will carry 35 tons of coal, which should enable her to steam 2,000 miles at 10 knots, and she is constructed on the turnabout principle, with a ram forward and a spur attached to the after rudder, and since she will steer as well when going astern as ahead, it is anticipated that she would prove a formidable foe if opposed to a fleet of hostile torpedo boats. Her speed is not named, but will undoubtedly be very

Fearless. (US Naval History and Heritage Command, NH 61044-A)

great. Being built in compartments, and also with longitudinal bulkheads, she will not be an easy craft to sink, and her high freeboard will, it is presumed, enable her to work her guns in any weather in which torpedo boats are likely to venture forth.

The usefulness and importance of craft of this character for defensive purposes can be well understood, and she will undoubtedly be a valuable auxiliary to any fleet, or squadron, cruising in waters where an attack by torpedo boats is possible.

Porpoise, one of the *Archer*-class cruisers. *(US Naval History and Heritage Command, NH 57870)*

The Admiralty did lay down two torpedo cruisers in 1884, *Scout* and *Fearless*. They were 220ft LBP and displaced 1,580 tons. Their twin shaft machinery could produce 3,200hp with forced draught, giving a maximum speed of 17 knots. They were armed with four 5in breech-loading rifles (BLR), eight 3pdr quick-firing guns, one above-water torpedo tube and two torpedo carriages. They were followed the next year by the eight vessels of the *Archer* class, which were slightly longer and carried six 6in BLRs instead of the four 5in mountings, and three 14in above-water torpedo tubes.

Also in 1885, Laird of Birkenhead laid down the first vessel to be given the designation 'torpedo gunboat', *Rattlesnake* (see front endpapers). At 200ft LBP, she was slightly smaller than *Scout*, but had a top speed of 19¼ knots under forced draught. She had a beam of 23ft, a displacement of 550 tons, and was fitted with four locomotive boilers and two triple-expansion engines producing 2,700hp, driving a twin shaft arrangement. The boilers were in two stokeholds and had a working pressure of about 140psi. The engines had a stroke of 18in

Rattlesnake. (US Naval History and Heritage Command, NH 76924)

and produced maximum horsepower at 310rpm. The shafts were made of Whitworth steel and the three-bladed propellers of manganese bronze. She could carry 80 tons of coal, giving a range of 2,800 miles at an economic speed of 10 knots.

She only had a single 5in gun and six 3pdr guns, but four above-water 14in torpedo tubes, one in the stem, one at the stern and one on each beam. Three near-sisters, *Grasshopper*, *Sandfly* and *Spider*, were built at the Royal Dockyards of Sheerness (one) and Devonport (two), but were not as successful as the prototype.

Rattlesnake was launched on 11 September 1886, and moved to Portsmouth in December for completion. Following the 1887 review at Spithead for Queen Victoria's Jubilee, and the subsequent manoeuvres, she became a tender to *Vernon*. She remained with *Vernon* until 30 November 1890, when she was paid off, remaining in reserve for ten years, although she did participate in some of the annual manoeuvres during that time. *Rattlesnake* was removed from the active list in December 1904, later being towed to the upper reaches of Portsmouth Harbour, where she was sunk whilst undergoing experiments with mines.

Grasshopper was floated out at Sheerness on 27 April 1886, but was not commissioned for service until 18 July 1889, although she had been temporarily commissioned for the 1888 annual manoeuvres. She was paid off again on 10 September, remaining in reserve until November 1901, although she did take part in some of the annual manoeuvres of that period. She operated in Irish waters, and, after undergoing a refit during the autumn of 1902, at the end of 1903 she became a tender to the torpedo depot ship *Warrior* (now preserved at Portsmouth) and her successor *Invincible*, subsequently renamed *Erebus*. Paid off in June 1904, *Grasshopper* was sold in the middle of 1905.

Sandfly was launched at Devonport on 30 September 1887. In 1890 she commissioned for service in the Mediterranean, leaving England in November to become senior officer at Gibraltar, remaining as such until early 1894. She paid off and remained there for ten years, before being removed from the Active List and scrapped. *Spider* was also launched at Devonport, slightly more than two weeks after *Sandfly*. During 1892–94 and 1896, she was tender to *Vivid* at Devonport, where she assisted with the instruction of students at the RN Engineering College, until replaced by *Sharpshooter* in

September 1898. She was sold by auction in May 1903 for £1,875, and broken up at Preston.

In an attempt to address the problem of low speed, the design of the next class was entrusted to the DNC, W H White. They were considerably larger, with a displacement of 735 tons. They were also 30ft longer than *Rattlesnake*, and fitted with a similar machinery outfit that was capable of producing more power: 3,500ihp according to Conway's, or 4,500ihp forced draught and 2,500ihp natural draught according to Armstrong. The result was not the desired increase in speed, and much trouble was experienced with the machinery, in particular the locomotive boilers.

The vessels were fitted with a long topgallant forecastle extending one-third of her length, but no poop. The officers' accommodation was aft on the lower deck, and there were two pole masts and two funnels. A bulkhead ran fore and aft between the two engine rooms, and the boilers and engines were protected from machine-gun fire by the coal bunkers. The armament comprised two 4.7in quick-firing guns and four 3pdr guns, mounted fore and aft, and five 14in torpedo tubes; a fixed stem tube and two twin trainable tubes mounted one on each beam.

The prototype vessel, *Sharpshooter*, was laid down at Devonport in either November 1887 (Parkes) or January 1888 (Conway's), and launched on 30 November 1889. Her entry into service was delayed by repeated failures of her

Grasshopper. (US Naval History and Heritage Command, NH 60495)

Gleaner, one of the later vessels in the *Sharpshooter* class. *(US Naval History and Heritage Command, NH 60488)*

boiler tubes. While returning from the 1892 manoeuvres, *Sharpshooter* suffered trouble with her boilers and she broke down off Land's End on 14 August. Experiencing high seas, she shipped 70 tons of water, which flooded her boiler rooms and extinguished the fires. She was towed to Devonport. During her life, she experienced further problems with her machinery, and in May 1895 began a series of trials of her Belleville boilers. The trials lasted for thirty-eight days over a four-month period. At the end of the trials, the captain of *Sharpshooter*, Lieutenant Commander A Dodgson, reported:

> In all cases the ship was manoeuvred as she might be in battle, the vessel cleared for action, and the men at their stations for general quarters. Full power for four boilers was used, giving a speed of 13½ knots, 190 revolutions, and 1450 indicated horse-power.
>
> The following manoeuvres were practised: Stopping frequently from full speed and starting again, without warning, after intervals of five minutes to 1½ hours, getting away at full speed from banked fires.
>
> All that was found necessary in the stokeholds was to close the draught plates of the furnaces, and open wide the tube box-doors, and in the engine-rooms to make a moderate use of the blow-off valves to the condensers when suddenly stopping. There was no priming at the engines. Fires were banked on the 9th December at 7pm, steam maintained all night at 150lb to 200lb till 8am on the 10th, when the ship was got under way and started immediately at full speed, and manoeuvred, as already mentioned, for six hours. On this trial, as a precautionary measure, a petty officer was stationed at the separator to ensure that its blowing-out apparatus did not fail, but the apparatus acted most satisfactorily, and the services of the petty officer were not once required. During the above trials the stokers employed were the men forming the first training class, who had been in the ship about a fortnight.

Sharpshooter ended the year at Portsmouth, training engine room staff. Having finished her career with the Royal Navy, in March 1914 she was renamed *Northampton* and became a training ship for boys moored near Temple Pier, London.

Salamander was also fitted with water-tube boilers by Mumford for experimental purposes.

TESTING MUMFORD BOILERS

***The Engineer*, 3 December 1897**

These boilers were very carefully tested under steam at the Culver-street Works, and gave an evaporative result which for speed and economy, but especially economy, has never been exceeded in practice by any express boiler.

The boiler is built up of a number of steel sections or 'headers', into the covers of which are expanded the ends of curved steel tubes. To secure perfect accessibility matters are so arranged that any group of tubes may be detached from the steam receiver at the top and the water chamber at the bottom, passed into the furnace, and taken out through the front. If there is not time to effect repairs, a spare 'element' can take the place of that removed, or failing this blank covers may be put on and steam got up again. The method of making the joints is most important, and has done much to secure the practical success of the boiler. No packing of any kind so-called is used; the joints are made with a single ring of copper wire about ⅛in thick. The flanges are very still, and the bolts strong. The jambing of the wire between the two planed surfaces produces a joint which is absolutely tight, requires no skill in the making, and can be broken without the smallest trouble.

Each boiler has 2,000 square feet of heating surface and 45 square feet of grate surface. A special feature of the boilers deserves attention. The products of combustion do not pass straight out among the tubes from the furnace to the external smoke casing, as in the Yarrow and Thornycroft boilers. Curved wrought iron baffle plates are carried on an inner row of tubes. These plates are very easily removed and replaced, and being in a manner protected by the water-tubes and kept cool by them, they are found to last a long time. The products of combustion have to pass from the front to near the back of the furnace before they can escape, which they do at each side, and return through the tubes to regular smoke-boxes at the firing end of the boiler, and thence to the uptake. It is the comparatively long run of the gases that renders the boiler so eminently economical.

In the present day it has come to be understood that the express boiler must have an automatic feed regulator. That employed on the *Salamander* is Mumford and Anthony's patent, part of a feed system which has been very carefully worked out so as to require the smallest possible amount of attention from those in charge of the boiler room.

To begin with, the feed-water is sent into the steam space – the best possible place, for reasons which ought to be well understood by everyone who has had experience at sea.

The feed is supplied by two sets of Mumford and Anthony's pumps. The pumps are of the vertical Duplex type. Steam cylinders and pumps are entirely of gun-metal. The steam cylinders are 11in in diameter, the pumps 7½in in diameter, with a stroke of 10in, constructed for a working pressure of 200lb.

The arrangements of the ports in the steam cylinders, which is protected by letters patent, compete the pump plungers to work in the same direction as if driven by cranks at right angles. Thus, one of the most important points in pumps is secured, viz, one or other of the plungers is always moving when the other is at the end of its stroke, thus a steady flow of water is maintained, avoiding jerks or sudden pressure in the discharge. It is impossible for both pistons to be at the ends of their strokes at the same time. In the steam cylinders there are only two moving parts, viz, the pistons – no slide valves, levers, pins, or tappets, to get out of order. Each piston serves as the valve for the admission and eduction of steam to the other, in addition to bearing its own duty as an ordinary piston, working the pumps direct, and this without any separate working part. The ports are so arranged that the pistons will start in any position.

There are no dead centres, and throughout a course of severe tests and lengthened trials, we understand that the pump has never been known to stick or stop of its own accord. This feature is absolutely necessary when working in connection with an automatic feed regulator, as the pump will at times be brought almost to a stand-still, and at others work at full speed, without regulating the steam valve or attention of any kind. We have ourselves seen pumps of this construction most severely tested with unqualified success, and during trials of the *Salamander*'s boilers we saw the whole of the feeding apparatus working with an ease and certainty that left nothing to be desired.

The feed-water passes into a small cast iron cistern fixed to the side of the ship under the deck. There is, we believe, in the *Salamander* one for each boiler, but one can be made to answer for two boilers. In the tank is a strong float. The water level in the cistern corresponds with that of the water in the boiler. At one end of the cistern is placed a transverse weigh shaft, which works steam-tight practically without friction, although one arm is inside the cistern and the other outside; the latter supports a balance weight, the other carries the float and the balanced valve. The amount to which the valve can fall, and so admit water to the boiler from the cistern, is determined by the hand wheel and screw, as shown. A glass water gauge is provided to show the level. We found on trial that this regulator is sufficiently sensitive to prevent a variation of more than ½in in the level of the water, but it does not carry on its duties with absurd delicacy. It appears to us to be a strong and efficient apparatus, quite capable of taking care of itself at sea, and that is no mean performance.

Finally, we may say that when we saw the *Salamander*'s boilers, both cold and under steam, and made ourselves acquainted with the methods of construction adopted by Mr Mumford, we came to the conclusion that the *Salamander* has got a most efficient and satisfactory boiler; not, we may add, a steam generating apparatus, but a boiler. Every seagoing engineer, at all events, will appreciate the difference, and we shall be very much surprised should its use be confined in the future to torpedo destroyers, or such like small craft. Indeed, many things suggest that it is better suited for large cruisers or battleships than it is for small craft, such as torpedo boats, in which a saving of weight in the boiler is paramount to almost every other consideration.

We may say, in conclusion, that the novel construction of the boilers, and the high claims for economy made by Mr Mumford, led the Admiralty to submit them to a very severe test, both under forced and natural draught, and the conditions of the contract were considerably exceeded in all respects.

Further experimentation took place with *Seagull* being fitted with Niclausse boilers, and *Spanker* with Du Temple boilers, and *Sheldrake* had her locomotive boilers replaced by Babcock and Wilson water-tube ones in 1899 at a cost of £28,000.

Altogether, twelve vessels were built to this design, the eight for the Royal Navy being constructed at Sheerness, Chatham or Devonport dockyards, and the other four being built by Armstrong, two for India and two for Australia. Four of the class, *Gossamer*, *Seagull*, *Skipjack* and *Spanker*, were converted to minesweepers in 1908/9.

Despite the failure of *Sharpshooter* to reach the desired speed, the Admiralty placed orders

Speedwell, a *Sharpshooter*-class vessel built at Devonport Dockyard. *(US Naval History and Heritage Command, NH 65914)*

for another eleven vessels, *Alarm* class, with the same principal dimensions, but with greater displacement. Armament also remained the same, except for *Jaseur*, *Jason*, *Niger*, *Onyx* and *Speedy*, which carried three 18in torpedo tubes, rather than the five 14in tubes of the previous vessels. Machinery remained the same, producing the same power, and so speeds generally dropped.

They were designed by W H White, CB, Director of Naval Construction, their particulars being 230ft long, 27ft beam, and displacement at 8ft 9in draught of 830 tons. *Circe*, *Alarm* and *Leda* were built at Sheerness Dockyard and engined by Messrs John Penn and Sons of Greenwich. They were fitted with triple-expansion three-cylinder twin engines, each driving a three-bladed screw propeller 8ft 3in diameter, and 9ft 6in mean pitch. The engine cylinders were 22in, 34in and 51in diameter respectively, the piston stroke of each being 21in. Steam was supplied by four boilers of the

Alarm. *(US Naval History and Heritage Command, NH 63000)*

Circe. (US Naval History and Heritage Command, NH 61366)

locomotive type, each 7ft 6in diameter in the barrel, and 15ft 9in long, there being eight furnaces in all, giving a grate surface of 182sq ft. The aggregate heating surface in the boilers, which were designed for a working pressure of 155psi, was 6,250sq ft, and the cooling surface in condensers of engines was 4,000sq ft.

Antelope was launched from No. 1 building slip at Her Majesty's Dockyard, Devonport, on 12 July 1893, eight and a half months after being laid down, owing to the great difficulty the naval authorities experienced in finding contractors willing to undertake the construction of the propelling machinery of the vessel under the conditions imposed, the responsibility of fitting her with propelling machinery, etc, eventually being undertaken by Yarrow. The launching ceremony was performed by Miss Florence Crocker, daughter of the chief constructor at Devonport Dockyard, and there were present at the function Rear Admiral Sir Algernon Lyons, naval commander-in-chief; Sir R More Molyneux, superintendent of the dockyard; and Mr G Crocker, chief constructor. *Antelope* was to cost £61,060.

In 1893 the official machinery trials of *Circe* were run off the Nore. The trials were attended by Mr Oram, representing the Admiralty, Mr Pattison, Sheerness Dockyard, and Mr J P Hall, the contracting engineers. After a preliminary run on Friday, 24 February to test joints and connections and get all in readiness, the vessel left Sheerness on Monday, 27 February to undergo a continuous eight-hour natural-draught trial, which was accomplished with the following results:

> With a steam pressure of 140lb per square inch, vacuum 27in, air pressure in stokeholds 8in, and the engines making a mean of 2,238 revolutions per minute, the mean indicated horsepower realised was 2,618, giving a speed of ship by log of 18.27 knots per hour; the contract power for this trial being 2,500-horse. The boiler tubes having been swept, and all joints and connections thoroughly examined, on Tuesday 28th, the vessel proceeded on the following morning, in very heavy weather, on a three-hours forced-draught full-power trial, which resulted in the stipulated 3,500 indicated horsepower contracted for being considerably exceeded, although the engines and boilers were, through the heavy sea that was encountered, very severely tested.

The official full-power trial, under forced draught, of *Leda* was successfully carried out on 11 September 1893, off Sheerness, the dockyard being represented by Mr Mattison, while Mr Samuel Rock represented the Admiralty, and Mr J P Flail the engineer contractors. On the forced draught full-power trial of three hours the machinery was required to develop and maintain 3,500 indicated horsepower with not more than 3in of air pressure in the stokeholds. This was satisfactorily exceeded on the trial of *Leda*, which obtained a mean of 3,601 horsepower with an average steam pressure in the boilers of 148lb, vacuum 27.5, revolutions 246. The mean air pressure in the stokeholds was 2.21, and the speed of the vessel was 18.3 knots. The furnaces of the boilers, which were of the marine locomotive type, were corrugated on the sides and top, on the principle of Mr F W Webb, manager of the London and North-Western Railway Company, and the fire-box ends of the tubes were fitted with ferrules on the Admiralty plan. On examination after the trials the boilers

Jason. (US Naval History and Heritage Command, NH 60130)

were found to have sustained no ill effects from the application of forced draught. The following details show the powers for the six half-hours as taken:

Half-hours	Indicated horsepower		Collective ihp
	Starboard	Port	
1	1,783.9	1,763 8	3,547.7
2	1,771.8	1,811 2	3,583.0
3	1,777.6	1,784 4	3,562.0
4	1,937.1	1,854 5	3,791.6
5	1,801.9	1,767 1	3,659.0
6	1,784.5	1,769 6	3,554.1
			21,607.4
Mean indicated horsepower for the three hours			3,601.2

Renard was built and engined by Messrs Laird Brothers, of Birkenhead, and on Thursday, 14 September 1893 she completed her official machinery trials off the Nore. The officials present were Mr Oram and Mr Emdin, for the Admiralty; Mr Mattison for Sheerness Dockyard, and Mr Betsey Bevis for the contracting engineers and shipbuilders; Captain Douglas, of the Steam Reserve, being in command. On Wednesday 6th the vessel underwent a full-power trial of eight hours' duration under natural draught, when the following mean results were obtained:

> With 0.83in of air pressure in the stokeholds, steam was maintained at 143.6lb pressure per square inch, the engines made 218 revolutions per minute, and developed 2,584 indicated horsepower, giving the ship a speed of 17.6 knots per hour; which, taking into account the state of the weather, was considered very satisfactory.

The weather – which in the meantime had been boisterous at sea – having cleared up, on the morning of the 14th *Renard* left the Nore for a three hours' full-power trial under forced draught, the mean results of which were that a good supply of steam of a pressure of 145psi was kept up with 2.7in of air pressure, and with a vacuum of 26½in the engines attained a speed of 254 revolutions a minute, and developed a total indicated power of 3,949 horses, 2,025 of which were given off by the starboard and 1,924 by the port engines; the resultant speed of the ship, which was drawing 8ft 1in forward and 11ft aft by log, being 19.4 knots per hour.

As 2,500 indicated horsepower for the natural draught and 3,500 for the forced draught was the power contracted to be developed on the speed trials of the *Renard*, it will be seen from the above recorded results that the actual powers realised were largely in excess of the requirements; that under forced draught being from the mean powers developed during the six half-hours of its continuance, which were 3,451, 3,992, 4,005, 4,028, 4,205 and 4,011, the highest yet attained in any vessel of the same class. There was slight priming of the boilers during the first half-hour, its effect being shown in the lower

Niger. (US Naval History and Heritage Command, NH 58644)

The launch of *Speedy*, the only torpedo gunboat built by Thornycroft. *(Vosper Thornycroft)*

power recorded; but with this exception, it will be seen that for two and a half consecutive hours the actual mean power realised was 4,048, or an excess of 548 over that contracted for, with the boilers at the finish of the trials absolutely tight and in a very satisfactory condition.

Speedy, which was designed and built by Thornycroft, using their own water-tube boilers, was different from the others. *Speedy* (Yard No. 281) was the largest vessel to have been built by Thornycroft, being 242ft LOA, and developing 4,703hp for a maximum speed of 20.55 knots. She was the only torpedo gunboat to have three funnels.

The Engineer described the machinery as follows:

> Her engines are triple compound, driving twin-screws, there are piston valves on the high pressure cylinders, which are unjacketted, steam is supplied by eight water-tube boilers with galvanised steel tubes. The masts, funnels, ventilators, and all fittings above the level of the forecastle deck will have to be removed to enable the vessel to pass under Hammersmith Bridge, which she will just be able to do at low tide. She will then proceed to the docks for a few days to be refitted, and then go upon her trials, which are to be of a very exhaustive nature.

She was launched on 18 May 1893, with boilers and engines on board, and hull complete and fully rigged, the displacement on launching being 577 tons. Among those present at the launch of *Speedy* were Lord George Hamilton, Sir Anthony Hoskings, Senior Naval Lord of the Admiralty, admirals Richards and Boys, Sir Nathaniel Barnaby, KCB, ex-chief constructor of the Navy, Captain Le Clerc, French naval attaché, Captain von Jedina, Austrian naval attaché, Captain Coles, United States naval attaché, Mr W H White, designer of *Speedy*, the Revd Lawford W T Dale, vicar of Chiswick, and Hamo Thornycroft, RA.

On a Tuesday morning in October 1893, *Speedy* left the Nore at 7am for an eight-hours' trial under natural draught. The trial, being of exceptional interest, was attended by the attachés of the French, German, Austrian and

Italian governments. The representative officials of the British Admiralty present were Mr Deadman and Mr Oxam; Mr Thornycroft and Mr Donaldson watching the trial on behalf of the builders and engineers. The result was a decided success, 3,043 indicated horsepower being developed by the engines – the contract being for 2,500 – with ½in of air pressure in the stokeholds.

Jason was fitted with new engines and boilers by the Fairfield Shipbuilding and Engineering Co Ltd in 1903. A series of official trials were carried out in May, on the Firth of Clyde. On the low-power trial a speed of 15 knots was attained with 1,185 indicated horsepower developed, and on the full-power trial of four runs over the measured mile at Skelmorlie the results were: mean indicated horsepower, 5,732; mean revolutions, 341; mean speed, 21.95 knots.

Speedy, *Circe*, *Jason*, *Leda*, *Niger* and *Hebe* were converted to minesweepers in 1908/9, *Antelope* following in 1915.

Before the results of the trials with *Speedy* were known, the Admiralty placed orders for yet another group of torpedo gunboats, the *Dryad* class. There were only five vessels in the class, with a length of 250ft LEP, 30½ft beam and a greater displacement of 1,070 tons. The results of speed trials were, once again, disappointing.

	Air pressure in stokehold	Horsepower	Revolutions	Speed
Dryad	2.28	3,709	242	18.2
*Halcyon**	2	3,546	248	17.7
Harrier	1.77	3,608	254	19
Hazard	2.19	3,734	260	19
Hussar	1.69	3,553	253	19.7

These vessels had both a poop and a topgallant forecastle, their funnels being sited far apart. They had two 4.7in quick-firing guns, one on the poop and one on the forecastle; two 6pdr guns mounted in forecastle sponsons, and two more further aft, one on each beam between the funnels. Their torpedo armament consisted of five 18in torpedo tubes, a stem tube and a twin trainable tube on each beam.

As displacement increased, so did the cost of the vessels, each of the *Dryad* class costing about twice that of the *Rattlesnake*.

With the successful development of torpedo boat destroyers, the days of the unsuccessful torpedo gunboat came to an end.

Hazard, the second of the _Dryad_ class to be launched, was lost in a collision in 1918. _(US Naval History and Heritage Command, NH 60579)_

*See Plate 7.

Hussar. (*US Naval History and Heritage Command, NH 60595*)

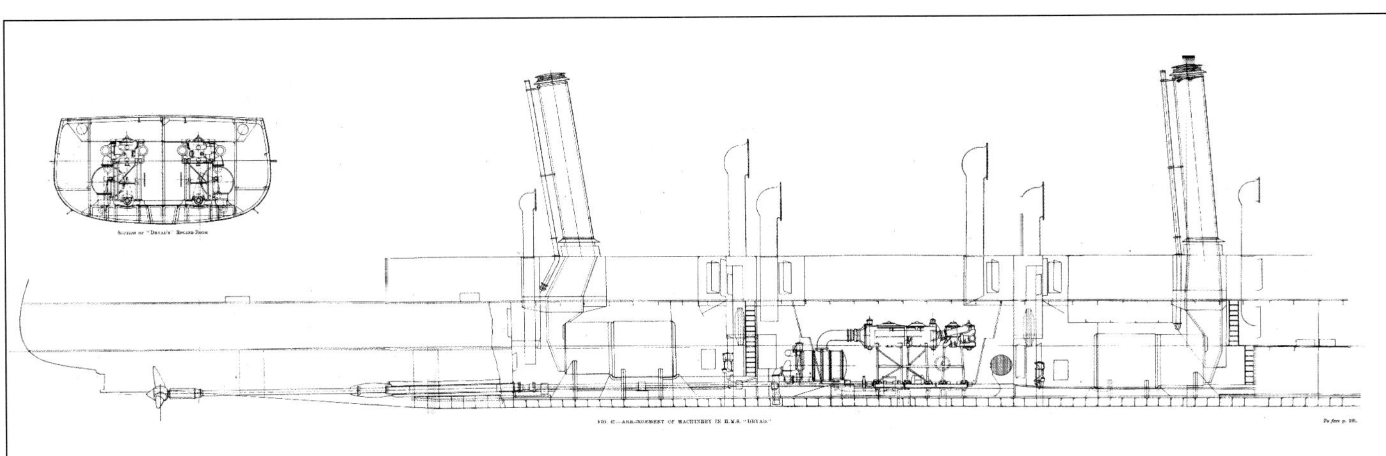

Arrangement of machinery in *Dryad.* (*Torpedoes and Torpedo Vessels*)

CHAPTER NINE

HMS *HECLA* AND HMS *VULCAN*

These two vessels were described officially as torpedo depot ships, ie, ships intended to accompany a torpedo flotilla to sea, carrying on their own deck a number of torpedo boats and their equipment, together with a full complement of stores for mining and countermining. *Vulcan* (see back endpapers and Plate 8) was also fitted as a factory or workshop, in which repairs could be effected to torpedo boats and mines.

Hecla was built and engined by Messrs Harland and Wolff of Belfast for the Atlantic trade in 1878, but subsequently purchased and adapted by the government at a cost of £126,190. Measuring 391.7ft in length by 38.9ft beam, *Hecla* had a displacement of 6,400 tons, on a draught of 24ft 3in. The engines, of 2,260 indicated horsepower, gave a maximum speed of 11.7 knots, and the bunkers held 2,200 tons of coal, allowing a radius of action, at 10 knots, of 26,400 miles. The armament consisted of four 64pdr muzzle-loaders, one 40pdr and one 5in breech-loader, eight machine guns, and four fixed torpedo tubes. She could stow away six second-class torpedo boats and three steam launches for minelaying, and carried some slight protection around her vitals, the machinery and boiler rooms being surrounded by coal armour. During the naval manoeuvres of 1885, *Hecla* accompanied the evolutionary squadron, and proved her *raison d'être* most clearly by repairing the various torpedo boats which came to grief.

In 1912 *Hecla* was rebuilt and re-armed with four 12pdr guns, and operated as a destroyer depot ship. She was sold to Ward of Preston in July 1926 for breaking up.

The first keel plates of *Vulcan* were laid down on 18 June 1888, and on 13 June the following year she was launched from Portsmouth

Hecla photographed early in her career, probably in the mid 1880s. This ship was purchased while building, being originally the merchant ship *British Crown*. The data with the original print lists the ship as carrying eight second-class torpedo boats, thirty Whitehead torpedoes, and five 64pdrs, one 40pdr, six Nordenfelt one-inch and two Gatling guns. *(US Naval History and Heritage Command, NH 88833)*

Hecla, note the torpedo boats on deck. *(US Naval History and Heritage Command, NH 60288)*

Dockyard. Of slightly greater displacement than *Hecla*, 6,620 tons on a mean draught of 23ft, the dimensions of *Vulcan* were length 350ft and beam 58ft. The framing of the hull was exceptionally strong, the stem- and sternposts consisting of large steel castings; the former of which shaped under the waterline into a formidable ram, while the bracket principle was applied within the extent of the double bottom. There was a protective steel deck extending the whole length of the vessel, having a minimum thickness of 2½in, and a maximum thickness of 5in on the slope. The principal armament, consisting of eight 36pdr quick-firing guns, mounted on Vavasseur's central-pivot system, was well protected by shields. These guns were placed in groups, four forward and four aft, on the upper deck, with machine guns fitting the intervening space amidships. On the main deck was a secondary battery of twelve 3pdr rapid-firing guns; and there were four torpedo tubes, two above water at the stem and stern respectively, and two fixed submerged tubes forward. There were also two above-water training tubes on the broadside, and the normal supply of torpedoes was thirty. *Vulcan* had a balanced rudder, which was controlled by hand from the upper deck, and by steam from the tiller compartment, bridge wheelhouse and conning tower. The steam gear was powerful enough to put the helm from hard-over to hard-over, or through an arc of 70 degrees, in the short space of thirty seconds, with the engines working at full speed ahead.

In addition to the usual supply of ship's boats, the vessel carried nine second-class torpedo boats, seven of which were under the direct handling of two powerful hydraulic

Vulcan just after launch. Note dockyard paddle tug alongside. *(Courtesy of the Naval Historical Foundation, Washington, DC, from Album of British Warships. US Naval History and Heritage Command, NH 75970)*

cranes, while the remaining two ran on trolleys into position for launching. Boats especially adapted for laying mines and countermines could be substituted for some of the torpedo boats, when required. The ship was fitted out to serve as a torpedo factory and laboratory, and general store-ship for mining, etc, and every part was well lit by electricity, the engines for which also worked four powerful search lights.

The propellers were rotated by two independent sets of three-cylinder compound engines, by Humphrys, Tennant, and Co, placed vertically in steel frames, the steam being supplied by four double-ended main boilers weighing about 40 tons each, and one single-ended auxiliary boiler, all built of Siemens-Martin steel, with corrugated steel furnaces. Before being accepted from the hands of the contractors, the engines had for four consecutive hours to maintain an indicated horsepower of 12,000 under forced draught, and 7,200 indicated horsepower for twelve hours under natural draught. The maximum speed under forced draught was estimated at 20 knots. The normal coal supply was 1,000 tons, disposed in bunkers in the hold and on the protective deck alongside the engine and boiler rooms, which gave a radius of action of about 12,000 miles at 10 knots, or 3,000 miles at the estimated speed of 18 knots. An additional amount of coal could be stowed in compartments abreast the hold bunkers, if desired.

Immediately after the launch, which was presided over by Mrs Gordon, wife of the Admiral Superintendent, *Vulcan* was taken alongside the wharf where her engines and boilers were standing ready to be lowered into their beds.

It was in the machinery for lifting the boats 'with ease and quickness' that *Vulcan* differed from other vessels of her class – see Appendix 5 for a full description.

Next to her boat-lifting gear, the most novel feature about *Vulcan* was the steam factory she had on board. *Vulcan* could reconstruct torpedo boats, both hull and engines, there being the necessary appliances on board for the purpose. On the upper deck was situated the smithy at the fore end of the deck-houses. In the centre was the principal forge, by Alldays and Onion. It was 3ft by 3ft 6in, which was large enough to do anything necessary for torpedo boat construction. The draught was obtained from a machine fan or by a hand-driven fan. In this department were the usual necessary appliances, such as anvils, vice benches, pipe-bending machinery, and so forth. It was originally proposed laying down a horizontal steam hammer, but it was afterwards thought that this might be too much for the ship, so an hydraulic forging press by Tannett, Walker, and Co was substituted. In this department there were also the necessary appliances for braziers' work.

The principal shop was on the protective deck forward, and there was a Fletcher's patent cupola, the pit for casting being at the side on the slope of the protective deck. Here iron and brass castings could be made of sufficient size for torpedo boat work. The blast for the cupola was obtained from a fan on the bulkhead. The forward boiler funnel served as a chimney. This

An engraving of *Vulcan* from a photograph taken by Mr West of Portsmouth. *(Engineering, 18 November 1892)*

The bow of *Vulcan*, showing the cap of the forward torpedo tube.

room contained the machine tools, consisting of five lathes, two planing machines, two shaping machines, two drilling machines, one slotting machine, one punching and shearing machine, one circular saw, and other necessary appliances. They were driven by a separate engine, the shafting being overhead. In this shop were two pairs of Willans engines, driving two Siemens dynamos of 4,000 amperes (A). There was another similar set of electric light machinery aft below the protective deck.

On the same deck forward on the port side was the capstan engine. In this compartment was the ship's ventilating fan, 4ft in diameter, driven direct by a Brotherhood engine. On the platform deck below was the submerged torpedo room, where the air-compressing machinery was situated. There were two sets of air-compressing engines here by Belliss and Co, and another set aft. There were two air reservoirs, also by Belliss, containing fifty tubes each. The pressure went up to 1,70psi. Either compressor could charge either reservoir, the whole being interchangeable in all ways.

There were two submerged torpedo tubes with shield bar and impulse gear of the service pattern. The torpedo was held by the bar until clear of the ship, so as to prevent it being deflected by the rush of the ship through the water – before it was clear of the port. The submerged torpedo tubes were very solid masses of brass. The tube with shield bar and impulse gear was composed of 5 tons 13cwt of brass, the sluice valve in the ship's side through which the torpedo passes weighed 1 ton 3cwt. These were made at Chatham. When it is remembered that the shield bar was made to protrude for a distance of 9ft at right angles from the side of the ship, and was designed to hold the torpedo up in a line with its course when the ship was going 20 knots, it will be seen that something solid was required. The bow and stern torpedo tubes were of ordinary construction, and very similar to those fitted in torpedo boats. They were fixed in the structure of the vessel, and therefore to direct the torpedo on a given course the ship had to manoeuvre. There were, however, two training torpedo guns in the waist. They were above water and pivoted in the side of the ship by a ball-and-socket arrangement. The full complement of torpedoes which the ship could carry was thirty, below the platform deck.

Another notable feature about *Vulcan* was the equipment carried for laying minefields. Below the platform deck, and under the machine shop, was the mine room. The mines were about 1,200lb in weight, and nearly 5ft high, and stood in racks, with an overhead railway for shifting them from part to part. There was a second mine room aft, a total of eighty-four mines being carried. Below the platform deck were also the small mining stores and magazines. Next were the hatchway of the main magazines and also to the small arms magazines.

Abaft the engine room on the platform deck was the hydraulic pumping room. The hydraulic machinery for working the boat derrick was aft. In the hydraulic room were two sets of air-compressing machinery by Belliss, the same as in the submerged torpedo room. In each of these hydraulic rooms there was also a 4ft fan with a Brotherhood engine, with another in the front room for ventilating forward. In the starboard hydraulic room was one of three war dynamos, placed below the protective deck. Under the hydraulic pumps were the suction tanks, built into and forming part of the structure of the ship. The steering engine was by Forrester, and was connected direct to the rudder head.

Vulcan carried the following boats: six second-class torpedo boats, a 53ft vidette boat, a 40ft steam pinnace, and a 30ft steam cutter. The boats not fitted with steam machinery were two 42ft mining launches, two 28ft cutters, one 36ft pinnace, one 27ft whaleboat, one 30ft gig, one 20ft gig, and two 14ft dinghies.

Vulcan was fitted with two sets of triple-expansion engines capable of exerting 6,000 indicated horsepower each, when working under forced draught, with an air pressure in stokehold equal to 2in of water; the combined weight of the machinery was about 1,100 tons. The sizes of cylinders to each set of engines were 40in, 59in, and 88in by 4ft 3in stroke, making 100 revolutions per minute at full power. There was a brass condenser for each set of engines, with 6,750sq ft of cooling surface to each condenser, and four sets (two spare) of circulating pumps for circulating water through the condenser, which could also pump from the bilge in case of a leak at the rate of 2,000 tons per hour collectively. There were four large double-ended boilers 14ft in diameter by 16ft 9in long for driving the main engines, and one smaller boiler 12ft 3in in diameter by 9ft 3in long for working auxiliary engines. The working pressure was 155psi above atmosphere. The boilers were fitted with corrugated furnaces with 655sq ft of fire-grate, and constructed of steel throughout. The auxiliary engines comprised two bilge pumps, two fire engines, two main feed engines, two auxiliary feed engines, steering engine, four sets of air-compressing engines and pumps, each set capable of compressing 20cu ft of air to a pressure of 1,700psi in seventeen minutes, with 90lb of steam pressure, three electric light

The workshop on board HMS *Vulcan*. *(Navy & Army Illustrated, 7 August 1896)*

A photograph of *Vulcan* taken on 5 December 1903, clearly showing the two large cranes.

engines, 400A and 80V each, two double distillers capable of producing 300 gallons of pure secondary water per hour collectively, capstan engine, workshop engine driving the machine tools, two steam pumping engines for hydraulic service, two 20-ton cranes, Fairbairn type, and eight fan engines for producing air pressure.

In 1892 alterations were made to the boilers, and in March 1893 she underwent trials of her machinery at the full forced draught pressure which the boilers were originally designed to withstand. The alterations consisted of fitting the new Admiralty ferrule to the tubes at the combustion chamber ends, replacing the tubes which had been removed, with the idea of improving the circulation of the water among the tubes, and giving it free access to the tube plates, and in lengthening the grates which had been reduced to prevent overheating.

A preliminary run was made on Friday, 10 March to test the adjustments of the machinery, and to see that all was in working order, a necessary precaution seeing that the ship had been laid up in reserve for a period of over fifteen months. *Vulcan* left the dockyard jetty at 9am, and by ten o'clock was so far clear of the harbour as to allow of 'Full speed' to be ordered. The air fans were adjusted to give a pressure of about 1.5in of water in the stokeholds, and at 10.20am the engines were developing upwards of 11,800hp, with 98½ revolutions. It was not considered advisable to open out too suddenly, considering the length of time the ship had been laid up, and consequently the engines were kept at about this power for the first half-hour of the trial. The speed of the air fans was then increased until a pressure of over 2in of water was steadily maintained in the stokeholds, the revolutions of the engines gradually increasing as the steam pressure went up, until at the end of the first hour about 102 was attained, the horsepower developed being 12,550. From this time to the end of the four hours' trial the working of the machinery and boilers was all that could be desired, the steam being steadily maintained, the engines working smoothly, and the required power obtained by slight alterations in the speed of the air fans, the ultimate result of the four hours' run being 12,032hp, 99.6 revolutions, 1.8in air pressure in the stokeholds, mean pressure of steam in boilers 148lb, 26.5in vacuum in the condensers, and the speed of the ship 20.2 knots per hour.

Subsequent examination of the boilers showed them to be quite sound and tight, the ferrules being quite uninjured. The grate surface was now 545sq ft, and the heating surface 19,160sq ft, the power developed being therefore 22hp per square foot of grate, and 627 per square foot of heating surface.

In 1902 she was reboilered and later became a submarine depot ship, during which time in 1915 her 4.7in guns were removed and four 3pdrs added. In February 1931 she became a training hulk, *Defiance III*, and survived until sold for breaking up in Belgium in December 1955.

APPENDIX ONE

EXPERIMENTAL CRUISE OF TORPEDO FLOTILLA

In April 1887 flotillas of torpedo boats were commissioned at their respective yards, and formed at Portland, with *Rattlesnake* as flagship and *Seahorse* as depot ship, for an experimental cruise of fourteen days.

The flotilla consisted of sixteen Thornycroft, four of Yarrow's and three of White's boats of 125ft in length, and *TB81*, built by White, of 150ft in length as leader, making a total of twenty-three boats of 125ft in length, one of 150ft in length, and *Rattlesnake*.

The object of the cruise was to give the officers and men thorough practice in handling the boats under various conditions, performing manoeuvres at different speeds, to test the efficiency of the several types of vessels, and to work out the following points, as far as circumstances would permit.

1. The efficiency of the arrangements made for commissioning, and the supply of stores.
2. The best formation for cruising day and night under all circumstances.
3. The best interval between boats and columns, and the best means of preserving station, regulating speed, and communicating changes of course, especially with men under cover.
4. The highest speed that can be maintained under various circumstances of sea and weather whilst keeping station.
5. The greatest number of boats that can be safely manoeuvred together in the dark without lights.
6. The best formation for attack.
7. On ships at anchor.
8. On ships under weigh, and also to force the manoeuvre.
9. On ships under weigh but more or less confined by narrow channels.
10. The best method of signalling by day and night, and what signals are necessary.
11. Sea-going qualities, habitability, and actual coal endurance at cruising speed.
12. Comparison of loss of speed in a moderate seaway with that of *Rattlesnake* and *TB81*, and also compare relative behaviour of different patterns of boats.
13. The value and disadvantages of bow tubes, including a comparison of the accuracy of the right ahead with broadside practice at high speed.
14. The average accuracy of the torpedo practice under service conditions at a measured range and target.
15. The deterioration of the torpedo from being kept in the boats, and the best means of testing and re-adjusting them.
16. The efficiency of all the gear connected with the tubes, including firing arrangement and director.
17. Effect of rolling on the practice.
18. Accuracy of practice with quick-firing gun at high speed in smooth water and at sea.
19. Use of electric search light in torpedo boats.

During this fortnight the boats were constantly exercised night and day in manoeuvring in large and small groups at different speeds, attacking *Rattlesnake* and ships at Portland under different conditions, running full-speed trials, and exercising firing guns and torpedoes.

On the termination of the fourteen days, the boats returned to their respective ports, and were kept ready in the Reserve to take part in the review and subsequent manoeuvres, with the exception of *TB72* and *TB35*, which were employed in working out the different points raised as regards accuracy of practice with torpedoes, etc, of which fuller details are given later.

As regards the different points to be elucidated in this cruise, the following short extracts from the report will show the general opinion of the value of these boats.

1. Commissioning the boats

Considering this was the first attempt at commissioning so large a number of boats, and that everybody was new to the work, the result was satisfactory, and will probably be improved upon on future occasions.

It appears that probably the time required to commission 28 boats will, with the existing arrangement, be about three times as long as to commission 8 boats, and so on in proportion.

It is most important that the indents be supplied immediately the boats commission, and that they contain only a list of articles actually put on board the boats.

Other defects in the arrangements noticed in commissioning these boats were:

Lay apart store inconveniently situated.
Stores too much scattered, and depot ships lying too far off the boats, causing much delay and inconvenience.
Stores placed on board before commissioning have to be accepted without survey.
No information supplied to the officer in command as regards stowage, valves, tanks, steering powers, &c. As regards this point, drawings of each boat, showing these details, will, in future be supplied on commissioning.

2. Best formation for cruising

Line ahead in columns of divisions when the number of boats does not exceed 16, after which flotilla order in squadrons of 8 boats each in the same formation.

3. Best interval between boats and means of communication

'Close order', that is, boats one boat's length apart from stem to stern in column and columns two boats' lengths apart, in fine weather, up to 12 knots speed.

'Open order', that is, boats three boats' length apart in column, and columns four boats' lengths apart in rough weather or at full speed.

This, however, depends on the nature of the manoeuvres it is intended to perform. In this flotilla only oblique movements were used; if rectangular movements are gone through, the columns must naturally be twice as many boats' lengths apart as there are boats in the longest column, which with a number of boats is undesirable, except for display. The best means of preserving station is found to be eye judgement, for regulating speed, the stop and throttle valves, though at low speed small alterations of speed are very difficult, and in Yarrow's boats without a circulating pump it is difficult to increase speed suddenly.

The best means of communicating changes of speed and course appears to be the whistle, but for night work two lanterns with coloured shades have been recommended for signalling purposes. It is not considered of much use to keep the men under cover except at the moment of attack, as there is little if any protection from anything except rifle fire.

4. Full speed can be safely maintained in open order in smooth water, and 12 knots in moderate weather, and it is not considered advisable to force them against a head sea.

5. Eight boats is the greatest number that it is desirable to work together at night without lights.

6. *Best formation for attack*

a) On ships at anchor: boats in pairs, in close order in line ahead, seems the best formation; though for boats armed with guns quarter line offers some advantages, but is more difficult to maintain. The distribution of the boats must depend greatly on the circumstances of each attack, but when possible an attack should be made from different directions, the boats approaching at moderate speed so as not to betray their presence by sparks or bow wave, full speed being reserved for the moment of discovery. If the channels of approach are restricted, it is hardly probable that an attack by the torpedo boats alone would be successful, but the assistance of rams is required (supported by boats armed with guns to protect them from guard boats), which would sweep away the enemy's net defences previous to the attack by the torpedo boats. Tide should be with, and wind against, the boats, if possible.
b) Against ships under weigh and free to manoeuvre, a squadron of boats should endeavour to surround the enemy so as to compel her to approach some of them bows on, the boats working in pairs. It would be

exceedingly hazardous, and would offer little chance of success in the daytime, except with a very large number of boats possessing a great superiority of speed over the enemy, but at night the chances of success would be much greater; but the difficulty of finding an enemy without lights is very great, and close quarters would be necessary for accurate torpedo practice on a dark night, against a ship under weigh.

c) When the enemy is confined in narrow channels over the edges of which boats can manoeuvre, the chances of a successful attack are greater and the boats should spread in pairs, so as to make attacks ahead and on the bow at a convenient moment. Unless aided by rain or thick weather, it is not probable that they could do so during the day, but at night they would have a decided advantage under these circumstances.

7. *Signals*

For day, flags semaphores, and whistles are efficient; for night, fixed and flashing coloured lights, Very's lights and whistles have been found to answer well.

The want of a proper boat's signal book suitable for manoeuvring torpedo boats has been much felt, but it is anticipated that the auxiliary signal book now under preparation will meet future requirements. During the cruises this year, instructions and signals somewhat on the following lines were used, and at the termination of the summer manoeuvres the following instructions and signals were drawn up by *Vernon* and forwarded to the Signal Committee, as a code which would be suitable for the manoeuvring of these boats. At the same time a pattern lantern with red, white and green shades, and flashing arrangement has been prepared by *Vernon* as a pattern lamp for night signalling in torpedo boats; and it has been submitted that two of these lamps be supplied to every torpedo and picket boat in the service

Instructions for conduct of Flotilla

1. The rule of the road is always to be observed to avoid collisions, except as between boats and ships, when the former are cruising at night without lights, in which case they get out of the way of ships.
2. A look-out is to be kept on the leading boat, if she makes any movement without signal, the other boats of the flotilla are to regulate themselves thereby, in order to keep their appointed stations. It is to be borne in mind that the safety of the boats composing the flotilla depends in a great measure on accurate station keeping, and the greatest care is to be taken on this point.
3. Should any boat find that she is unable to keep her proper station, she is not to persist too long in endeavouring to do so, but is to haul out of line and form astern of her own division, doing all she can to keep up with the remainder of the flotilla, without in any way exposing herself.
4. In a fog, or at night, when it is necessary to ascertain one another's whereabouts, the boats are to sound their fleet numbers on their steam or mouth whistles, following in succession the motions of their leader.
5. Manoeuvres will be performed obliquely, or at unequal speeds, unless contrary orders are given.
6. Boats altering course together are invariably to preserve their compass bearing and distances, being guided by the movements of the boats towards which they are to turn to avoid fouling.
7. Boats altering course in succession are invariably to preserve formation. When a large turn has to be made, following boats should be careful not to turn inside of the next ahead.
8. The columns on that side to which the turn is being made will reduce speed as requisite, but not below 6 knots, and the others will increase speed until all have come round to the point required, each boat following in its leader's wake.
9. Way should always be kept on boats.
10. When manoeuvring, Yarrow boats (except *TB79* and *TB80*, which are a new pattern) should give full helm, other boats regulating helm and speed as requisite to turn on similar arcs.
11. No boats to pass through a column.
12. Close order signifies boats in column to be one boat's length apart from hull to hull. Open order three boats' lengths apart.
13. When cruising at night without lights, squadrons of boats will invariably form in columns of divisions in line ahead, columns

two boat lengths apart and boats in close order, senior column on the right. Alterations of course short of 8 points will be made by whistle; all alterations of speed by whistle.

Signals

The flotilla will be organised by Fleet numbers as usual. Boats will be denoted by their official numbers as pendants, the numeral pendant being used for 0, church pendant as 1st substitute, and answering pendant for 2nd substitute. The Army and Navy Signal Book will be used.

Pendants used either singly or in combination with flags for general purposes –

1. Compass, *over* numeral flags: Alter course together to Starboard, number of points indicated.
   Compass, *under* numeral flags: Alter course together to Port together, number of points indicated.

Note. The above signals only apply up to 16 points, and the compass table must be altered, compass 17 being N, and so on consecutively by East and South, to West and North.

2. Repeat.
3. Organisation: When hoisted with numeral flags indicates number of divisions flotilla is to be organised in.
   With blue burgee: Flotilla is to be organised in squadrons – Each division of previously existing organisation will then become a squadron; its subdivisions becoming divisions and being sub-divided by rule.
   If hoisted with 'negative' existing organisation is annulled.
4. *Special* Pendant *over* Numeral Flag: Alter course *in succession* to *Starboard,* the number of points indicated.
   Special Pendant under Numeral Flag: Alter course *in succession* to *Port,* the number of points indicated.
5. Rendezvous in case of parting company when shown with signals from local table.
6. Military.
7. Horary, but used as in general signal book.
8. Close) When hoisted with divisional flags, direct columns to open
9. Open) or close two boats' lengths each time.

Note. Open or close pendant singly, indicates boats in column are to open or close each other by one boat's length.

Numeral pendant: When hoisted with alphabetical flags, A, B, or C, denotes relative bearing of guides of columns.

Answering: Substitute for 2nd pendant, as when required to make 100 (or 63 + 37) pendants.

Church: Speed pendant when hoisted with numeral flags indicates speed in knots Fleet are to proceed at. Singly at sea – Man overboard. By Senior Officer – Have anchored. Also substitute for upper pendant.

Single Flag Signal

To be obeyed as soon as seen, as they may be kept flying for a continuance. For corresponding night signals see below.

Flag signal	Signification
1	Attack enemy ships.
2	Retire.
3	Chase
4	General recall.
5	Keep enemy in sight.
6	Attack enemy ships.
7	Disabled (defect to be indicated at once).
8	Enemy is in sight.
9	Prevent enemy escaping.
0	Get up steam for full speed and prepare to attack.

Fog Signals

Will be made with syrenette, as ordinary flashing signals.

Manoeuvring Signals

To be obeyed when hauled down.
Single flags for general purposes as usual, but in addition.
D. Addresses Commanders of Divisions or Squadrons.
Signal Flags to be used to denote Forming Orders for Torpedo Boats.

1 Line A Ahead
2 Divisions B Abreast
3 Sub-divisions C Quarter Line

Alphabetical superior to Starboard.
Alphabetical inferior to Port.
Columns to be two boats' lengths apart.
Special pendant over blue burgee, assume flotilla order.

Note. Flotilla order is Flag Ship in centre and Squadrons disposed as follows:

I. Four cables on Starboard beam of flag.
II. Four cables on Port beam of flag.

III. Four cables Astern beam of flag.
IV. Four cables Ahead beam of flag.

When in flotilla order, alterations of course are invariably to be made by Flag and Squadron Commanders together, but boats of Squadrons are to alter in succession, thus preserving formation of each Squadron.

If desired to increase distance apart of Squadrons, or the reverse, the open and close pendant will be shewn with D, signifying a change of distance of one cable each time. Bearings and distances of Flag and Commanders of Squadrons being invariably preserved.

Whistle Sounds

In all alterations of course, whether made by signal or not, the whistles are to be used as follows, either by day or night. (NB New pattern whistle.)

On Round end of Whistle.

Two shorts, I am directing my course to Port.
One short, I am directing my course to Starboard.

When the boat is in her course, the leader gives the opposite sign to signify steady.

On Flat end of Whistle.

Long blast, I am decreasing speed.
Succession of long and short, I am increasing speed.

On either end of the Whistle. *Succession of shorts*, Stop at once.

On Steam Whistle, 3 blasts, I am going astern.

Night Signals

Night Signals will be made at night by:

1. Ordinary Flashing Signals by Light.	Executive signal for signals made with flashing lights as in General Signal Book; those made with Very's Lights are to be executed when last light goes out; those by fixed coloured light goes out; those by fixed coloured
2. By Fixed Coloured Lights or Very's Lights.	

Rocket and Blue Light – Disabled.
Two Rockets – Lost the Flotilla.
Blue Light and Blank Cartridge – Man overboard.

Style of Signal	Night Signal By Very Lights	By Coloured Lamps	Corresponding Flag Signal	Specification
Single coloured lights or I Very light. Usual formation signals, lights to be kept burning as guide to next astern.	I White	I White	I. A.	Single column line ahead.
	I Red	I Red	2. A.	Columns of divisional line ahead to port.
	I Green	I Green	A. 2.	Columns of divisional line ahead to starboard.
		Light Extinguished	81	Out lights, preserve formation.
Single lights flashed.		I White flashed	–	Ordinary flashing signal.
Preparative signals.		I Red flashed	8	Enemy is in sight.
		I Green flashed	0	Prepare to attack.
Enemy signals, 2 lights of same colour.		2 Reds	I	Attack enemy's ships.
		2 Reds (Upper one flashed.)	7	Attack enemy's boats.
		2 Greens	2	Retire.
		2 Greens (Upper one flashed.)	9	Prevent enemy escaping.
		2 Whites	3	Chase.
		2 Whites (Upper one flashed.)	5	Keep enemy in sight.
Usual signals required when cruising. 2 lights of different colours or 2 Very's lights.	Red, White	Red over White	123	Anchor instantly.
	Red, Green	Red over Green	99	Stop engines.
	Green, White	Green over White	129	Weigh.
	Green, Red	Green over Red	–	Proceed to rendezvous.
	White, Red	White over Red	16 4 pt.	Alter course in succession 16 points to port.
	White, Green	White over Green	4 pt. 16	Alter course in succession 16 points to starboard.
Usual signals required when cruising, but of less importance. 2 lights of different colours, the upper ne being flashed or 3 Very's lights.	White, Red, White	White over Red (White flashed)	8 4 pt.	Alter course in succession 8 points to port.
	White, Green, White	White over Green (Green flashed)	4 pt. 8	Alter course in succession 8 points to starboard.
	Red, White, Red	Red over White (Red flashed)	–	Make fast to buoy or or jetty.
	Red, Green, Red	Red over Green (Red flashed)	–	Proceed dead slow.
	Green, Red, Green	Green over Red (Green flashed)	157	Next astern come within hail.
	Green, White, Green	Green over White (Green flashed)	–	Prepare to get under weigh.
	Red, White, Green		4	General recall.

Night Signals for Torpedo Boats

Night Signals proposed with 2 lamps on ensign staff, fitted with Red, White, and Green shades, and flashing arrangement, according to pattern lamp prepared in *Vernon*, with corresponding signals by Very's Lights, which may be used when concealment is no object.

A pattern lamp has been ordered to be sent to Admiralty, and the system, or some modification of it, will probably be approved of for torpedo boat signalling.

Private Signals proposed between boats and boats, or boats and ships in war time

A single sign of 5 or more characters, flashed by ordinary flashing light, to be answered by another sign of similar number of characters.

Thus - —- —- - - —- Challenge.

—- - - —- —- Answer.

Sea-going Qualities and Coal Endurance

8. The sea-going qualities of the boats, if not overladen and managed with judgement, are good; but the men's mess deck in rough weather soon becomes unfit for habitation, rendering the boats unsuited for making voyages with a fleet, though they are very suited for coast and harbour defence.

The coal consumption at full speed appears to be – White's, 25 cwt per hour; Thornycroft's and Yarrow's 19 cwt; and at a speed of 12 knots, the usual cruising speeds, varies, in all the boats tried, from 5 to 7 cwt per hour, but the supply of fresh water to the boilers seems insufficient in all the boats.

Loss of Speed and behaviour in a seaway

9. A very moderate sea makes it undesirable to exceed 10 knots, *TB81*, of 150ft in length, having a slight superiority, whereas the *Rattlesnake* is not affected by a moderate sea, as though wet where going against it, has ample protection from water entering, and strength to withstand the shock of sea.

The advantages gained by the Thornycroft's boats from their fine entrance, and not having stem tubes, is very marked: the other boats, especially Yarrow's, throwing up so much water and spray as to make them very conspicuous and uncomfortable. The White's boats, in a heavy sea, would probably be better than the others, owing to their increased beam and stability.

Torpedo Practice

10, 11, and 14. This is dealt with later.

Deterioration of Torpedoes

12. No deterioration has been observed from keeping the torpedoes in their tubes, but excessive practice has been found to have a slight effect on the depth keeping of the Fiume torpedoes, owing to the wear of the numerous bearings of the diving rod, and the inferior quality of metal used in the construction of their internal parts.

It has, however, been proposed that in future, when the boats are commissioned for exercise, that only two torpedoes be supplied for practice.

The best means of testing and adjusting torpedoes is by using them from the stem tube (where fitted) at slow speed.

Efficiency of Tubes

13. As a rule the fittings of the tubes and gear is satisfactory, but, in a few instances, defective trippers, clamping gear, training gear and firing gear, have caused accidents to torpedoes and failures in practice.

15. The practice from the Nordenfelt machine guns and 3-pounder quick-firing guns is described as good; better practice being made end on than on the broadside.

16. The electric search lights are useful for searching out or reconnoitring a harbour and for signal purposes but the beams from two boats should not be crossed at distances over 500 yards for efficiently illuminating the entrances to a port, on account of the small power of the lights.

In addition to the above points, which had to be specially reported on, it was also noticed:

1. That each boat should have a week's cruise independently before joining a flotilla, to give the crew a chance of becoming thoroughly acquainted with their vessel, and that the commissioning trials of her torpedoes should never be omitted, as, owing to there being no means of effecting repairs on board, it is very important to test everything well before starting.

2. That the depot ship should be supplied with steam boats for facility of communication between her and the different boats.
3. That wherever boats are to be stationed in war times, suitable cambers or wharves, with convenient coaling and watering places, should be prepared.
4. That the engine-room staff should be increased by one leading stoker, and that more training is necessary than the majority of these men get in torpedo boat work, and that the deck hands should be trained to perform stokehold duties.
5. That it is highly desirable to keep a number of these boats in constant use at the home ports, commissioning them, and exercising their crews in all their duties during the training-brig cruising season.
6. Two signalmen should be borne in the boats of the divisional leaders.
7. Staff necessary for the officer in command of a large flotilla, in addition to the depot paymaster and his staff, should be:
   1 signal officer
   1 clerk or writer
   1 fleet or staff-engineer
   1 assistant-engineer
   1 carpenter or skilled carpenter's mate.
   and a proportion of spare hands should be attached to the depot ship, to take the place of sick men, especially as regards the engine-room department.
8. It is very desirable that the depot ship be an improved *Hecla*, and not a makeshift without any torpedo appliances, and that the depot staff be appointed four clear days before the boat's commission.
9. That the kit of officers and men be clearly laid down in the instructions, so as to ensure uniformity.

As a result of the cruises during the year, the following improvements in the fittings of the boats will be carried out.

Yarrow's Boats: A small deck wheel fitted; bunkers floored with steel instead of wooden plates, which have occasionally caught fire; steering gear improved as regards leads of chain; chart locker to be fitted.

Thornycroft's Boats: Deck wheel fitted, so that it can be used from both foremost and after conning tower.

White's Boats: Chart locker to be fitted; ventilation of engine-room improved; handles of water-tight doors improved.

In All Boats: Standard compass fitted with azimuth circle and aneroid barometer supplied. Magazine doors strengthened.

The following improvements have also been recommended, and are under consideration:

Yarrow's boats to be fitted with circulating pump for surface condenser, and small pump for carrying the condensed steam back to the boiler. Signal lockers to be near the mast.

Two special lamps, with red and green shades, to be supplied for signal purposes.

The method of keeping the store accounts in torpedo boats is, however, still under consideration, and will probably be still further simplified.

TRIAL OF BOW FIRE IN A SEAWAY

TB35 and *TB72* were specially commissioned to carry out practice in a seaway, and were dispatched to Portland for this purpose, it being considered a more favourable locality for this practice than Portsmouth. After waiting a long time for a favourable opportunity, during which other equally important experiments were carried out, three runs were obtained in a rough sea and long heavy swell, the stem tube being used on each occasion to fire a Mark V RL torpedo.

One run was obtained from each type of boat (White's and Yarrow's), steaming 14 knots against the sea, the boats pitching heavily, and the torpedoes being fired at the moment when the bows were completely immersed in a wave.

Both torpedoes ran well, with a 3oz charge for impulse, keeping their depth and passing 20 yards right and under the target respectively, at a range of 450 yards, and were recovered uninjured.

One run was then obtained from the Yarrow boat, *TB72*, with the same torpedo, at 13 knots, with 3oz impulse, with the sea abeam. The torpedo, which was discharged as the boat rolled heavily to starboard, just came to the surface, owing to the high impulse, took its depth again and ran well, passing about 10 yards to the left of the target in a 400 yards range.

No opportunity was obtained for similar practice from the revolving tubes, the boats had to return to Portsmouth to take part in the Naval

Review but it can be safely deduced from these experiments that the torpedoes can be discharged and be expected to run well in any weather in which it is likely that the boats will be called upon to use them.

ACCURACY OF PRACTICE FROM REVOLVING TUBES

Whilst waiting for an opportunity to carry out the above-named trials, the boats were employed running their torpedoes to ascertain the general accuracy that might be expected from these boats. For this purpose, at least three consecutive runs were made from each position with a well-adjusted torpedo, at a target 100 yards long, conspicuously marked every ten yards, the range being 400 yards, and the boats proceeding at high speed. The deflection used was that which previous running from a Thornycroft's boat had proved to give good practice, and was not altered during the three runs, the object being to ascertain if it was constant, and also to calculate it for future practice for each type of boat. Unfortunately, the faulty fitting of the compressors in some of the positions of training rather spoilt the results from them, as the recoil of the tubes was so great as to reduce the velocity of discharge and render the deflection erratic. The results are briefly as follows: the boats running at full speed from 15 to 17 knots.

Yarrow boat, *TB72*.

70° before the beam – All three shots passed within two yards of the same spot at 400 yards, being deflected 10°.

40° before the beam – Nine out of ten shots made passed within 20 yards of the same spot, being deflected 16°.

Abeam – Three shots at same spot being deflected 15°.

20° before the beam – Two out of three shots at same place being deflected 20°, the third shot not being deflected quite so much.

20° abaft the beam – Three shots within 15 yards of the same place, with 8° deflection.

70° abaft the beam – Torpedoes deflected forward about 5°, and ran to same place, but the forward deflection is attributed to faulty compressors allowing the tube to jump.

White's boat, *TB35*.

The compressors in this boat were very faulty, but the tubes were lashed to assist them, and when they did not kick the results were very good; at 70° abaft the beam three runs passed within five yards of each other, with no deflection.

In positions where the stop on the turret took the recoil instead of the compressors, the results were:

Abeam – Three out of five runs at same spot, with 20° deflection, one deflecting less.

20° abaft the beam – Four out of five shots within 25 yards of each other, with 12° deflection; fifth shot bad and unaccounted for.

From these experiments, it is evident that, with properly fitted tubes, very accurate practice can be made, if the right deflection is allowed, and which may be taken to be as in the following Table, for a speed of 15 knots.

Training of tube	White	Yarrow	Thornycroft
70° before the beam	10	10	10
40° before the beam	16	16	15
20° before the beam	12	20	20
Abeam	15	15	15
20° abaft the beam	12	10	10
70° abaft the beam	0	0	0

APPENDIX TWO

DISPOSITION OF FIRST-CLASS TORPEDO BOATS

The 1883 annual report from *Vernon* stated that eight vessels were stationed overseas: *TB7* and *TB8* in Gibraltar; *TB9*, *TB10*, *TB11* and *TB17* in Malta; *TB18* and *TB20* at Hong Kong.

The 1884 report gave the disposition of the nineteen boats in commission as: *TB1* at *Vernon*; *TB2* and *TB5* at Devonport; *TB3*, *TB13* and *TB19* at Portsmouth; *TB4* at Chatham; *TB6* and *TB15* at the Cape of Good Hope; *TB7* and *TB18* at Gibraltar; *TB8* and *TB20* at Hong Kong; *TB9*, *TB10*, *TB11* and *TB17* at Malta; *TB12* at Portsmouth and *TB14* at Chatham, both preparing to move to Bermuda.

In 1886 *TB1* was still attached to *Vernon* but was considered only suitable for harbour service. Likewise, *TB2* and *TB5* remained at Devonport where both were operational. *TB3* and *TB19* also remained at Portsmouth but the condition of *TB19* was 'doubtful', and *TB13* had moved to Devonport, attached to torpedo school ship *Defiance*. *TB4* at Chatham was at fourteen days' notice, but *TB6* to *TB11*, *TB15* to *TB18* and *TB20* were all operational and remained at the same overseas stations as two years previously. *TB12* and *TB14* were both in Portsmouth where they were to be tried with oil fuel and a Nordenfelt smoke consumer, respectively. *TB21* and *TB22* had joined the force at Malta, but the other new boats were in Great Britain, some still being completed and some undergoing rebuilding of their bows.

In 1890 concern was expressed at the small number of boats available for use in the United Kingdom – seven at Portsmouth (*TBs 3*, *19*, *23*, *25*, *41*, *42* and *75*); nine at Plymouth (*TBs 2*, *24*, *34*, *45*, *51*, *52*, *53*, *54* and *55*); ten at Sheerness (*TBs 4*, *12*, *63*, *64*, *65*, *67*, *68*, *72*, *73* and *74*); and none at either Chatham or Pembroke. *TB1*, *TB5*, *TB13* and *TB14* were only suitable for instructional purposes, the last two being based at Plymouth and Portsmouth, respectively. Overseas, there were nine boats in Malta (*TBs 9*, *10*, *11*, *21*, *22*, *43*, *44*, *46* and *56*); four in Gibraltar (*TBs 7*, *46*, *48* and *70*); six in Hong Kong (*TBs 8*, *20*, *35*, *36*, *37* and *38*), four at the Cape of Good Hope (*TBs 6*, *15*, *28* and *29*); two in Esquimalt (*TBs 39* and *40*); four in Bermuda (*TBs 30*, *31*, *32* and *69*); and two in Halifax (*TBs 61* and *62*). *TB26* and *TB27* were at Chatham, awaiting orders to move to Jamaica. *TB17* and *TB18* were only suitable for instructional purposes, and were stationed in Malta and Gibraltar, respectively.

In addition, *TBs 49*, *50*, *66*, *71*, *76*, *77*, *78*, *79*, *80*, *81*, *82*, *83*, *84* and *85* were at Portsmouth, and *TBs 57*, *58*, *59*, *60*, *86* and *87* were at Plymouth, all ready for mobilisation.

Of the ten new boats delivered during 1895, six were sent to Gibraltar (*TBs 88*, *89*, *91*, *92*, *93* and *97*), increasing the total stationed there to eleven. The distribution of the others remained similar to that in 1890, but six boats (*TBs 100*, *102*, *103*, *104*, *105* and *106*) moved to Bombay, and *TB101* to Calcutta.

Prior to the manoeuvres of 1899, those torpedo boats destined to participate, together with three torpedo gunboats, gathered together at the torpedo school ship, *Defiance*, at Devonport, for exercises. They formed into three divisions of eight boats, each under the command of one of the gunboats, and were divided into six sub-divisions –

1st Division	2nd Division	3rd Division
Gossamer	Spanker	Jason
TB83, TB63, TB64, TB65	*TB81, TB71, TB76, TB77*	*TB86, TB52, TB53, TB55*
TB74, TB68, TB72, TB73	*TB84, TB66, TB79, TB42*	*TB45, TB57, TB58, TB49*

101 torpedoes were successfully fired at fixed targets and 49 at moving targets. There were 24 lost shots due to torpedo defects and 12 due to drill errors.

APPENDIX THREE

COMPARATIVE TRIALS OF SECOND-CLASS TORPEDO BOATS

Comparative and exhaustive trials took place during 1888 with four second-class torpedo boats of the latest designs by different builders, with a view to determining the best form of boat.

The boats tried were *TB12*, wood, a 56ft turnabout boat, built by White of Cowes; *TB19* and *TB50*, second-class steel torpedo boats, built by Yarrow; and *TB99*, second-class steel torpedo boat, built by Thornycroft.

The boats were principally tried to compare:

a) Sea-going qualities and handiness;
b) Speed;
c) Armament;
d) Strength to withstand rough usage;
   which, together with length, stability, and especially displacement and weight of armament, are points of great importance in a boat which has to be hoisted in and out of a seagoing vessel.

Details of *TB69*, which may be taken as a pattern of the old type, have also been included, though she was not subjected to any further trials, which were principally carried out with *TB49*, *TB50* and *TB12*, wood.

(a) Seagoing qualities and handiness

TB49 and *TB50* present the following peculiarities: Their deadwood is cut away, and the keel rises aft for nearly one-third of their length the rudder is large with a low centre of effort, the lower blade of the propeller being below the rudder. The screws are right-handed.

The boats turn very rapidly, especially to port, and can be steered fairly well when going astern, except in a strong breeze, but they are not so handy going astern as *TB12*, turnabout boat, whose peculiarities are well known; nor as *TB99*, with Thornycroft's twin rudders.

In *TB49* and *TB50*, a great heel occurs if the helm be righted suddenly after being hard over at speed, especially when under port helm, and this is, perhaps, the only serious defect in the design of the boat. This heel can, however, be avoided, by righting the helm gradually. They have also a slight list to port in smooth water at high speeds owing to the thrust of the propeller, and heel to the wind, being high out of the water.

These points are against good practice with the revolving tube, necessitating careful management just before discharging the torpedoes.

Their greatest beam is at the water line, which is objectionable in boats which have to lie alongside ships or jetties.

They are also very fine forward, which causes heavy pitching in a seaway, but reduces the spray thrown up to a minimum.

Their seagoing qualities are good, especially when going head to sea, when they are comparatively dry to *TB99*, and can be steered conveniently, but when running they steer rather unsteadily.

TB99 behaves well in a seaway, except for the dense clouds of spray thrown up by the bluff bow, which render it almost impossible to steer in a moderate seaway. The open stern sheets with which she is fitted appear unobjectionable, except that there is no shelter for crew and ammunition.

TB12, wood, is a very good sea boat, stiffer than the others, owing to her greater beam, fuller lines, and more flare out above water, but her internal arrangements are not so good, the bow hatch not being watertight, the boiler portion of the boat not being decked in, and the after position of conning tower is objectionable for steering from, being obstructed by the funnel and the crew when working the torpedoes. The open stern sheets would also hold a great deal of water, if a heavy sea was shipped, and the watertight compartments are large and not sufficient in number, but the side compartments may be put against this as regards buoyancy. The want of a bulkhead before the boiler is, however, much felt, as the heat and steam render fore compartment uninhabitable.

The boats were on several occasions steamed in company in moderate weather, and on 6 July *TB12*, *TB49* and *TB50*, were steamed from the Warner light to the Dean tail buoy and back, a distance of 6.3 knots, in a WSW wind, force 7, with moderate swell and sea, which was about 3 points on starboard quarter going out, and on the port bow returning. A considerable swell was experienced on nearing the Dean tail buoy, and on the return trip the short steep sea on the edge of the banks tested the seaworthiness of the boats severely.

The following table gives the details of speeds obtained on this occasion, the torpedo armament being complete. The poor results obtained as regards speed may be partly attributed to the engine-room staff being new to the boats, and unable to keep full pressure of steam, the proper crews having been recently mobilised, but this is only what is likely to happen in the exigencies of war:

Boat	No. of men on board	Coal carried (cwts)	Time Going (min sec)	Returning (min sec)	Total time (min sec)	Mean speed (knots)	Draught of water Forward (ft in)	Aft (ft in)	Remarks
12	8	34	15 2	21 10	36 12	10.48	2 1	4 8	Speed had to be
49	10	30	15 0	24 16	39 16	9.6	2 1	4 0	eased after
50	8	30	16 0	21 0	36 0	10.5	2 1	4 0	rounding buoy.

The boats otherwise behaved well under these circumstances, but the speed of *TB49* had to be eased after rounding the buoy, owing to the violent pitching burying her forward. *TB50* contrasted very favourably in this respect, probably owing to her greater length, but it would probably have been impossible to drive them at any higher speed had the sea been any worse; as it was, the heavy spray thrown up on the return trip rendered steering a matter of difficulty.

The torpedoes could have been used with careful management, but the practice from the revolving tubes would have been probably less accurate than from the dropping gear.

TB12 shipped a considerable quantity of water, and a small quantity entered the stokehold of each boat through the ventilator of the fan engine. The boats, however, proved themselves seaworthy, but *TB49* and *TB50* yawed a good deal when running, and *TB49* was evidently inferior to *TB50* in all respects. *TB12* in form and proportions appeared the best, though the position of the conning tower was unfavourable, and that of *TB49* and *TB50* is much preferred. Such conditions as these are obviously not favourable to the action of this type of boat, which would be most useful in thick weather and smooth sea.

(b) Speed

To compare the speeds of the different boats on service, trials somewhat similar to the above, but in more moderate weather, were carried out on several occasions, the speeds on a run from Warner to Bullock patch buoy and back, a distance of 12.1 knots in a slight swell and sea, with a WSW wind, force 5, being: *TB12*, 11.2 knots; *TB49*, 12.34 knots; *TB50*, 12.57 knots.

On another occasion on a run of 6.3 knots under very similar circumstances, *TB12* obtained a speed of 11.3 knots, and *TB99*, 11.8 knots.

These results show a slight superiority of speed in moderate weather for the steel boats, which also show higher speeds in smooth water under the conditions of measured mile trials.

As regards the machinery:

– The engine room of *TB49* is very cramped.

– The engines of all the boats have been found efficient, but the triple-expansion engines are far superior to the compound ones, and the boilers of *TB49* and *TB50* were found to prime much less than that of *TB12*.

(c) Torpedo armament

The only designs of armament yet considered as being able to be carried by these boats are: Dropping gear, fixed stem tubes (1 or 2), and single revolving tube.

The comparative advantages and disadvantages are as follows:

Advantages

Dropping gear	*Fixed stem tube*	*Single revolving tube*
• Two torpedoes carried with extreme lightness, and in good position. • No impulse required. • Well known in Service. Any pattern of torpedo can be used, but preferably those of good stability and efficient controlling gear. • Torpedo armament easily removable. Boat's bows may be built so as not to throw up spray.	• With certain torpedoes very accurate practice can be made. • Tubes being fixed involve less chance of error at director. • One tube and torpedo is a light armament. • Torpedoes well protected and not liable to injury when laying alongside a ship. • Electrical contacts and tube well protected against spray.	• Greater tactical advantages owing to large arcs of training. • Any pattern of torpedo can be used. • Lighter than other forms where 2 torpedoes are used. • Can be mounted in best position of boat for good design. • Easily removable. • Can run past a ship, discharging her torpedo without altering course. • Boat's bows can be built so as not to throw up spray.

Disadvantages

Dropping gear	*Fixed stem tube*	*Single trainable tube*
• Tendency of torpedoes to dive, and possibility of tongs hanging. • Practice not so good as revolving tube, except with stable torpedoes and good controlling gear. • Torpedoes not so well protected when lying alongside as ship. • Danger to boat if torpedo dives and strikes a hard bottom, but this is small. • Boat must be steered steadily just before firing, and must turn away after firing.	• One torpedo only can be carried efficiently. • Heavy weight in bows renders her conspicuous from spray, and blinds the coxswain in a very moderate sea. • Torpedoes must have good stability and controlling gear for good practice. • Danger to boat if torpedo dives and strikes the bottom; this is small. • Boat must be steadily steered just before firing, and turn away after firing. • Not so well known in the service as other methods. • Cannot be removed.	• One torpedo instead of two, as in dropping gear. • Deflection alters with heel of boat, and practice in a seaway would not be as good as other methods. • Possibility of breaking up the torpedo, if it is fired when the boat has a heavy list. • Electrical contacts and tube not so well protected against spray as in the stem tube.

A large amount of practice has been carried out from each boat, both experimentally to test the accuracy of fire, and by classes under instruction, in which the general working of the tubes and gear is well tested as regards strength and general efficiency.

The results of the experimental practice in fine weather is slightly in favour of the single revolving tubes in *TB49* and *TB50*, but it is considered that in a seaway (good torpedoes being used in each case) that the best and most reliable practice would be made from the fixed stem tube, and then from the dropping gear.

Owing, however, to its effect on the seaworthiness of the boat, the *Vernon* cannot recommend the stem tube as the armament of these small boats, and the revolving tube is considered the best, provided that the boats possess the necessary stiffness to ensure the torpedo being safely ejected in a moderate sea. This stiffness is not possessed by *TB49* and *TB50*, nor do the builders hold out any hope that it can be obtained, so this type of armament, otherwise satisfactory, has been abandoned and dropping gear will be the armament of the 10 new boats now building by Yarrow. An improved form of dropping gear has been designed by *Vernon*, with the object of it being fitted to these boats, which are of very similar, though slightly improved, construction to *TB50*, the beam having been increased to 9ft, and the greatest beam being above the water line.

Subsequent practice with dropping gear, fitted extemporarily to *TB50*, using Marks VI and VII RL IV Fiume and Berlin torpedoes, showed that excellent practice could be obtained from these boats with dropping gear.

(d) Gun armament

It is considered generally, both in *Vernon* and in seagoing ships, that these boats should carry, in addition to their torpedo armament, a gun of equal penetration to the one-inch Nordenfelt for their defence against other boats, and this will be arranged for in the new boats now building. The best position is considered to be the top of the conning tower.

(e) Constructive strength

There is little doubt that, weight for weight, the steel boats possess more strength, speed, and stowage room than the wooden boats, and that any serious damage to the plating is more easily repaired in steel than wood, and that the steel boats are less liable to damage from resting on crutches inboard, and leaks are less easily set up.

For these reasons steel is preferred as the material for their construction.

Summary of Recommendations

On the above trials it was recommended that:

a) Second-class boats should be capable of carrying simultaneously a light gun and torpedo armament.
b) The best armament would be a torpedo tube like *TB50*, if the boat could be constructed with the necessary stiffness, and the tube centre carried at a height of not less than 4ft 6in above the load water line when fully equipped, together with a 2-barrelled one-inch Nordenfelt (or Maxim gun of equal power) on the fore conning tower, kept as low as possible by a suitable mounting. If the necessary stiffness cannot be obtained, the torpedo armament should be dropping gear, arranged, if possible, to hold the torpedoes higher for firing and lower for stowing, and on the whole the balance appears to be in favour of this armament.
c) High speed is of great advantage, but stability should not be sacrificed to obtain it.
d) The boats should be built of steel, and decked throughout.
e) The greatest beam should not be at the water line, but near the deck, and not less than 9ft for a 60ft boat.
f) The form of bow and conning tower should be similar to *TB50*.
g) No side scuttles should be fitted, and the hand rails should be strong and serviceable.
h) The draught of water might be increased 6in with advantage.
i) Other points of details requiring alteration are: Better communication from conning tower to engine room and to deck. A tiller or hand wheel aft. Door to conning tower to open outwards.

So far as present experience goes, *TB49* and *TB50* are very satisfactory, and a great improvement on the old type of second-class steel torpedo boats.

In the beginning of December, *TB100*, second-class steel torpedo boat, of similar construction to *TB99*, except that she has open bow sheets abaft the conning tower, made the voyage from Portsmouth to Devonport in charge of Lieutenant Carey. She was delayed some time at Torquay owing to rough weather, the open head sheets proving objectionable in a seaway, and the bluff bow due to the pair of torpedo tubes causing such sheets of spray as to make steaming difficult, and constant baling forward necessary. This occurred with no torpedoes on board, and appears conclusive against repeating the type of *TB99* and *TB100*, second-class boats, although they are very useful and convenient for harbour service.

Ten boats of similar design to *TB50*, but with increased beam, are now being built by Messrs Yarrow and Co. Their armament will be dropping gear and a machine gun.

APPENDIX FOUR

QUICK-FIRING GUNS

Small-calibre, quick-firing guns were developed as a means of defence against torpedo boats. Initially, machine guns, such as those developed by Gatling, Gardner, Nordenfelt and Maxim, each of which was adopted by the Royal Navy, were considered sufficient.

As early as 1877 Mr Nordenfelt produced a one-inch gun, designed for use against torpedo boats, and worked with a breech mechanism and lever in the same manner as his rifle calibre gun. With four barrels it threw projectiles weighing 7 drachms at a rate of about 216 a minute, and was considered powerful enough to stop any torpedo boat at that time, and, accordingly, for many years it was supplied to all vessels as an anti-torpedo-boat gun, wherever it was possible to provide positions for it.

But while England adopted Nordenfelt guns in the first instance for repelling torpedo boat attacks, France and other countries adopted a revolving gun, the invention of Mr Hotchkiss. Mr Hotchkiss constructed various revolving guns, but his 37mm (1.46in) calibre gun met with most approval; the projectile being over one pound in weight could be used as a shell, and it was no doubt considered that shell would be more generally effective against torpedo boats than solid projectiles.

A 37mm quick-firing gun on a torpedo boat mount.

Torpedo boats, however, increased in size, and their boilers were arranged so as to be protected by coal, so it became necessary to provide guns which would discharge heavier projectiles with a high velocity, but with the same rapidity of fire. Both Mr Nordenfelt and Mr Hotchkiss devoted themselves to the task, with the result that they produced the first quick-firing guns throwing 3lb and 6lb projectiles, which fulfilled all the necessary conditions; the guns of both makers being equally well adapted for the purpose in view.

As the torpedo boats increased in size, the quick-firing guns, being relatively light and simple to operate and maintain, became part of their armament for their own defence, as well as part of the armament of larger vessels for defence against torpedo boats.

Quick-firing guns ought rather to be called quick-loading guns, because it is in the method of loading that the great advantage of the system lies, brass cartridge-cases being used instead of silk cloth. Although heavier than cartridges in silk cloth, yet the brass cases have the advantage of being cartridges and obturators at the same time, and of allowing a gun to be reloaded with a fresh charge immediately after firing, as sponging or washing out can be omitted without danger; and they can, moreover, do duty as a rammer for pushing the projectile home, a duty which certainly could not be performed by means of a silk-cloth cartridge. In the 3- and 6pdrs and smaller natures of quick-firing ordnance, the powder and projectile are in one case, and the term 'simultaneous' loading is used in regard to them, as against 'separate' loading, used in the larger quick-firing guns, where there are two operations, the projectile being entered first, and then the powder in its case.

From the 3- and 6pdrs between twenty-five and thirty unaimed shots can be fired by a trained man per minute, and fifteen rounds have been fired at a target in a minute, twelve out of the fifteen being hits.

Both the Nordenfelt and Hotchkiss 6pdrs are supplied to the Navy, as the same ammunition can be used for both descriptions of guns, but the 3pdrs are all Hotchkiss.

The Hotchkiss 3- or 6pdr gun is made up entirely of steel, in two principal parts, the barrel and the jacket, the latter being shrunk on the former, the two being locked together by a ring or hoop screwing on to both.

The breech of the gun on the exterior is enlarged from the rear of the powder-chamber, and somewhat squared, in order to give a large bearing surface to the breech-block.

The jacket carries the breech mechanism, the breech-block belonging to what is known as the wedge system; it is worked by a two-handled lever on the right of the gun (below), its distinctive feature being that it works vertically, and in opening is allowed to fall freely. The mechanism of the breech-block is very simple, the various functions required of it being: (a) to open and close the breech; (b) to fire the guns; (c) to extract the empty cartridge case. The block moves vertically, and falls of its own weight; therefore the mechanism for opening and closing has to lift the block straight up in closing, and to keep it either from falling open when closed or from falling out of the gun when open. It is lifted

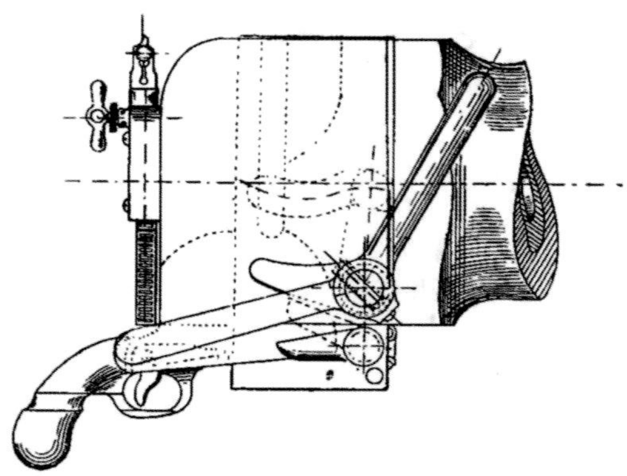
Longitudinal Elevation.

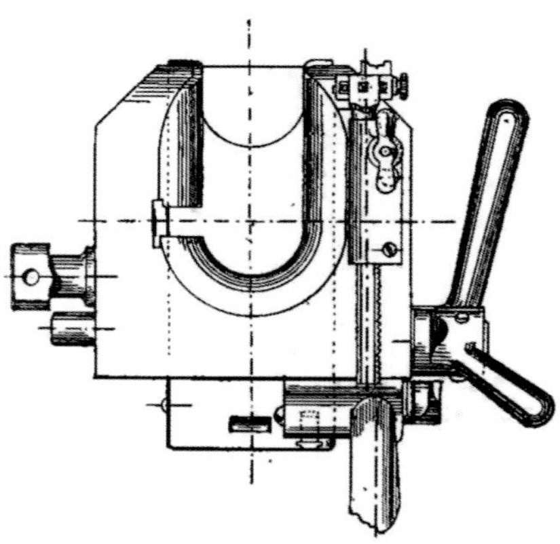
Rear Elevation.

Breech mechanism of Hotchkiss 3pdr quick-firing gun.

by means of a crank having a stud on the end, which works in a slot-way on the right side of the block, the block resting entirely upon it; when, therefore, the crank is turned, the stud sweeps down or up through its arc and the block is carried down or up with it. A stop-bolt screwed through the left side of the breech keeps the block from falling out of the gun. When the breech is closed the block is kept from falling down by the crank being slightly past the vertical to the front, and also by a light automatic spring catch on the handle. To load, one man opens the breech by turning the lever from right to left, and another pushes the cartridge into the chamber. The breech is closed again by the reverse motion to opening, the lock in the breech-block being cocked by the action. Loading in no way interferes with the firer, who can all the time be keeping his sights on the object to be fired at, elevating or training by means of the shoulder-piece, which is one of the distinctive features of Mr Hotchkiss's guns (below).

The gun is fired by a trigger, there being a hammer precisely similar in shape and action to the hammer of a sporting rifle. The hammer is pivoted on an axle, called the rocking-shaft, which is hung to the lower front part of the breech-block; on the end of this shaft, projecting from the right side of the breech, is a short lever or cocking-arm, and on the crank axle is another short lever or cocking toe. When the crank is turned, in opening the breech, the toe presses on the arm and thus revolves the rocking-shaft, throwing the hammer back.

The empty cartridge cases are extracted by a small bar of steel with a stout claw on the end, which engages in a slot-way in the breech-block, so that the down-and-up movement of the block gives an out-and-in movement to the extractor; the empty cases are thrown well to the rear of the gun. Only percussion firing is used, electric firing not having been found desirable in so small a gun.

It is to Elswick again that the Navy is indebted for the mountings of these guns, as, after a competitive trial in which several inventors submitted designs, the Admiralty selected the Armstrong recoil mounting for the 3pdr, and finally adopted the same mounting for the 6pdr.

As it was contemplated to use these guns for field service, trunnions were essential, with the result, however, that the mountings were not quite as compact as they might have been with trunnionless guns, but the mounting as devised has been thoroughly successful and has stood the test of many years, not one single instance of failure has been recorded. The mounting is made up of three different parts: the upper carriage, the revolving bracket, and the pivot. The upper carriage is one gun-metal casting, consisting of the frame and four cylinders, one cylinder to absorb the recoil and another to contain the spiral running-out spring being arranged on each side of the gun. The trunnions of the gun are fixed into 'trunnion boxes', which are connected in front to the recoil pistons, and in rear to the springs. The recoil cylinders are bored out with a slight taper, so that although there is considerable clearance round the pistons when at the front end of the cylinders, the former fit the latter at the rear end. Thus, when the gun commences to recoil, the liquid can pass freely from one side of the piston to the other, but as the piston travels to the rear the clearance gradually diminishes until the energy of recoil is absorbed, a fairly constant pressure being maintained throughout recoil. A connecting channel between the two cylinders made through the casting insures the pressure being equal in both.

The upper carriage is also fitted with trunnions, and it is about these that the gun and carriage oscillate when elevation is given the trunnions on the gun being only used as a connection to the carriage. The shoulder-piece is attached to the carriage (on the left side), thus none of the concussion or motion due to the recoil of the gun is felt by the firer.

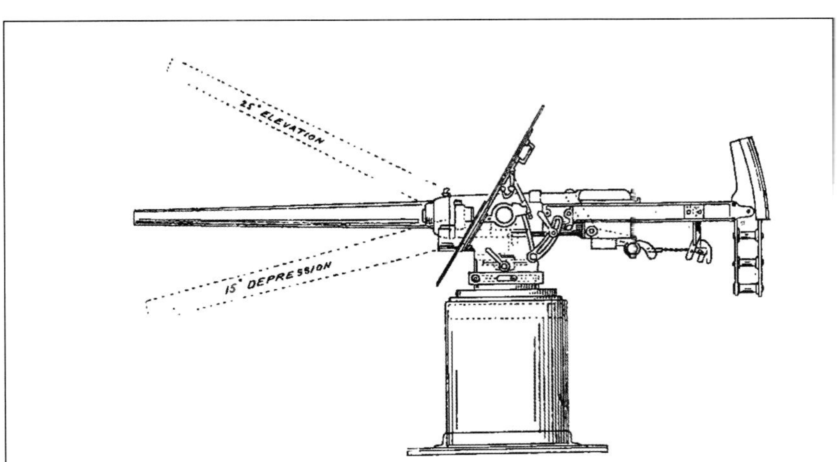

6pdr Hotchkiss quick-firing gun on Elswick automatic recoil mounting.

The brackets supporting the carriage trunnions are in one steel casting, which fits on a pin rising from the pivot; by this means rotation for training may be obtained. A gun-metal ring, put in place in two halves, and fitting over flanges on the revolving bracket and on the pivot, forms the 'clip ring'.

The recoil mounting for the 6pdr differs slightly from that for the 3pdr, because the Admiralty desired to have a mounting suitable for the Nordenfelt guns as well as for the Hotchkiss guns, and these have different external dimensions. The spring cylinder in the 6pdr mounting are underneath the recoil cylinders instead of directly in rear. To save space there is also a different arrangement of gland for the piston-rods.

The 6pdr guns had a muzzle velocity of 1,773ft/sec, with that of the 3pdr guns being slightly higher at 1,867 or 1,927ft/sec.

APPENDIX FIVE

THE DAVITS OF HMS *VULCAN*

The weekly publication *Engineering* on 18 November 1892 contained the following description of Vulcan's boat lifting gear.

Vulcan is arranged to carry six second-class torpedo boats, besides a couple of countermining launches and a steam pinnace. It is in the machinery for lifting these boats with ease and quickness that *Vulcan* differs most essentially from other vessels of her class. This consists of two large hydraulic cranes, or, to speak more correctly, two gigantic hydraulic davits, designed and constructed by Sir W G Armstrong, Mitchell, and Co.

The diagram on page 176 shows the arrangement of these davits. Fig 1 is a side view, the davit being swung fore and aft. Fig 2 is a cross-section taken athwartships. Fig 3 is a plan, and Figs 4 and 5 views of the hydraulic mechanism to a larger scale. These hydraulic davits have a lifting power of 20 tons and command a radius of 38ft, and as they are placed they have an out-reach of 29ft from the side of the vessel. The total height is 65ft. The jibs are of steel, and turn in sockets, one fixed to the deck and the other to a seating built upon the frames of the vessel as shown in the drawings. Each jib weighs 27 tons, and it will easily be understood

Vulcan hoisting out a torpedo boat.

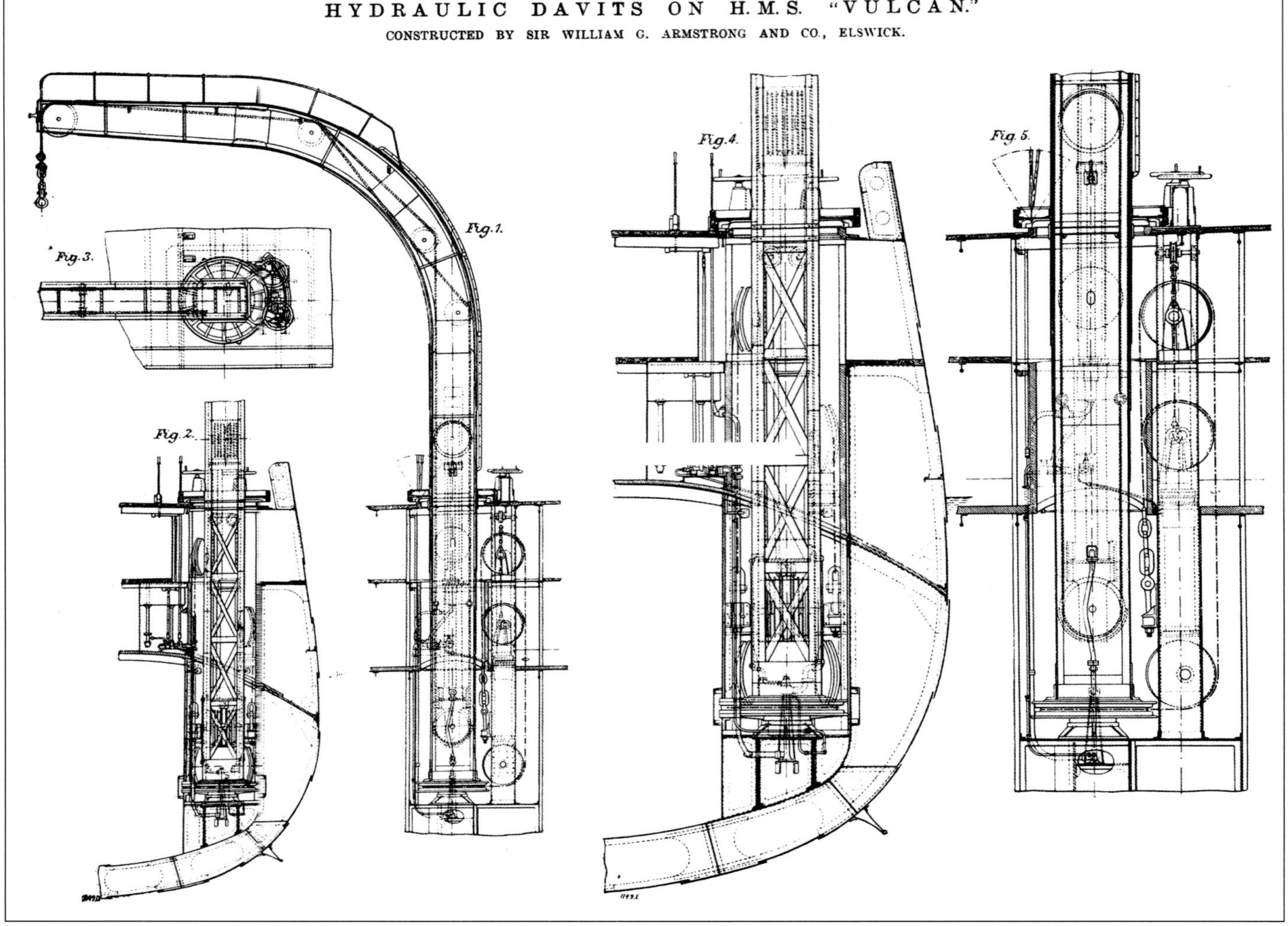

Hydraulic davits of HMS *Vulcan*. *(Engineering*, 18 November 1892*)*

that so great a weight carried at such a height – to say nothing of the pendent torpedo boat – requires to be secured very firmly to the vessel. About 30ft of the pillar is contained within the hull, the upper, main, and protective decks being pierced for the purpose. The foot is taken by a special steel casting bolted to the double bottom, which is naturally strengthened and stayed to withstand the unusual stress thus put upon it. The socket in the upper deck, which also is specially strengthened for the purpose, is composed of a steel ring sufficiently solid to resist all the canting tendency due to the lifting of weights or the momentum of the davit in a seaway. The jibs are built up of steel plates and angles on the box girder principle, and depend for their strength on the resistance offered to bending by steel plates placed edgeways, and stiffened at intervals by cross-plates and angles. The lifting machinery, as will be seen by the illustrations, is in the pillar, and largely beneath the protection deck, that part which is above being within an armoured tube provided for the purpose, and also to protect the opening in the armoured deck, the latter perhaps being the most important function. There are two cylinders of unequal diameter fitted with rams, the stroke of which is 10ft. The diameter of the large cylinder is 17½in and of the smaller one 5½in. Both rams have attached to their upper parts a crosshead which carries four sheaves as shown. There are also four corresponding pulleys at the bottom of the ram. This, of course, is an ordinary arrangement. The ordinary working pressure is 1,000lb per square inch, and the thrust exerted on the crosshead is about 118 tons. The ropes are of steel wire and are 5½in in circumference. They, or specimen lengths, have been subjected to a tensile test of 90 tons without receiving damage. These ropes are so reve as to form two complete sets of pulleys having two fixed and two running ends, the latter passing over two suitable fairleads at the outer end of the jib, and being connected by a crossbar which carries the ordinary swivel and hocks for making attachment to the weight to be lifted. It has already been said that there are two cylinders of unequal diameter, one 17½in and the other 5½in. The latter is provided for keeping the lifting rope and slings taut when the boat is attached. When there is any movement of the sea, and it is seldom indeed that there are not waves, this arrangement is almost a necessity, for the lifting of a heavy boat is a most difficult operation, and attended with considerable risk, however smartly the duty may be carried on. The small ram is not powerful enough to lift the boat, being only about 2½ tons capacity, but is sufficient to keep a strain on the rope and so take up all slack. The arrangement of valves is such that the main ram cannot be brought into play until the small cylinder has put the strain on. There is also provision for the escape of water from the cylinder when the ram is driven back by the falling of the boat on the waves.

The slewing motion is obtained by means of two cylinders fitted with rams 16in in diameter, and having a direct thrusting power of 90 tons. These cylinders are placed vertically beside the pillar of the crane. The head of each ram carries a pulley. A chain is provided, one end of which is attached to one of the cylinders, and from thence passes over the pulley at the head of the ram working in that cylinder. It then descends, and passing over a guide pulley takes a turn round a drum attached to the bottom of the pillar as shown. A similar chain passes up from the drum over another guide pulley, and then up over the pulley on the head of the other ram, and finally down beside the cylinder to which the end is attached. It will be seen that by raising one ram and lowering the other the chains will cause the drum on the foot of the pillar to revolve and thus swing the davit. This part of the mechanism is of much more than the usual power and strength in order to provide for the heel of the vessel. The turning cylinders and the valves in connection with them are arranged so that the jib is under control in both directions, but as an additional safeguard against taking charge and to provide for times when the water and pressure may be shut off, powerful brakes, actuated by a couple of handwheels on deck, are provided. The turning range is 250 degrees, which is sufficient to enable a boat to be picked up from alongside and placed in almost any position on deck. The davits being placed 40ft apart it is obvious that they can only serve the side on which they are placed respectively, but in order to provide for all contingencies – through one davit becoming disabled – the six torpedo boats are stowed in crutches fixed on movable trolleys which run on rails placed athwartships. Wormwheel gearing is provided for traversing the boats from one side of the vessel to the other.

In addition to the two torpedo boat davits described, the same firm has fitted hydraulic lifting, topping, and slewing gear to a derrick on the ship. This is adapted for dealing with launches up to a weight of about 10 tons. The lifting arrangements are similar in principle to those adopted for the hydraulic davits, and are shown in the diagram on page 178. The cylinders are placed vertically near the heel of the derrick. The topping machinery also consists of a cylinder with a plunger, multiplying sheaves, and a flexible wire rope, but the cylinder is telescopic so as to economise space; the load of 10 tons can be lifted through the full lift of 25ft from the water level at the rate of 90ft per minute. The topping of the derrick with the load can be done at the rate of 20ft per minute. The slewing into position is effected by means of hydraulic bollards. In the official tests this derrick was required to hold up, turn into position; and lower a weight of 20 tons, in order to test the strength of all the parts. There are four turning bollards or vertical winches worked by hydraulic power. These are provided for hauling purposes and give a direct pull of 30cwt.

The hydraulic davits were tested before being taken over in three ways. The first test consisted of lifting the full working load of 20 tons through the full lift of 40ft at the rate of 90ft per minute, traversing it through the full range at a speed of 45ft per minute, and then lowering the load. A load of 25 tons was then lifted, traversed and lowered through the full range. The last test consisted of holding a load of 40 tons, traversing it through the full range, and then lowering it.

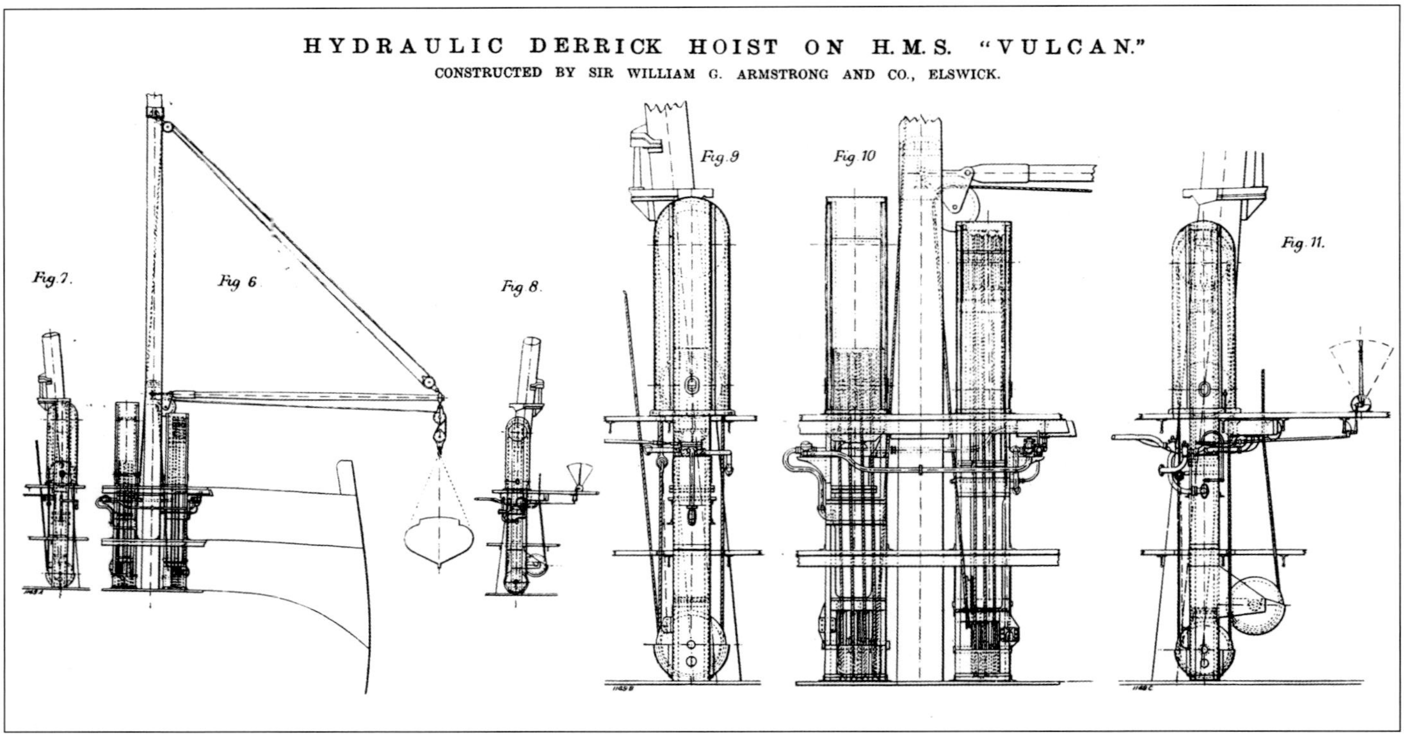

Hydraulic derrick of HMS *Vulcan*. *(Engineering, 18 November 1892)*

The tests were carried out to the satisfaction of the Admiralty authorities.

The pumping engines for working the cranes and derrick hoist are in duplicate, and are of the compound horizontal tandem type with direct-acting pumps. The two high-pressure cylinders of each engine are 13½in in diameter, and the two low-pressure cylinders 27in in diameter. The steam pressure is 100lb per square inch. The engines are specially designed for working without an accumulator, and are fitted with hydraulic governors for regulating the speed according to the demands for water. When the hydraulic gear is not in use, an automatic arrangement shuts off steam, so that the engines only work three revolutions per minute. There is also an automatic auxiliary valve to admit steam to the low-pressure cylinder when required. When the engines are working slowly, and there is no draught on the pressure water, the surplus is discharged through spring-loaded escape valves.

APPENDIX SIX

TURBINIA

Turbinia first came to the attention of the public when she turned up unannounced at the Navy Review for the Diamond Jubilee of Queen Victoria at Spithead, on 26 June 1897, in front of the Prince of Wales, foreign dignitaries, and Lords of the Admiralty. As an audacious publicity stunt, *Turbinia*, which was much faster than any other ship at the time, raced between the two lines of Navy ships and steamed up and down in front of the crowd and princes, while easily evading a Navy picket boat that tried to pursue her, almost swamping it with her wake.

Charles Algernon Parsons had invented the modern steam turbine in 1884, and set up the Parsons Marine Steam Turbine Company in 1893. He had the experimental vessel *Turbinia* built in a light design of steel by the firm of Brown and Hood, based at Wallsend on Tyne.

The Admiralty was kept informed of developments, and *Turbinia* was launched on 2

Turbinia at speed.

Turbinia under construction.

August 1894. Preliminary trials were made on 14 November 1894, using a single propeller of 30in diameter. This suffered excessive slip, and a four-bladed propeller was next tried, with no improvement. Various other types were tried, the best results coming from three propellers on the one shaft, but still the slip was too high and the vessel's speed unsatisfactory. The problem was diagnosed as cavitation, a term applied to a phenomenon first noticed by Sir John I Thornycroft and S W Barnaby in 1893, during trials of a 27-knot *Daring*-class torpedo boat destroyer. However, a top speed of more than 34 knots was achieved. The turbines were directly driven, geared turbines not being introduced until 1910.

Although torpedoes were never fitted to *Turbinia*, she was often referred to as a torpedo boat. In May 1897 *The Engineer* gave the following description:

> She is 100ft in length, 9ft beam, 3ft draught amidships, and 41 tons displacement. She has three screw shafts, each directly driven by a compound steam turbine of the parallel flow type. The three turbines are in series, and the steam is expanded – at full power – from a pressure of 170lb absolute, at which it reaches the motor, to a pressure of 1lb absolute, at which it is condensed. The shafts are slightly inclined, and each carries three screws, making nine in all. The screws have a diameter of 18in, and when running at full speed they make 2,200 revolutions per minute. Steam is supplied from a water-tube boiler, and the draught is forced by a fan, mounted on a prolongation of the low-pressure motor shaft, the advantage of this arrangement being that the draught is increased as the demand for steam increases, and also that the power to drive the fan is obtained directly from the main engines.
>
> Up to the present the maximum mean speed attained has been 32¾ knots, as the mean of two consecutive runs on the measured mile. These runs were made after about four hours' steaming at other speeds, and the boat on the day of the trials had been fifteen days in the water. It is anticipated that on subsequent trials, after some alterations to the steam pipe, still higher mean speeds will be obtained. As it stands, however, the indicated horsepower realised is 2,100, and the consumption of feed-water per indicated

horsepower hour 14½lb, and the speed the fastest of any vessel irrespective of size. The weight of the main engines is 3 tons 13 cwt. Total weight of machinery, including turbines and auxiliary engines, condenser and boiler, the propellers and shafts, the tanks and the water in boiler and hot well, 22 tons. Thus nearly 100 horse power is developed per ton of machinery, and nearly 50 horsepower per ton of displacement of boat. In the *Turbinia* the stresses on the boiler and machinery are, as far as possible, according to the Board of Trade rules, and the scantlings of the hull are heavy for a boat of her size and class.

Mr Froude commented that the arrangement of the propellers in the *Turbinia* was not all that could be desired, and thought that better results could be obtained if the engine could be geared down and an ordinary propeller used at normal speeds. Likewise, Sir W White commented on the difficulty of reversing, and pointed out that it necessitated a second motor, or sets of motors, for going astern. He brought forward a suggestion that a vessel should be first tried with a Yarrow or Thornycroft engine and then with a Parsons, so that it should be possible to make some trustworthy comparison between the two means of propulsion. Mr Parsons responded that the difficulty of reversing was not very great, as by the addition of an extra weight of ¾ ton he could, and was about to put in, an extra motor, which would propel the vessel astern at 12 knots speed. On *Turbinia*, provision had been made whereby she could reverse at 3-knot speed.

The following paper was read by the Hon Charles Parsons at the thirty-eighth session of the Institution of Naval Architects on 8 April 1897.

The Application of the Compound Steam Turbine to the Purpose of Marine Propulsion

It has been suggested by Sir W H White that a paper giving some account of the application of the compound steam turbine to the purposes of marine propulsion might be of interest to the members of this Institution. The date of this paper is perhaps somewhat premature, as the *Turbinia*, the first boat fitted with turbine engines, has not yet completed her experimental trials, but as the results so far ascertained are in some respects remarkable, this perhaps may afford some excuse for their publication. The manufacture of the compound steam turbine was first commenced in the year 1885 with the construction of small engines for the driving of dynamos; successive improvements were made, and larger engines constructed, but up to the year 1892 the consumption of steam was not such as to justify the application of this class of engine to the purpose of marine propulsion, though on account of its light weight, small size, and high speed of revolution it presented greater advantages over ordinary engines for certain classes of work.

In the year 1892, however, a highly developed compound turbine, adapted for condensing, was constructed for the Cambridge Electric Supply Company, and when tested by Professor Ewing, FRS, showed a consumption of steam equivalent

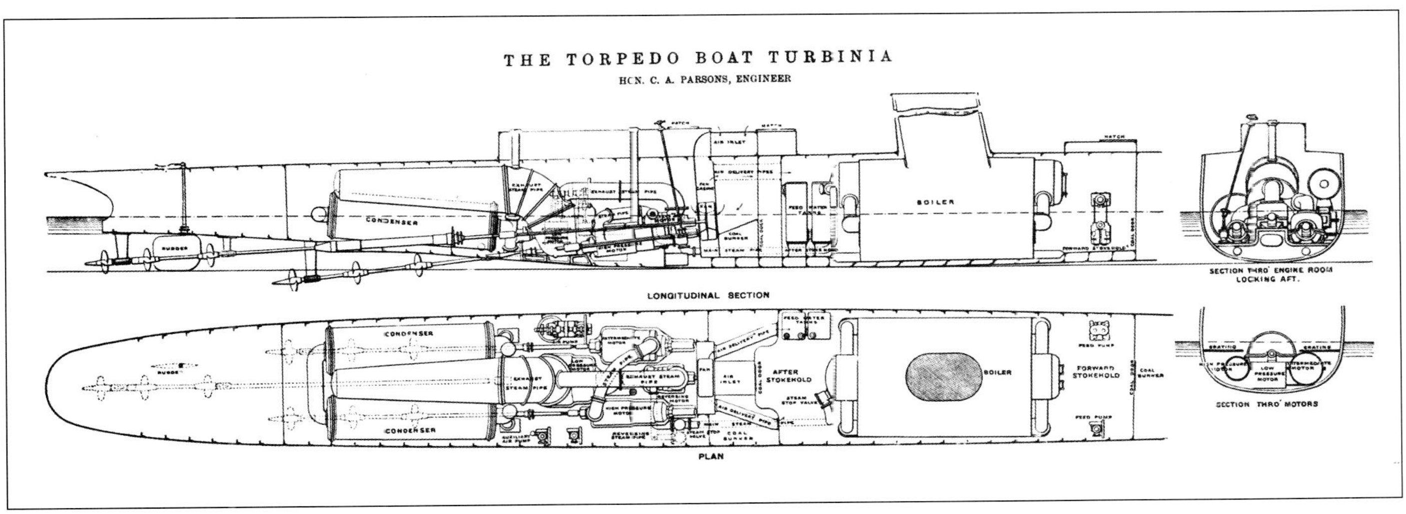

An arrangement drawing of *Turbinia*. (*The Engineer*, 28 May 1897)

to 15.1lb per indicated horsepower per hour, the boiler pressure being 100lb, and the steam superheated to 127 degrees Fahrenheit above the point of saturation. More recently, compound turbine engines have been constructed up to 900 horsepower, both condensing and non-condensing, and consumptions of steam as low as 14lb per indicated horsepower with saturated steam, and 100lb boiler pressure, have been ascertained in engines of 200 horsepower, and still lower consumptions in engines of larger size. Many of the original engines are still doing good work; some, especially the larger sizes of 500-horse and upwards, are frequently kept at work for several weeks without stopping. The returns of the Newcastle and District Electric Lighting Company show a yearly cost of upkeep of 2½ per cent per annum, and the total horsepower of turbines now at work in England exceeds 30,000 horsepower.

In January 1894, a syndicate was formed to test thoroughly the application of the compound steam turbine to marine propulsion, and a boat was designed for this purpose. In view of the large amount of alteration that would probably be required before a satisfactory issue was reached, and the large amount of time and expense necessarily involved, it was decided to keep the dimensions as small as possible, but not so small as to preclude the possibility of reaching an unprecedented rate of speed, should all the parts work as satisfactorily as was anticipated. The fulfilment of these anticipations was, however, much delayed, and almost frustrated, by a difficulty which, though foreseen, proved to be of a much more serious character than was anticipated. This difficulty was that termed by Mr R E Froude 'the cavitation of the water', or, in other words, the hollowing out of vacuous spaces by the blade of the screw, and this pitfall for the designers of screws for very fast vessels, though indicated by theory to exist, came upon us in the case of our very fast running screw, taxed beyond the usual extent, in its most aggravated form. When the boat and machinery were designed the trials of the *Daring*, which first drew attention to this difficulty, had not taken place.

The *Turbinia* – as the boat is named – is 100ft in length, 9ft beam, and 44½ tons displacement. The original turbine engine fitted in her was designed to develop upwards of 1,500 actual horsepower at a speed of 2,500 revolutions per minute. The boiler is of the water-tube type for 225lb per square inch working pressure, with large steam space and large return water legs, and with a total heating surface of 1,100 square feet, and a grate surface of 42 square feet; two firing doors are provided, one at each end. The stokeholds are closed, and the draught furnished by a fan coupled directly to the engine shaft. The condenser is of large size, having 4,200 square foot of cooling surface; the circulating water is fed by scoops, which are hinged and reversible, so that a complete reversal of the flow of water can be obtained should the tubes become choked. The auxiliary machinery consists of main air pump and spare air pump, auxiliary circulating pump, main and spare feed pumps, main and spare oil pumps, also the usual bilge ejectors; the fresh-water tank and hotwell contain about 250 gallons. The hull is built of steel plate, of thickness varying from 5⁄16 in the bottom to 1⁄16 in the sides near the stern, and is divided into five spaces by water-tight bulkheads. The deck is of steel plate.

Trials were made with screws of various patterns, but the results were unsatisfactory, and it was apparent that a great loss of power was taking place in the screw. To investigate the question thoroughly, a spring torsional dynamometer was constructed, and fitted between the engine and screw shaft, measuring the actual torque transmitted. The measurements conclusively proved that the cause of failure lay entirely in the screws, and, with the object of further investigating the character of this waste of power, a series of experiments were made with model two-bladed screws of 2in diameter, revolved in a bath of water heated to within a few degrees of the boiling point, and, in order that the model screw should produce analogous results to the real screw, it was arranged that the temperature of the water and the head of water above the propeller, as well as the speed of revolution, should be such as to closely resemble the actual conditions and forces at work in the real screw, the object in heating the water being to obtain an increased vapour pressure from the water, so as to permit a representation of the conditions with a more moderate and convenient speed of revolution than would otherwise have been necessary.

The approximate weights are:

Main engines	3 tons 13 cwt
Total weight of machinery and boiler, screws and shafting, tanks, &c	22 tons
Weight of hull complete	15 tons
Coal and water	7½ tons
Total displacement	44½ tons

The screw was illuminated by light from an arc lamp reflected from a revolving mirror attached to the screw shaft, which fell on it at one point only of the revolution, and by this means the shape, form, and growth of the cavities could be clearly seen and traced as if stationary. It appeared that a cavity or blister first formed a little behind the leading edge, and near the tip of the blade; then as the speed of revolution was increased, it enlarged in all directions until, at a speed corresponding to that in the *Turbinia*'s propeller, it had grown so as to cover a sector of the screw disc of 90 degrees. When the speed was still further increased, the screw, as a whole, revolved in a cylindrical cavity, from one end of which the blades scraped off layers of solid water, delivering them on to the other. In this extreme case nearly the whole energy of the screw was expended in maintaining this vacuous space. It also appeared that when the cavity had grown to be a little larger than the width of the blade, the leading edge acted like a wedge, the forward side of the edge giving negative thrust.

From these experiments it would appear that in all screws, of whatever slip ratio, there will be a limiting speed of blade, depending upon the slip ratio and the curvature of the back – in other words, on the slip ratio and thickness of blade; beyond this speed a great loss of power will occur; and that, should the speed of ships be still further increased, the adoption of somewhat larger pitch ratios than those at present usual will be found desirable.

It is not proposed here to trace further the losses of power by cavitation, but, generally speaking, the effect is felt in the case of the real ship, not in the racing of the screw, but in loss of propulsion effect. In the model experiments however, in hot water, the effect was both loss and propulsion effect and also racing, as would naturally be expected from the fact of greater vapour density of the water in the latter case rendering the cavities more stable. A series of model experiments on cavitation in cold water on the lines described would be extremely interesting, and probably instructive, but would require more elaborate, powerful, and extremely high-speed apparatus than was at our disposal. It would also seem that the limitation imposed on slip ratio tends in favour of larger pitch ratio for very fast vessels.

The single compound turbine engine was now removed from the boat and replaced by three separate compound turbines, directly coupled to three screw shafts, working in series on the steam, the turbines being the high-pressure, intermediate, and low-pressure, and designed for a complete expansion of the steam of 100-fold, each turbine exerting approximately one-third of the whole power developed, the three screw shafts now being of reduced scantling. By this change the power delivered to each screw shaft was reduced to one-third, while the division of the engine into three was favourble to the compactness and efficient working of the turbines. The total weight of engines and the speed of revolution remained the same as before. The effect on the screws was to reduce their scantling, and to bring their conditions of working closer to those of ordinary practice. The thrust of the propellers is balanced by steam pressure in the motors. The rest of the machinery remains the same, though some changes in arrangement were necessary. The usual *lignum-vitae* bearings are used for the screw shafts. The engine cylinders lie closely to the bottom of the boat, and are bolted directly to small seatings on the frames of sufficient strength to take the thrust of the propellers. The centre of gravity of the machinery is consequently much lower than with ordinary engines.

At all speeds the boat travels with an almost complete absence of vibration, and the steady flow of steam to the motors may have some influence on priming; at any rate, no sign of this has yet occurred with ordinary Newcastle town water. No distilling apparatus has been fitted. The boat has been run at nearly full speed in rough water, and no evidence of gyroscopic action has been observable, though such a result would be anticipated from the known small amount of these forces under actual conditions; indeed the *Turbinia* has so far proved herself an excellent sea boat. The oiling of the main engines is carried on automatically under a pressure of 10lb per square inch by a small pump worked off the air-pump engine; a small independent duplex oil pump is also fitted as standby. The main engines require practically no attendance beyond the regulation of a small amount of live steam to pack the glands and keep the vacuum good.

The advantages claimed for the compound steam turbine over ordinary engines may be summarised as follows: (1) increased speed, (2) increased economy of steam, (3) increased carrying power of vessel, (4) increased facilities for navigating shallow waters, (5) increased stability of vessel, (6) increased safety to machinery for war purposes, (7) reduced weight of machinery, (8) reduced space occupied by machinery, (9) reduced initial cost, (10) reduced cost of attendance on machinery, (11) diminished cost of upkeep of machinery, (12) largely reduced vibration, (13) reduced size and weight of screw propellers and shafting.

Appendix

Trials of the Turbinia. In December of last year several runs were made on the measured mile, and the maximum mean speed obtained after due allowance for tide was 29.6 knots per hour, the mean revolutions of the engines being 2,550 per minute. Since then new propellers of increased pitch ratio have been fitted. Further trials were made on 1 April. The mean of the two consecutive runs gave a speed of 31.01 knots per hour, the mean revolutions of the engines being 2,100 per minute, the fastest run being at the rate of 32.61 knots per hour. The utmost horsepower required to drive the boat at the speed of 31.01 knots is 946, as calculated from experiments on her model, made at Heaton Works, on the method of the late Mr William Froude.

Assuming the ratio of thrust horsepower to indicated horsepower to be 60 per cent (which appears to be the ascertained ratio for torpedo boats and ships of fine lines), the equivalent indicated horsepower for 31.01 knots is 1,576. The feed-water supplied to the boiler was measured by a Siemens water meter previously calibrated under the working conditions, and found to be substantially correct. These measurements were made when running at a speed of 28 knots, and the consumption at 31.01 knots has been calculated from those measurements according to the known law between steam pressure and consumption, and by the observed steam pressures on the engines at the respective speeds. The consumption at 31.01 knots is approximately 25,000lb per hour, or 15.86lb per indicated horsepower. It should be observed that the assumption of the thrust horsepower being 60 per cent of the indicated horsepower presupposes that the propellers are of the best form attainable, and should those now fitted be superseded by others of higher efficiency, as is possible, and indeed probable, then the figures of consumption per indicated horsepower will be correspondingly improved, and the speed of the boat increased. The consumption of steam at 11.4 knots speed has been measured by meter, and found to be 2,700lb per hour, or equivalent to a coal consumption of about 24.6lb per knot.

Conditions of running of *Turbinia* at 31.01 knots speed.

Mean revolutions of engines	2,100
Steam pressure in boiler	200lb
Steam pressure at engines	180lb
Vacuum at exhaust of engines	13½lbs
Speed of boat	31.01 knots
Calculated thrust horsepower	946
Calculated indicated horsepower	1576
Consumption of steam, reduced to basis of 31.01 knots	25,000lb
Consumption of steam per indicated horsepower per hour	1516lb
Total weight of machinery, including boiler, condensers, engines, auxiliaries, shafting, propellers, tanks, water in boiler, and hotwell, in working order	22 tons
Indicated horsepower per ton of total machinery	72

Owing to adverse weather, these trials have been much delayed, and had finally to be made under unfavourable circumstances. They are, however, believed to substantially accurate.

On Saturday, 10 April the *Turbinia* attained the highest velocity ever reached by a steam vessel, making an average of 32¾ knots on the measured mile.

For details of the annual report of 1887 from HMS *Vernon*, see Chapter 5.

APPENDIX SEVEN

ALUMINIUM TORPEDO BOATS

Although the Royal Navy did not acquire any aluminium torpedo boats, they did show interest in a second-class torpedo boat built for the French navy by the British shipbuilder Yarrow. In *Alfred Yarrow, His Life And Work*, this boat is mentioned as one of the 'notable' vessels produced by the company:

> An interesting second-class torpedo-boat was constructed by the Yarrow firm for the French government in 1892. The authorities in Paris invited tenders for a special type, which it was desired should serve as a tender to the battleships in the French navy. The government stipulated that the length should be limited to 60ft, but they demanded a speed of over 20 knots, with a lifting weight of under 10 tons. The French constructors did not submit any proposal, stating that the conditions could not be complied with. The Yarrow firm offered to carry out the requirements of the government, suggesting that the hull be built of aluminium, which is lighter than steel. After the contract was given, the French firms were somewhat vexed at its being placed out of the country, and represented to the minister that if they had been told that aluminium would have been accepted, they could have conformed to the conditions demanded. But the authorities pointed out that it was open to every firm to have proposed aluminium, as no stipulation had been laid down as to what material should be used for the hull.
>
> The order for this sample boat was successfully completed, but, on being taken over by the French authorities, it was left in Cherbourg Harbour, and the hull began to deteriorate, which was due to one of two causes.
>
> For some time she was moored in the dock alongside a wooden vessel, the bottom of which was coppered. The vessels being in salt water, a galvanic action may have taken place between the two boats and the aluminium hull would naturally be the one attacked.
>
> Another explanation of the trouble has been given: it is well known to those who travel that, in continental villages, washing operations are generally carried on by the peasant women in running water, and a considerable quantity of soap is necessary. It appears that a stream used in this way flowed into the dockyard where this little boat was moored, and consequently the water became alkaline. An alkali will attack aluminium and, if sufficient washing took place in the stream, it might account for the deterioration of the boat's hull.
>
> Had the French authorities taken the precaution to have the boat lifted out of the water and properly painted, as would have been the case had she been built of steel, no such deterioration would have occurred. Unfortunately, this mischance brought the use of aluminium as a boatbuilding material into disrepute.

Both heat and alkalis were recognised as significant problems, and hence aluminium was not used in areas likely to be exposed to significant heat.

A great deal of experimentation had been undertaken by Yarrow to determine the exact material to be used – plates to be 50 per cent thicker than steel, with 6 per cent copper, rolled to a medium extent of hardness, and cold 'shaped'. Trials showed that corrosion would be less than 4 per cent per annum for an unpainted surface, provided that there was no galvanic action due to other metals being in contact with the aluminium.

An illustration of the second-class torpedo boat built for the French Navy. *(Alfred Yarrow, His Life and Work)*

The publication *The Engineer*, dated 5 October 1894, included a detailed description:

Ten tons with steam up and coal in the bunkers; twenty and a half knots speed; 300 horsepower. Ten years ago – perhaps five years ago – the man who suggested the possibility of producing a boat which could live in a sea and satisfy the conditions embodied in the first lines above would have been regarded as a lunatic by those who had not watched the progress of events. On Saturday last Mr Yarrow demonstrated on the Thames the possibility of producing such a vessel when, with a small party of guests on board, he ran an aluminium torpedo boat, which he has just completed for the French government, from Greenwich Pier to Crossness and back. The boat which has not yet received either a name or an official number, is the largest vessel yet built of aluminium. Indeed, she is the largest structure of any kind yet produced in that metal, a small yacht and an arctic boat, recently illustrated in our columns, being her only predecessors. The torpedo boat is of the second-class. She is 60ft long, and 9ft 3in beam. Thus she has 9in more beam than the English 60ft boats, a most important improvement in many respects. The object of what is termed a second-class torpedo boat is to be carried on the deck of large men-of-war, to be lowered in the water and to act, when necessity requires, as a scout to watch the movements of the enemy's torpedo boats, or for the use of the ship for landing and embarking the officers. The ordinary armament of a second-class torpedo boat consists of one or two machine guns placed forward and a torpedo launching tube aft.

It is self-evident that lightness of construction is of paramount importance in craft of this kind, not only because reduced displacement secures increased speed, but, considering that the boat has to be lifted and lowered by the tackle available on board the ironclad or other vessel, it is clear that the weight to be handled should be reduced to a minimum. Moreover, as these boats are placed high up on a ship's deck, any reduction of top weight increases the stability of the ship to which they are attached. In the English Navy a large number of these second-class torpedo boats is used to form part of the standard equipment of all men-of-war. The French naval authorities, however, up till last year had not adopted them, and, as they were desirous of introducing them into their navy, they invited tenders for the best torpedo boat of this class which modern improvements enabled constructors to build, to serve as a type to be followed in the future. The primary conditions imposed were good sea-going qualities and lightness, combined with the highest obtainable speed. The proposal submitted by Messrs Yarrow and Co was the one accepted, as they were prepared to guarantee a higher speed and lighter weight to be lifted than any other firm, mainly in consequence of having determined to adopt aluminium for the construction of the hull. The boat illustrated is the first aluminium vessel built for the French government.

Comparatively little has hitherto been known about aluminium as a structural material, and before adopting it Messrs Yarrow and Co carried out a series of elaborate experiments on the metal to obtain information. The great and uniform success of this firm in all their ventures is largely due to the elaborate system of experimenting carried out at Poplar. The trials of aluminium referred to its stiffness, best working temperature, corrosion, &c. It was found, in the first place, necessary to alloy the metal, by which its tensile strength was raised from 9 tons per square inch to about 113 tons. The alloy is mainly 6 per cent of copper. As regards stiffness, &c, a general result was arrived at. All scantlings were increased 25 per cent over that allowed for steel, and as aluminium weighs about one-third of steel, it follows that a reduction of about one-half was effected in the weight of the hull, which was reduced from about four tons for steel to about two tons for aluminium. In order to arrive at some precise information concerning corrosion, two aluminium plates were accurately weighed, and then secured on the sides of a wooden coppered sailing ship, the copper being removed and replaced by the aluminium. This ship made a voyage round the world, then the aluminium plates were removed, weighed, and found to have suffered no appreciable loss. The great foes to aluminium are alkalis, which attack it powerfully, and heat. It fuses at a moderate heat, and loses much of its strength at comparatively low temperatures. In the case of a torpedo boat there is no trouble incurred in avoiding both sources of risk. No plates or angles were touched by the fire; everything was bent cold. The frames are a little closer together than they would be if of steel. The extra cost of material in the use of this particular boat being £1 000 as compared with that of steel. In return there is a saving of about two tons in weight and a gain of about 3½ knots in speed over vessels of the same class and dimensions in the British Navy which steam under the like conditions at 17 knots. The boat is built in the usual way, and triple-riveted with aluminium rivets. Her machinery consists of a set of triple-expansion engines, driving an aluminium bronze propeller at 580 to 600 revolutions per minute. These engines are balanced without bob weights, on Mr Yarrow's principle, at two points only, the balance weights being fitted at properly calculated angles to the cranks. The boiler is of the ordinary Yarrow water-tube type.

The official trial took place on 20 September, the French government being represented by a Commission, of which Captain L Clerc was the president. We give below a copy of the official report of the trial:

Official Trial of Aluminium Second-class Torpedo Boat for the French government by Yarrow and Co. Dimension, 60ft by 9ft 3 in

The trial consisted of a continuous run of two hours' duration in the estuary of the Thames. Weather, calm; number of persons on board, seventeen; total load on trial, three tons.

No. of run	Steam in boiler	First receiver	Second receiver	Vacuum in ondenser	Air pressure in stokehold	Revolutions per minute	Time on knot	Speed	First means	Second means	Mean of means
				(in)	(in)		(m s)				(knots)
1	185	72	12	24	2½	600.36	2 42	22.222	20.893	20.807	
2	185	72	12	24	1¼	598.80	3 4	19.565	20.721	20.566	
3	175	72	12	24	2	593.40	2 45	21.877	20.412	20.229	
4	175	62	11½	24	1½	578.16	3 10	18.947	20.187	20.341	20.503
5	180	65	11	24	1½	586.80	2 48	21.428	20.496		
6	185	70	12¼	24	1¾	591.48	3 4	19.565			

During the trial of two hours' duration the engines made 70,948 revolutions, being at the rate of 591.2 revolutions per minute, corresponding to a mean speed during the entire run of 20.558 knots per hour. The boiler – Yarrow's patent water-tube – made ample steam without priming, and the engines worked without any heating. The vibration was very slight, and not appreciable.

During all the trials of this boat, the absence of vibration and of noise in the engine-room has been most noteworthy. On Saturday she was run at various speeds from dead slow up to the highest attainable, and at none was the slightest vibration to be felt in any part of the boat forward, aft, or amidships. The only thing of the kind perceptible was a species of purring thrill. Part of this is no doubt due to the construction of the engines; but much remains to be explained by the metal. Although aluminium is in some forms one of the most sonorous in existence, in the shape of a torpedo boat it is wanting in that resilience and vibratory stiffness peculiar to steel. This largely explains the comparative silence of the engines. In a thin steel hull every sound is magnified, in the aluminium boat it is deadened – the new metal behaving apparently very much like wood. Nor is this silence without its value. Such a boat as this of which we write might be able to creep alongside an enemy and take him unawares, where the ordinary boat would be detected in the stillness of a night by the clank of its machinery.

The 1895 annual report from HMS *Vernon* included the following report:

Aluminium Torpedo Boats

It is known that the Torpedo Depot ship *Foudre*, launched last month at Bordeaux, is intended to carry on her deck eight torpedo boats of 14 tons; three of these little craft have been delivered, the five others are going to be laid down shortly – of the three first, one is of aluminium and was built in England by Yarrow, the others are of steel and come from the works of Creusot.

The intention of the Ministry of Marine was to have the last five built of aluminium. The Yarrow boat has given entire satisfaction as regards speed – and has even surpassed by several knots the speed expected at her trials – but it has been quite different as regards preservation. She had scarcely arrived at Cherbourg before rather serious deterioration of the keel was discovered, and after a sojourn of two months in the Arsenal, these deteriorations had increased to such an extent that the hull was considered useless. The plates of the side, (bordering plates) for example, have such deep erasions in several places that they no longer offer the least resistance, they crumble away under one's nail, and may be penetrated without difficulty; and the evil extends over such large surfaces that the renewal of the entire hull is necessary. In reality the aluminium employed has behaved very badly, not only under the action of sea water but also under that of sea air; it has, in fact, been proved that the deteriorations are very great above the water-line. Some people assert that these phenomena of corrosion should be attributed to the employment of an aluminium in which is present foreign matter, that they would not have existed if a pure metal had been employed, and they rely, to support their opinion, on trials made in the United States with aluminium plates of various compositions; those in which no impurities existed would, they say, have endured perfectly a sojourn of several months in sea water. But this metal cannot be depended on, and before adopting it for naval construction it must be subjected to numerous trials: and it is for this reason that the Ministry of Marine has given up the idea of building of aluminium the five last torpedo boats of the *Foudre*; these little craft will be made of steel. As for the Yarrow boat, if she is to be used, she must have a new hull.

BIBLIOGRAPHY

Abelsen, Frank, 'The Torpedo Boat Rap', *Warship 38* (Conway Maritime, 1986)

Admiralty, *Torpedo Drill Book* (HMSO,1914)

Anon, 'The Spar Torpedo', *Navy & Army Illustrated*, 6 September 1902

Armstrong, G E, *Torpedoes and Torpedo-Vessels* (George Bell, 1896)

Atteridge, A Hilliard, 'Torpedoes', *Popular Science Review*, vol 12 (1873)

Barnaby, K C, *100 Years of Specialized Ship-building and Engineering* (Hutchinson, 1964)

Barnes, Eleanor C, *Alfred Yarrow, His Life and Work* (Edward Arnold, 1924)

Borthwick, Alastair, *Yarrow and Company Limited, 1865–1977* (Yarrow Shipbuilders)

Branfill-Cook, Roger, *Torpedo: The Complete History of the World's Most Revolutionary Naval Weapon* (Seaforth, 2014)

Briggs, Mark, 'TB 191 – A Tasmanian Torpedo Boat', *Warship 2012* (Conway Maritime)

Brown, D K, *Warrior to Dreadnought* (Chatham Publishing, 1997)

Brown, David K, 'Steam Torpedo Boats of the Royal Navy', *Warship 2005* (Conway Maritime)

Collard, Ian, *Cammell Laird: The Naval Ships*, vol 2 (Tempus Publishing)

Colledge, J J, and Ben Warlow, *Ships of the Royal Navy* (Casemate, 2010)

Dingle, Nicholas, *British Warships 1860–1906* (Pen & Sword Maritime, 2009)

Dittmar, F J, and J J Colledge, *British Warships 1914–1919* (Ian Allan, 1972)

Fock, Harald, *Fast Fighting Boats* (Nautical Publishing, 1978)

Gardiner, Robert (ed), *All the World's Fighting Ships, 1860–1905* (Conway Maritime, 1979)

————, *All the World's Fighting Ships, 1906–1921* (Conway Maritime, 1985)

————, *Steam, Steel and Shellfire: The Steam Warship, 1815–1905* (Conway Maritime, 1992)

Gillett, Ross, 'Acheron and Avernus', *Warship 22* (Conway Maritime, 1982)

Harris, Daniel, 'Swedish Steam Torpedo Boats', *Warship 2000–2001* (Conway Maritime)

Hinds, Joe, *The Ship Killers*, vol 2: *1280–1899*; vol 3: *1900–August 1939* (Nimble Books, 2009)

Hooper, John *Captain Henry Jackson of HMS Defiance* (John Hooper, 2007)

Hunter, James W, 'Last Line of Defence: a brief history of the torpedo boats and torpedo boat support facilities of Colonial New South Wales', *The Great Circle*, vol 37, no 2 (2015)

Illustrated London News, 6 February 1875

Jane, Fred T, *All The World's Fighting Ships, 1898* (Jane's Publishing, 1986 edn)

————, *Jane's Fighting Ships 1906–7* (David & Charles, 1970 edn)

————, *Jane's Fighting Ships, 1914* (David & Charles, 1968 edn)

Lyon, D J, 'Torpedo Warfare: A Successful Prediction', *Warship 27* (Conway Maritime, 1983)

————, 'Some Thornycroft Designs', *Warship 28* (Conway Maritime, 1983)

Lyon, David, *The Ship*, vol 8: *Steam, Steel and Torpedoes: The Warship in the 19th Century* (National Maritime Museum, 1980)

Perkins, Richard, *British Warship Recognition: The Perkins Identification Albums*, vol V: *Destroyers, Torpedo Boats and Coastal Forces, 1876–1939* (Seaforth, 2017)

Poland, E N, *The Torpedomen: HMS Vernon's Story, 1872–1986* (Portsmouth Naval Heritage Trust, 1993)

Sleeman, C W, *Torpedoes and Torpedo Warfare* (1889, Naval & Military Press reprint)

Thornycroft Activities (1930)

United States Torpedo Station, Newport, *Handbook for Seaman Gunners* (1908)

Williams, David L, *Maritime Heritage – White's of Cowes* (Silver Link Publishing, 1993)

Williams, David L, and Richard P de Kerbrech, *J Samuel White & Co, Shipbuilders* (History Press, 2012)

Wisemann, Tom, 'Danish Tumleren Torpedo Boats', *Warship 1990* (Conway Maritime)

Woolley, A Sedgewick, 'On Spar Torpedo Warfare', *Engineering* (9 April 1875)

INDEX

All ships are British unless otherwise stated.

Profile of the design for the torpedo depot ship, HMS *Vulcan*, 1888.
(© National Maritime Museum, Greenwich, London)

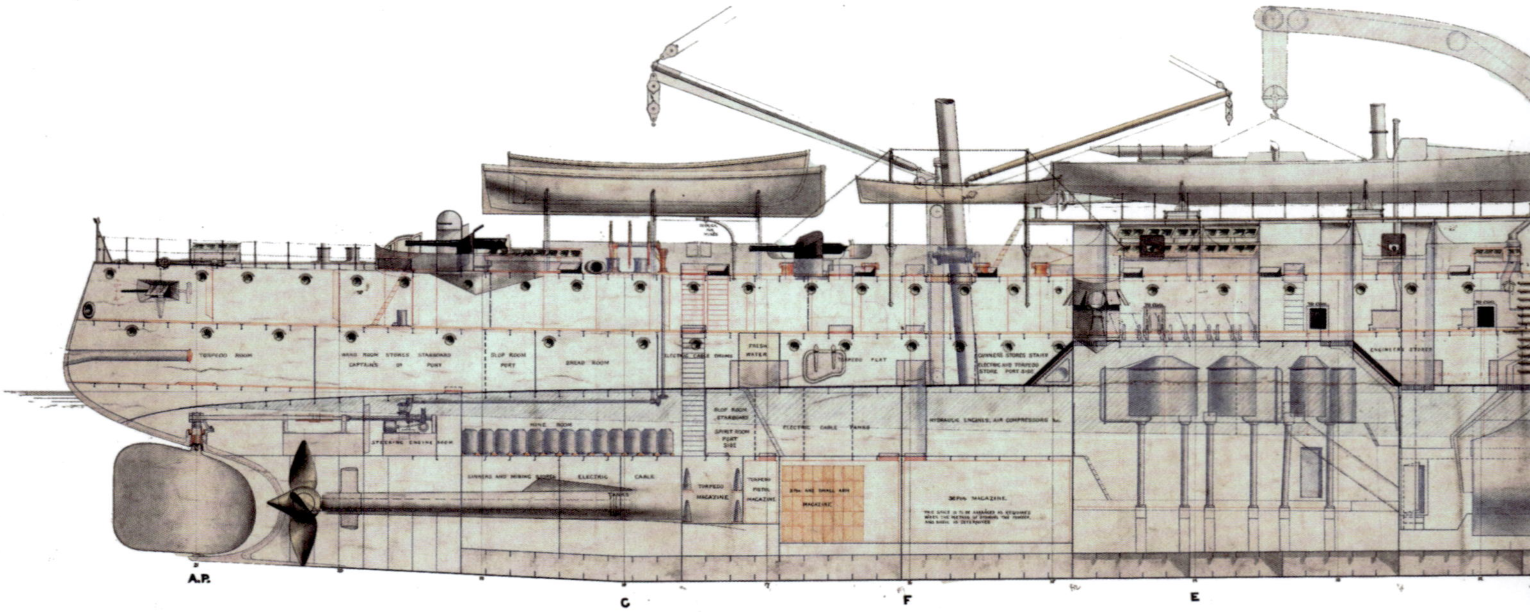

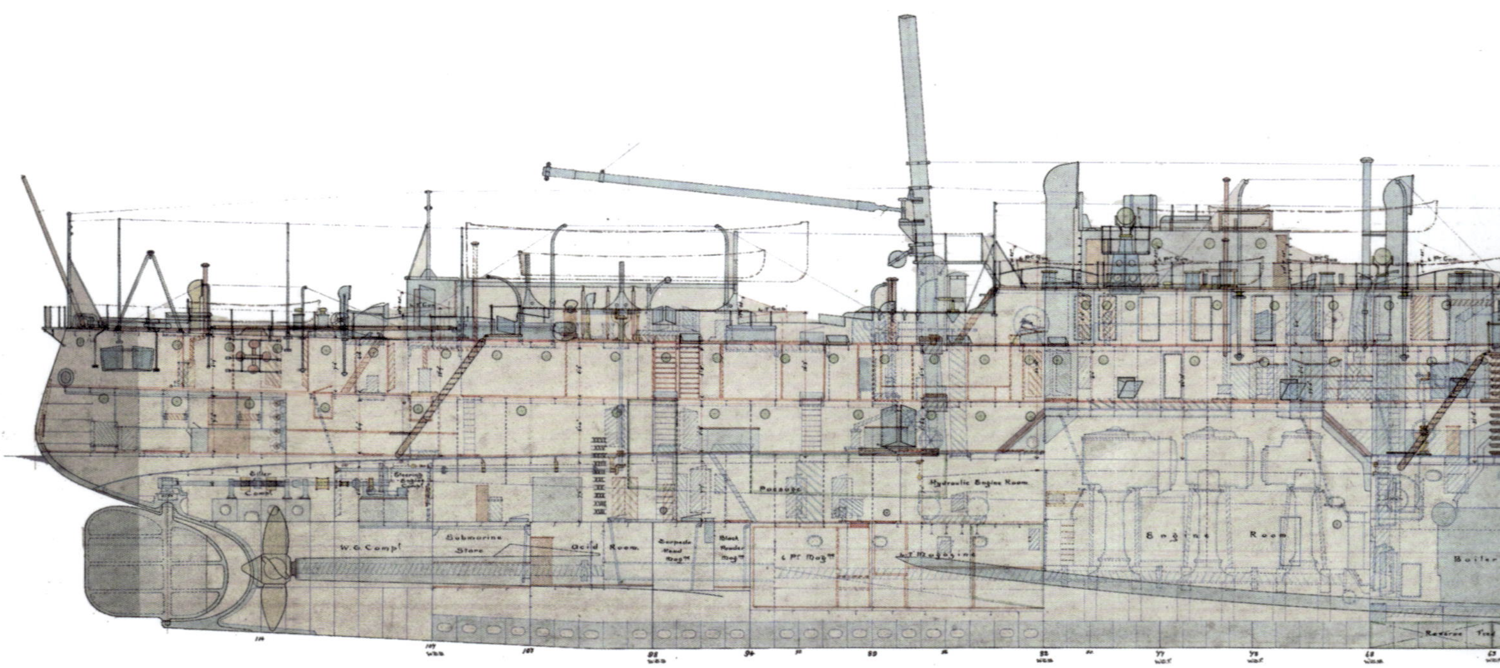

As-fitted profile of the torpedo depot ship, HMS *Vulcan*, 1909. The distinctive cranes have been omitted and the torpedo boats are not shown on deck, as in the profile above. There are also noticeable differences in the boiler arrangements.
(© National Maritime Museum, Greenwich, London)